The Imported State

EDITORIAL BOARD

Jean-Marie Apostolidès

K. Anthony Appiah

Louis Brenner

Ngwarsungu Chiwengo

Jocelyne Dakhlia

Hans Ulrich Gumbrecht

Sandra Harding

Françoise Lionnet

Hervé Moulin

Gayatri Chakravorty Spivak

Mestizo Spaces
Espaces Métissés

V. Y. Mudimbe
EDITOR

Bogumil Jewsiewicki
ASSOCIATE EDITOR

The Imported State

The Westernization of the Political Order

Bertrand Badie

Translated by Claudia Royal

STANFORD UNIVERSITY PRESS
STANFORD, CALIFORNIA

Stanford University Press
Stanford, California

© 2000 by the Board of Trustees of the
Leland Stanford Junior University

The Imported State: The Westernization of the Political Order
was originally published as
L'état importé: L'occidentalisation de l'ordre politique
© 1992, Libraire Arthème Fayard.

Assistance for the translation was provided by the
French Ministry of Culture.

Printed in the United States of America on acid-free, archival-quality paper.

Library of Congress Cataloging-in-Publication Data

Badie, Bertrand.
  [Etat importé. English]
  The imported state : the westernization of the political order / Bertrand Badie ; translated by Claudia Royal.
    p. cm. – (Mestizo spaces)
  Includes bibliographical references and index.
ISBN 0-8047-3387-2 (alk. paper)
  1. Developing countries–Politics and government. 2. Dependency.
3. Political development. 4. International relations. I. Series.
JF60 .B24313 2000
320.9172′2–dc21   99-087857

Original printing 2000

Last figure below indicates year of this printing:
09 08 07 06 05 04 03 02 01 00

Typeset by James P. Brommer in 10/13 Bodoni Book

To the memory of my father, Monsour Badie

Contents

	Introduction	1
PART ONE:	The Exportation of Political Models	5
1.	The Logic of Dependence	9
2.	The Universalist Claim of the State	48
PART TWO:	The Importation of Political Models	89
3.	Importers and Their Strategies	93
4.	Imported Products	131
PART THREE:	Failed Universalization and Creative Deviation	165
5.	Internal Disorders	169
6.	International Disorders	201
	Conclusion	233
	Notes	239
	Bibliography	249
	Index	261

Introduction

History has not come to an end. The twentieth century has seen the fall of several totalitarian regimes and the end of colonialism, at least in the classical sense. The move toward independence produced a temporary proliferation and uniformity of states pretty much everywhere on the planet. It promoted the formation of a vast "third world," to use a misleading term, that was seen as a stage of apprenticeship leading to membership in the mainstream world. The final stage was to lead to democracy, which, for lack of any other model, seemed to be the ultimate goal of History.

However, these developmentalist visions are languishing in the last of their illusions, while the dreams of convergence and the myth of a uniform, continuous advance vanish into thin air. The social sciences are now solidly postdevelopmentalist, which at least makes them more lucid. Time has done its work: the paths taken by countries in Africa and Asia over the last third of a century have not conformed to the expected models. No states based on Enlightenment ideals have blossomed; political competition has not led to progress; the visions of what the state should be have found no common ground. However, the answer to the question of why this is the case does not lie in this disillusioned assertion, which, by itself, is not enough to reopen the matter for analysis. Such an analysis would lead only to other questions; empirical investigations reveal the paradoxes of a planned globalization and its unexpected effects on developmental processes.

"Globalization" is the establishment of an international system tending toward unification of its rules, values, and objectives, while claiming to integrate within its center the whole of humanity. Never before seen in history, this process seems naturally to support and even confirm the hypothesis of convergence. In fact, it reveals the limits of such a hypothesis by exposing several inconsistencies: by stimulating the importation of Western models into societies in the South,* it reveals its inadequacy; by inciting peripheral societies to adapt, it raises hopes of innovation that may very well be false; by rushing the process of world unification, it encourages the rebirth and affirmation of individual characteristics; by endowing the international order with a center of power more structured than ever, it tends to intensify conflict. By seeking to bring historical development to an end, it suddenly launches History in varied and contradictory directions.

The first of these inconsistencies is not the least. The years following decolonization clearly revealed the failure of all mimicry in the constitutional area. Everything indicates, however, that mimicry has not ceased and that it has even intensified. Even stranger, importation often prevails over exportation, since the elite in Southern societies continue to borrow, even while loudly condemning the practice. It is as if the logic of globalization goes from error to error, depriving peripheral societies of the means to correct themselves. This vicious circle is, of course, related to a network of forces, but we can hypothetically say that it is further nourished by strategic considerations, and notably by the advantages from which certain members of the elite profit.

Thus the non-Western societies are perpetually torn between a logic of adaptation and a logic of innovation. The first is considered "realistic"; it is certainly rational in the short term. The second coincides intellectually with thoughtful reflections on long-term effects. Practitioners and sociologists often try to reconcile them, in particular by assigning innovative features to those practices stemming from a forced hybridization. Such a synthesis is dangerous; it is especially fragile because the two systems of thought derive, in fact, from contradictory strategies: in the context of massive and relatively uncontrolled importation, innovation becomes the natural emblem of protest and casts doubt on the authorities more than it reinvents them. Thus revivalist calls also rouse to action, since they are more accusatory and populist than programmatic and constructivist. As

---

*Translator's note: The term "South" is used throughout this text to refer to the generally poorer, "third world," non-Western countries, found most often in the southern hemisphere, in contrast to the richer, developed countries in the "North," that is, Western Europe and North America. In addition, the term "princes of the South" refers to the more tribal, clannish, or familial, but more specifically, local rulers in opposition to the "princes of the North," those leaders who represent the state as it has evolved in the Western world.

producers of divergences, such calls exacerbate the gulf between the governors and the governed. They reveal and dramatize the process of westernization, preventing the banalization of everything that proclaims itself universal.

Globalization, then, goes hand in hand with the glorification of singularity. This association is even more curious in that the first is demanding, offering many promising resources: the unification of the international system is based on solid technical means that promote mobility, communication, interpenetration; it aims at the effective reduction of particularities as well as membership in a common juridical, political, economic, and even ethical order. The individuality that confronts it lacks the advantage of power: it can certainly mobilize resources unavailable to the center, but it thrives in particular on blockages and oppositions stirred up by any kind of cultural homogenization.

Henceforth, globalization reconstructs the very idea of dependence. Even supposing a unified international order fortified by a complex process of a diffusion of models, globalization implies the prior existence of a power structure driving international relations. Complex in its unity, this structure is not determined by any single factor, nor can it be considered exclusively economic. It cannot be reduced to a simple play of actors, and particularly not to a "plot by the dominating forces." Its principal property is the creation of networks as well as utilities that unite the players of the "North" and the "South," who possess very diverse interests and objectives. Provoking power, globalization also creates its own opposition, engenders its own conflicts, and sets up its own divergences. Finding visibility in its claim to unify models, it confers on the tensions it generates a primarily cultural tone.

Contradictory in its realizations, utopian in its pretensions, naive in its postulates, denounced, occasionally demonized, generator of often violent conflicts, cultural dependence remains, even grows, and increasingly controls the international scene. Behind all these ambiguities appears perhaps the essential hypothesis: beyond these dysfunctions, sometimes because of them, cultural dependence disposes of a not insignificant political capacity, one that determines how the international system functions, and specifically how peripheral societies evolve. As a result, it is effective and functional, as much for those who export its cultural models as for those who import them, as much for what it realizes as in how it manages its failures. From this universalization made up of successes and setbacks, of resistances and tensions, new histories unfold, ones that perhaps bring innovations into the center of non-Western societies, just as they do into the center of the international system.

PART ONE

The Exportation of Political Models

Political models are not necessarily exported consciously; nor is such an exportation part of a plot or, even less, a "Western stratagem," as a certain facileness of language or an overzealous, often poorly conceived third-worldist view would have us believe. Yet for two centuries at least, political thought, institutions, and practices, as well as legal codes and economic theories, have migrated from the shores of Europe or North America toward the south and east. Colonization or conquest have often, but not always (far from it), served as vectors, as the examples of the Ottoman empire, China, and Japan reveal. The most effective exportation has often been the most diffuse, carried by the configuration of power that has structured a worldwide, international order since the end of the eighteenth century, activated and reactivated by the claim to universalism that characterizes the Western political construct.

The dynamic of dependence and universal identity naturally reinforce each other and help unify the West, at least in an analytical sense. As the center of the international system they have globalized, the Western societies, from Western Europe to North America, occupy the same position of power and are linked by the same political language. Though their conceptions of law differ, their judicial exports obscure those differences, as the example of India suggests. Quite obviously in competition with each other, and even stimulated by rivalry in influence and conquest, these states nonetheless provide the societies they approach, or who request help from them, with formulas that partake of the same cultural universe, that help consolidate the same international order, and that give rise to the same dissonances within the receiving collectivities.

Similarly, exportation practices are not always identical, even if these differences apply more to the methods of colonization than to the process of diffusion as a whole. With its strong state control, France applied the method of direct administration in its colonies, thus spreading a political and administrative culture that nonetheless differed from what was practiced at home. Since Great Britain was less state controlled, it relied on the practice of indirect rule, which allowed it to better handle precolonial relationships of authority. These differences, however, faded with decolonization and the subsequent construction of new states. They fade even more when one looks at westernization from a global perspective: then everything happens as if the dynamic of importation, as well as the constraints and tropisms that affect it, outweigh the conditions proper to each mechanism of importation so as to standardize the results and to better legitimize their genuinely universal claims.

1. The Logic of Dependence

One can easily observe the principle of national sovereignty empirically. It is not necessary that a society be colonized in order to demonstrate its dependence on another; nor does a seat in the United Nations suffice for a state to claim full sovereignty, its legal status notwithstanding. This fundamental flaw in our system of international law is more than just academic: knowledge of the mechanisms that obliterate sovereignty allows us to resolve the enigma of power in international relations and to understand how certain political models travel, spread, and take root in other countries–in other words, how they can emigrate from the countries that dominate the international order.

Latin American social scientists have significantly systematized their reflections on this process.[1] In the 1950s South America was considered an anomaly: independent but under domination, the Latin American nations represented the bad conscience of the postwar international order; as the place where the international order seemed the most categorical, these nations fell victim to sociological mechanisms that clearly violated most of the articles in the United Nations charter. Underdevelopment no longer provided an excuse, since the situation continued to deteriorate: a temporary situation was fast becoming chronic. The opposition between the formal and the real–which no one could ignore–led to the hypothesis of doubling: behind a formal *integration* into the international political system, the Latin American nations felt the effects of an *incorporation* into the center of an international capitalist system. What the political order formalized, the economic order dismantled.

The Failure of an Economic Vision

The entry of the sociology of dependence into the domain of the social sciences was all the more sensational because it brought with it several postulates. One was the unity of the sciences of society, because only the dissociation of economic and political approaches could support the illusion of national sovereignty. Another was the international dimension of development, since a purely internal analysis could dangerously obscure the real reasons for economic backwardness by attributing it to cultural factors. Finally, there was the determining nature of transnational relations that disrupt borders and sovereignties, that place the study of power in both national and international contexts, and that reveal the existence of a worldwide unifying capitalist system endowed with a center and a periphery. In this view, the periphery appears to be manipulated on at least three fronts. Drained by the center, it feeds the economic development of the hegemonic powers. Structurally backward, its worsening underdevelopment serves the interests of the center and reinforces the conditions of its domination. Held in check by the functions assigned to it by the international division of labor, it supports a development from which it obtains no benefit.

In sum, this economic vision took hold because of its functionalism: the order of dependence was forged and reproduced without any challenge to its effectiveness or its ineluctable logic. The individual actor becomes useless and exploitable: he has no control over the mechanisms that suppress the sovereignty of his native country; whether he chooses to collaborate or protest, his choice will have no effect on the collective order. The prince of the South becomes an irresponsible puppet. No act of will can either stop or speed up the processes regulating the international economic order.

This thesis surprised no one. Several decades earlier, Marxist analysis claimed to have detected the economic processes that began the dynamic of dependence. Following the Ricardian tradition, Lenin had already developed an economic theory of imperialism by noting the functional necessity of an absorption of surplus.[2] According to this theory, since surplus is linked to industrial development and the fusion of industrial and financial capitalism, it manifests itself as a profusion of excess capital that gravitates to less-developed countries, where profits would be at their highest. This new financial dynamic thus marks the beginning of the world as divided among the powers of the northern hemisphere, making imperialism the "highest stage of capitalism." Lenin's explanation has been a disappointment, however, because most of the flow of capital remained confined within the developing world, even when imperial expansion reached its apex. Moreover, of all the capitalist countries, Germany was the one that best corresponded to Lenin's understanding of imperialist tendencies; yet Germany was the European country least involved in colonial conquest.

In the tradition of Adam Smith, Rosa Luxemburg proposed an alternate interpretation that seems no more convincing.[3] Increasingly focused on the opposite contradiction of production and consumption, she saw capitalist economy as characterized by an urgent need to acquire new markets that would absorb the production that a too-moderate increase in purchasing power could not consume. Thus colonial conquest supported the exportation of goods. Her analysis is disappointing because it underestimates the role of the state, which beginning with Keynesianism, brought about a different and more effective redistribution of the functions of production and consumption. Imperialism could certainly have had the market effects she assigns to it. But it would be incorrect to mistake this possibility for a necessity and to see this hypothetical dependence [of capitalism on colonial expansion] as a long-term, stable, a priori fact, not subject to other uses or capable of either changing purpose or fulfilling several purposes.

It would, of course, be incorrect to dismiss the recent reworkings of the economic paradigm. Notably, Cardoso has decisively shown how relations of dependence can be modulated as a function of the strategies of those in power at the center of an international system.[4] The construction of an American hegemony thus broke with the nineteenth-century imperial model and abandoned agricultural production to peripheral countries in order to entrust industrial production to the center. This division of labor was upset by the United States' innovative formulas of dependence through enclaves that directly organized and controlled investment and production sites at negligible cost in the very center of the developing world. The political order was transformed: in the peripheral societies, power lost even more of its deliberative function, the enclaves became even less subject to the external forces of sovereignty, and the hypothesis of incorporation lost even more ground.

This perspective is provocative because it is a little more humane: there are actors in it, and they have relevant strategies, and the processes of dependence are presented as unstable. However, though the model becomes viable, it remains marked by the same heaviness that encumbered economic determinism. Incorporation into the international capitalist system alone is supposed to control the entire mechanism of dependence. Moreover, the peripheral political elite is unable to escape the logic of the system. While the central actor takes part in decision making, the peripheral one seems, on the contrary, completely passive, condemned to lose more and more of his autonomy and forced to perform repressive functions that bring him absolutely no benefit.

This economist logic, however, resembles a colossus with clay feet. Numerous historical and sociological observations easily demonstrate the fragility of a theory that prevails only by its scope and globalizing pretensions. Hans Morgenthau and, later, Raymond Aron drew up a long list of contradictions and denials of all sorts that historians of the colonial period kept artificially viable.[5] The two most imperialist nations, France and Great Britain, are also the ones that, from an economic point of view, were the least in need: France, because of its low economic and demographic increases, and Great Britain, because its age and its development sheltered it from tensions that it could, in any case, regulate with its dominions more than with its colonies. In addition, the colonial enterprise only rarely received support from the economic elite, as the debates in Third Republic France surrounding the conquests of Tonkin and the African continent reveal.

But history confirms that political mechanisms have significantly affected colonial development. Since politicians directed and organized imperial expansion, it developed synchronously with political and diplomatic proposals and strategies at the national level. The Franco-Italian rivalry sheds light on the circumstances surrounding the conquest of Tunisia, just as the Franco-German rivalry reveals the modalities of conquest in Morocco. The Congress of Berlin carved up Africa according to the competitions among the nations of Europe, which merely reproduced the age-old imperialism inextricably linked to the concept of state-controlled government. Since Tilly's work, we know that the postfeudal international order led each state to seek simultaneously the maximum territorial resources to protect itself and, by competitive confrontation, to find the means to strengthen its own institutionalization.[6] The Peace of Westphalia in 1648 created a Europe frozen in borders so intangibly fixed that this very intangibility became an established principle in which competition could occur only externally. As Schumpeter affirms, expansion thus became an end in itself, the simple geographical displacement of the will to dominate for the sake of dominating.[7] The parallel with the modern logic of dependence seems striking. The economic advantages of this logic notwithstanding, the political foundations of dependence may be seen from two perspectives: the central role played by the political actors in the construction of this relation, and the effective and deterministic mediation by the state in establishing its logic.

Observing the actor's role helps somewhat to demythologize the matter: obviously, it leads one to limit determinism, to question the relevance of deterministic perspectives; it also introduces an element of liberty that was obscured by the postulate of forced incorporation into the international economic system. More palpably, it disproves the hypothesis, obviously too simple, of unequivocal relations between dominant and dominated, since it suggests that dependence evolves at least partially from a convergence of strategies that bring together, in a functional exchange, the elites of the North and the elites of the South. Galtung's works have opportunely drawn our attention to this fact. He hypothesizes that imperialism could develop to its full capacity only if the individuals and collective actors on both sides of the borders that, within the very heart of the international system, separate the center and the periphery maintain a certain harmony.[8] Such a harmony presupposes an active convergence of the interests of the elites in the center with those of the elites in the periphery. It further implies that the conflicts between elites and masses are more acute at the periphery than in the center. Finally, it requires that the interests of the masses in the center conflict with those of the periphery. One can see clearly what takes shape beneath these apparently simple characteristics: on one hand, a strategy of at least partial collaboration between the princes of the South and the princes of the North that requires, among other things, that dependence be equally remunerative for the former; on the other, the reproduction, indeed the increase, of the gap between elites and masses of the South, thus separating the social spheres and the official political scene in such a way as to perpetuate the condition of dependence. Similarly, this model was followed in the elements deployed since the Congress of Baku, when the Third International sought to combat imperialism specifically by trying to reconcile the proletariat of the North with the popular masses in the South. From all these points of view, the processes of dependence remain fundamentally a composite of the strategies of power and the strategies of mobilization, and thus a veritably political objective.

Dependence by the State

The same logic governs the preeminent role of the state. The Northern states produce dependence, of course, by the very fact of their competition, but also by the effect of the political and diplomatic strategies they use to accumulate power. Moreover, dependence arises from the very confrontation of their capacities with those of the developing "states." Callaghy's formula, applied to these "states," is significant, since it depicts them as "lame Leviathans,"[9] thus underscoring the powerful imbalance existing between the state's claims to govern the entire social order and the actual weakness of its performance. This imbalance relates to several elements, each of which individually sustains the effects of dependence and whose makeup noticeably worsens those effects.

The neopatrimonial construction of power is both a major trait of developing societies and a decisive element in the connection between princes of the South and those of the North.[10] It describes a weakly observable phenomenon, found as much in Africa as in Southeast Asia or the Middle East: the prince's strategy consists in appropriating for himself the political space and, based on that, the principal resources belonging to private social spaces. Though initially personal, this practice quickly becomes collective, in order to benefit equally both close associates and the whole of the state bourgeoisie, whose survival depends primarily on its capacity to find a place in the patrimonial logic. When this phenomenon is viewed from a moral perspective, as it often is, it is viewed pejoratively. However, it derives essentially from social mechanisms that cannot be dissociated from the conditions of dependence.

Neopatrimonialism stems, in effect, from the paucity of internal resources available to the political system, relative to the abundance of external resources. The Western state has come about in part by performing the function of fiscal extraction, while civil society possessed, in turn, an effective counterpower thanks to a system of representation that enabled the populace to vote on the issue of taxes. The modest, often insignificant role played by taxation in financing the expenses of the Southern nations tends to deprive the populace of a means to exert pressure on and exercise control over the government. As the entity administering relations with the exterior, then, the state becomes the principal provider of resources. Acquired in the processes of international negotiations, these resources reinforce the dependence of the elite in the peripheral nations relative to the elite in the Northern nations, while simultaneously endowing the latter with a super-strength relative to the social spaces they supposedly govern.

At the same time, neopatrimonial logic derives strength from the segmentation characterizing the society it must contend with.[11] The history of the individualization of social relations is largely tied to the course of development in the West, where the state, civil society, and the bond between citizens find their fullest significance. In this history, the hinge between state and society is not neutral; the multiplicity of horizontal alliances and divisions that structure state and society constrain political interactions and define the conditions under which such interactions will take place, power will change hands, and debates will be organized. From this point on, in the West the political actor is no longer the master of his environment. In the peripheral societies, however, the persistence of community alliances and the precedence given to traditional identifications over civil ones create, in those societies, a layering effect in both the extra-political spaces and the microcommunity spaces, as the progress of tribalism and the proliferation of particularisms reveal. Thus insulated from those individuals without political status, the professional man of power in a peripheral society is far more capable than his Western counterpart of appropriating social goods and rearranging the border separating the public and the private to his own advantage.[12]

Management of this border is facilitated by the convergence of several factors. First, power is itself constructed on a communal mode: either the tribe attains the ranks of a political class or the presence of a monocratic system stimulates the formation of clans. Through, for example, the *dowreh* in Iran or the *shillal* in Egypt, the holders of power control all the channels, permitting them to cross freely from private to public space.[13] The absence or the meagerness of horizontal alliances, particularly of interest-based organizations, promotes the proliferation of vertical channels: a party of the Arab nation, the Ba'ath Party, thus became in Syria the party of the Alaouite minority and in Iraq the party of the Takriti clan; a party formed to promote a new progressive political class based on socialist and nationalist ideals, the Tunisian Neo-Destour was transformed little by little into the party controlled by the Sahelians. Similarly, family alliances between political and economic elites in Lebanon were structured like clans, while the traditional legitimists allied with the royal families in the conservative monarchies in Morocco or, formerly, in Iran participate actively in governmental and business affairs. In Saudi Arabia, the merchant class takes part in the areas controlled by the royal family all the more willingly because the royal family guarantees it a monopoly in financial and economic activities, and this in a country where foreign companies have no legal access to the local market.[14]

From this point of view, opulence has the same effect as precariousness or even poverty. If the former activates patrimonialism by the abundance of contracts it dispenses and goods it controls, the latter profits from a different but equally effective means. In the center, the limited resources belonging to the state incite the political actors to diversify their assets: state control in Ivory Coast of the office regulating coffee prices is not only an instrument of control for the political center but also an extremely effective way to finance state expenses and, consequently, to provide for the needs inherent to bureaucratic excess. More generally, corruption has increased because there are far too many civil servants and they are all paid far too little; at the same time, the prince attempts to involve the largest number of educated young men in government institutions in order to make them loyal to himself. This strategy follows the example of Gamal Abdel Nasser, who decided that all university graduates could apply for employment in the public sector. In this vicious circle, the more civil servants there are, the less they are paid and the more they are drawn to seek compensation, through social connections, in the appropriation, however modest, of social benefits. At the other end of the spectrum the expectations are identical. The sociologist Banfield had earlier shown convincingly that precariousness was a rational source of clientelism.[15] In other words, the more limited the resources, the more an individual seeks to build direct relations with a superior belonging to the central political elite. This logic allows the individual to hope for some gain that he will not have to share as he would have had to in a horizontal structure based on a coalition of interests. Valuable as well as functional on both sides, the clientelist approach keeps the borders fluid, even to the point of effectively blurring the lines between public and private.

Here too, dependence is both cause and effect. The precariousness of resources relates largely to the effects of economic dependence; a more or less strong segmentation of society is itself partially linked to the circumstances of colonial conquest, whereas the resulting colonial administration tended to perpetuate, even at times to protect, the communal tribal order. In short, neopatrimonialism most certainly results from a combination of economic factors and political strategies. In return, these characteristics reinforce the bonds of dependence: the segmentary nature of the social order favors the dynamics of incorporation into the international economic system. The construction of microcommunal economies, whether informally or through their direct management by family communities, paves the way for the establishment of the enclaves Cardoso analyzes. It encourages the reproduction of a dual economy, half of which is largely immune to the logic of the marketplace, and half of which is part of the global economy.[16] As a result, in Zimbabwe, for example, the opposition is divided between large-scale commercial agriculture, controlled by a small minority of whites holding 39 percent of the land, and a communal agriculture covering 42 percent of the land and providing livelihood for 53 percent of Zimbabwe's population. Not only does this distribution directly support Zimbabwe's efforts to participate economically at the international level, it also promotes a neopatrimonial strategy fulfilling several functions necessary to the maintenance of Zimbabwe's economy. It establishes a formula of compromise and coexistence between the white minority and the state, wherein the latter continues to allot essential subsidies to the former in exchange for the financing of its bureaucratic machinery. Similarly, in terms of the black peasant class, this neopatrimonial strategy allows the state to maintain a minimal relationship with the local economies that escape every attempt at central regulation. Because it has no recourse to the various types of stimulation at the disposal of economic political forces, the political elite must resign itself to affecting these local economies through clientelist relations and interpersonal networks. The Land Acquisition Bill, not passed until March 1992 by the Harare parliament, anticipates, of course, an expropriation of large landholdings and a redistribution of land. It is significant, however, that its passage was so late that its application remains uncertain and that it is perceived as a threat to Zimbabwe's economy.[17]

It would certainly be risky and reductionist to cling to the binary vision of one sector aligned with a dominating and expansionist exterior opposed to another sector of dominated and regressive self-consumption. For one thing, the latter benefits from infrastructural funds produced by the former. Through their own development, white agriculture and industry have constructed within Zimbabwe a communications network from which the black economy continues to benefit. Moreover, by imitation and emulation, the power of the exporting economic sector has undeniably rebounded on the traditional sector, which has provoked the black peasantry to coalesce, to organize itself into cooperatives, and to benefit from a more performative technical knowledge. Like Nigeria, a country equally exposed to the stimulation of a modern economic enclave, Zimbabwe is well connected in a network that limits the segmentizing tendency of social spaces. However, this network is of minimal significance because the power of the white sector in Zimbabwe short-circuits any initiatives by the black agricultural community that might endanger its influence. Both white and black partners cooperate directly under conditions that are individually very advantageous, but which contradict the collective interests of the black peasantry.

The whites propose to buy from the blacks part or all of their produce at prices lower than those asked by the commercial cooperatives, but which still remain advantageous to the large-scale white farmer who can find his supplies close at hand at a lesser price. The division of labor between commercial agriculture and supplementary agriculture thus continues with the active support of a state that benefits from it, since it optimizes its resources in the short term and protects its own network of clients.

The neopatrimonial focus of political systems is also guaranteed by the essentially political identity of those who govern. Whether they come from the entourage of princes in traditional monarchies or from the ranks of the liberation movements in formerly colonized societies, these people exercise their power by means of skills and resources that only increase their isolation from the social spaces. Founding fathers of states have thus often fallen victim to their own creation, which, whether acquired through a war of liberation or a smooth, gradual gaining of independence, loses its own substance as the princes confront the daily life of managing states that more often than not lack resources. When they have benefited from a traditional devolution of power, the monarchies can reproduce their legitimacy only by relying on a history less and less compatible with the requirements of socioeconomic modernization. In the first case, the prince tries to compensate for the erosion of his authority by a heavy symbolic investment, which leads him to present himself, as did Habib Bourguiba, Félix Houphouët-Boigny, or Ahmed Sukarno, as the "father of the nation," and thus found his patrimonial domination both personally and affectively. Alternatively, this focus is combined with a proliferation of ideological symbols that confer a political identity on this domination: Marxism in Zimbabwe, socialism in Nasser's Egypt or Nehru's India. The ideological compensation picks up where the mobilizing effects of the national liberation struggle leave off, but it takes on an aspect all the more formal in that this anticapitalist focus allows the existence of a powerful international economic sector that escapes state control. Its only relevance is therefore political and internal, thus promoting the reproduction of the neopatrimonial order. In the case of monarchies, the prince is led to diversify his strategy, reserving his traditional discourse for the rural areas and compensating for his deficit of legitimacy within urban society by a recourse to clientelist techniques, as can be seen in the example of Morocco. In both these cases, the inability of the governing elite to acquire a representative capacity, that is, to define itself either as the expression of certain categories of social interests or as the bearer of a socioeconomic modernizing process, leads to the confirmation of neopatrimonial formulas as well as to their growing delegitimation within the social spaces.[18]

This delegitimation is all the more evident in the increasingly ambiguous attitude that the political elites seem condemned to take toward economic development. On one hand, economic development is a goal that every head of state must pursue, yet each such head of state must also impose his hierarchical authority on the peripheral leaders who uphold traditional values. On the other hand, an overly active policy of development risks producing several negative results: it would valorize the competence of the technocratic elite relative to that of the fragile political elite, break up social spaces and favor the constitution of a civil society capable of counterbalancing the political system, and indeed, neutralize neopatrimonial strategies, which would in effect lose their essential effectiveness in the context of an active modernization, where the resources of power would be otherwise divided and where the nonpolitical elites would have direct access to the center.

Fearing the formation of a rival elite causes the princes to pursue various strategies: the active control of the education of young diplomats, whom they absorb directly into the various administrative agencies of their regimes; the limitation of direct access by nongovernmental organizations (NGOs) to the social spaces in which they hope to promote development; the establishment of themselves as a necessary intermediary in the negotiation and channeling of foreign aid for development; and the prioritization of this aid toward financing government expenses, in order to thus cover costs incurred by the neopatrimonial managing of power. It is probably at this level that the contradiction between neopatrimonialism and development is most evident. But what is also especially clear, and most patently so, is the link between this type of political order and dependence. It is not simply the case that this dependence relation is made stronger when the process of economic emancipation in the peripheral areas is moderated, indeed retarded, by neopatrimonialism; this dependence relation is built upon an *active* solidarity and a convergence of interests between the elites of the North and those of the South. This relation has nothing mechanical about it: on the contrary, the political elites of the South relegitimize their regimes and mobilize their people politically by denouncing imperialism. Nasser's nationalization of the Suez canal or Mossadegh's of the Anglo-Iranian Company, or even Bourguiba's reconquest of Bizerte or Nehru's of Goa are cases in point. In the early 1960s, Sukarno, Kwame Nkrumah, and Ahmed Sékou Touré all made great use of the symbols of the struggle against imperialism. However, economic initiatives and symbolic actions cannot overturn a cluster of factors long in place and constituted by a solid material reality: the political weaknesses of a developing state, the scarcity of resources available to the elites by virtue of their strictly political identity, and the narrowness of means available to them to remain in power and contain social pressure.

Politics thus becomes a decisive element in constructing dependence relations. The "dependentist" school incorrectly rejects politics as accessory or derivative, in favor of an economic thesis that leads to deformed, even caricatural, analyses of the state's role, which are very broad and often contradictory. In a systematic-functionalist perspective, Immanuel Wallerstein notices that the logic of international domination renders powerless any state emerging at the periphery whose dynamic could, by its independence and sovereignty, thwart the interests of world capitalism. In a similar reasoning process, André Gunder-Frank considers the peripheral state a puppet that merely maintains the juridical and political illusion of an independence that the economic context renders in all respects impossible.[19] Inversely, Cardoso does not challenge the hypothesis of a peripheral state that, conversely, would be, according to him, called upon to assume the repressive functions destined either to cause those it administers to accept the logic of the international division of labor, or, in new modes of dependence, to make them respect the direct submission of certain economic sectors to the interests of international capitalism.[20] The extreme form of the school of dependence, the neomercantilist school, goes so far as to rehabilitate the peripheral state by presenting it as the sole possible rampart against the inflow of power coming from the international environment.[21]

The debate seems futile and distorted. It struggles to reproduce a sociology that relegates the state to a simple superstructure equipped with an "autonomy" more or less "relative." More profoundly, it rests upon an instrumental and functional conception of a politics that has no reason for being: in developing countries, in this view, the political order is not constituted to engage in repression in the name of those in power or even to keep up illusions or appearances that can serve their interests. Such a hypothesis leads immediately to extreme conclusions; those who hold it posit either the existence of an invisible hand devoted to imperialist interests and regulating the international order to its benefit, or assert that cynically and with absolute complicity the princes of the South, have placed themselves, without a second thought, at the service of the Northern princes the moment independence has been achieved. Taken to its logical conclusion, this conception leads to the absurd: an anti-imperialist symbolism that inspires deceptive practices meant to better hide the effects of dependence and thus make them more effective. As for political structures, they would be, depending on which analysis one consults, either simple facades or clumsy instruments of coercion.

This vision has produced several dead ends. Initially, it supported the erroneous hypothesis of a correlation between dependence and authoritarianism. Clearly, the link between development and authoritarianism is contestable; the oil boom that so greatly benefited the countries of the Arabian peninsula, Iran, and Libya, only confirmed their growing authoritarianism. Moreover, the efforts of Guillermo O'Donnell to associate authoritarianism with the reinforcement of links with foreign capitalism and the rise of populism with the promotion of economic nationalism proved doubly dangerous.[22] First, because it would be presumptuous to see the appearance of the dictatorships that have marked Latin America at the end of the second millennium as indicating a regression of the mechanisms of dependence. Second, because it would be excessive to systematically associate the populist vogue with a simple manifestation of economic nationalism. Since the beginning of the 1980s, Latin American populism has become increasingly successful, as the elections of Alberto Fujimori as president in Peru and Carlos Menem in Argentina have shown. In both cases, populism has set in motion an economic policy that exacerbated the conditions of economic dependence in the countries concerned. Besides, in all these cases, nationalism holds a secondary place, far behind a more profound reaction of censorship within official policy, of government officials, and in the state itself, which reveals a profound tension between society and neopatrimonial political structures. As such, this phenomenon occurs in Africa through the combined resurgence of tribalism and sects; in the Moslem world and the Indian subcontinent it occurs through the diverse revivalist expressions or through particularist resurgences with intentionally vague outlines. To ignore the antipatrimonial orientation, centered initially on government leaders, which characterizes these populist movements amounts to a denial of the dense international political relations among the developing societies. To single out their xenophobic orientation and make it the mark of a popular challenge against dependence leads one to forget that the denunciation of the foreign is a current dimension of populist-type social movements, mentioned above, notably by Eric Hobsbawm.[23]

Similarly, underestimating the political mediation of dependence phenomena makes it difficult, even impossible, to analyze the "newly industrializing nations" (NIN).[24] The rise in these countries of an economy of exportation does not correspond with the thesis of "development from underdevelopment" advanced by the "dependentists"; moreover, this rise obscures the demarcation between the world of the dominators and that of the dominated, only adding to the confusion created by the existence of a communist world and that of the Southern countries rich in natural resources. Economic heterogeneity is such that, in the North as in the South, any binary distinction becomes effectively schematic, rendering economic variables apparently insignificant. Further, amendments proposed by the sociology of dependence are unconvincing. Regarding the economic success of certain southern societies, Cardoso refers to a "dependent-associate development"; here he diverges from the untenable thesis of an irreversible deterioration of economic conditions within the periphery of the international system. However, this hypothesis is largely fictional: contrary to what had been generally thought, notably in a "neoclassical" perspective, the success of the NINs owes little to the pressure of an international economic system, to the regulating and incorporating effects of the world market, and even less to the establishment of any kind of international division of labor. The performance of the new industrial powers is a function of political factors, state financial support, tax breaks, their own political protectionism, and especially their very repressive social policies.[25] States and the political elite have contributed substantial funds, which modify the economic situation noticeably and even the effectiveness of an economic dependence that, without having disappeared, is substantially weakened and altered because the rise of the NINs has even begun to limit technological dependence, as in India or South Korea, and financial dependence, as in the latter.

However, equally revealing, these states have not departed from a single one of the political attributes that we have emphasized. By choosing a political strategy of development, they maintain basic control of it and decrease only in the most illusory sense the overvaluing of politics relative to social space. Because of the very characteristics of this strategy of development, they also maintain the principal characteristics of their neopatrimonial orientation, even strengthening some of them. Attempts to industrialize based fundamentally on very active but very selective policies of exemptions, credits, preferential tariffs in the public sector, and budgetary subsidies give the state the means to accomplish its patrimonial tutelage even more vigorously. State control of the banking sector and credit establishments–or, at least, their direct and indirect control–derives from the axis of the reinforcement of the power elite's patrimonial potential. Similarly, new data coming from the economic transformations of the NINs do not noticeably change the political dependence of their states. This is true, as the examples of Korea and Singapore have shown, but also as can be seen in the "little dragons" like Thailand, the most industrialized countries of South America, and especially Brazil.

A political rereading of dependence relations thus solves the problem of certain incoherences that the diversification of the peripheral economies introduced into classical theories of dependence. Similarly, it eliminates the clumsy category of the "semiperiphery" used by such authors as Wallerstein, who must take account of the impossibility of dividing the "international economic system" into *a* center and *a* periphery. Where should the Mediterranean economies, or those of Central Europe or Scandinavian Europe be placed? Dependence analyzed in terms of location in the interior of a presumably unified system suggests the existence of intermediary positions that only add confusion and incoherence to the explanation. On the other hand, interpreting dependence in terms of actors and political strategies frees one from systemic determinisms and from needing to resort to largely incomprehensible subcategories.

Abandoning systemic constraints is probably the most serious achievement. Neither impotent puppets nor cynical accomplices, the political elites can appear henceforth in the plenitude of their strategic accomplishments. These cannot be appreciated in economic terms, but rather as a function of a history and sociology that separate them from the domain of economics. Their initiatives must, then, be understood in a double sociopolitical context. On one hand, these initiatives have their own national context, composed of a segmented social order, vertical social relations, and a political scene the elites claim to monopolize and control without competition but which is, in fact, structured according to cultural and institutional models that isolate them from society. On the other hand, there is the international environment, which controls the sources of internal finances in these societies, but which also determines the rules of interstate interaction, international norms, international influences, diplomatic orientations, and, therefore, the conditions of access to the international scene. Faced with this double constraint, strategic convergences occur: separated from internal social spaces and challenged in their legitimacy, these elites are well advised to invest in the international scene and to seek patronage from the Northern princes, from whom they can thus obtain protection and resources that will permit them subsequently to reinforce their positions in the center of their own society. But, reciprocally, this clientelist strategy encourages them to systematize their patrimonial practices. This occurs for two reasons: on one hand, because it provides them with resources capable of making these practices effective; and on the other, because their increasing focus on the exterior and their reinforced clientelism widen the gap separating them from their internal social spaces, thus reducing the institutional capacities of communication between governed and governing, and making recourse to neopatrimonial tinkering inevitable. Thus the solidarity between internal and external politics appears profound, verifying the hypothesis of the political foundation of dependence.

Patron States and Client States

Dependence functions more as an interaction than as a system. Rather than determined intangibly by factors beyond human will, it is perpetually created and recreated according to procedures that are in the final analysis very like the clientelist model. This model has been developed to account for internal conditions and to characterize a type of possible relation unifying the governing and the governed within a single society. The links are then defined as personal, dependence-creating, and based "on a reciprocal exchange of favors between two people, the patron and the client, who control unequal resources."[26] The logic of exchange, this inequality, just like the verticality of the relation, applies perfectly to interstate relations. At the same time, its individual construction poses certain problems that could make this conceptualization metaphoric.

Quite evidently, dependence presupposes an exchange of favors: the "patron state" allots to the "client state" goods necessary to its survival according to a procedure identical with what occurs at the level of internal societal functions. In turn, the client state brings favors all the more diverse, whether they concern the use of its territory or the symbolic power it holds as a state on the international scene. The transfer of territorial rights from the patron state corresponds, first of all, to what an abundant literature formerly called the "looting of the third world," referring principally to its diverse and abundant natural resources. It is also known that this transfer fits into the geopolitical aims of the patron state and concerns the granting of military bases or simply of "facilities" for crossing the client state's territory. These two are often demanded as exclusive rights, as Great Britain did with Persia following the Afghan wars in the nineteenth century.

But it is remarkable that in modern times this transfer logic tends to become outrageously diversified, as is revealed by the extension of the practice of the "trash state," in which the client allows the patron to dump industrial waste on its land and in its waters. This kind of agreement concerns in particular the Gulf of Guinea and the Horn of Africa.[27] The client state can just as well withhold the rights available to it as an actor in the international community. The right to vote granted to the francophone countries of Africa is a current practice within international institutions, as revealed, for example, by their refusal to approve the resolutions condemning French policies in New Caledonia presented before the United Nations General Assembly in 1986 and 1987.

The *inequality* of relations is just as evident. It is founded, of course, on a disparity of resources, but also on a difference of location within the international scene: in the internal order, the patron's role comes from his presence at the center of the system, or at least from his proximity and easy access to the center. The relation is henceforth unequal in that abandonment by one's partner has more serious consequences for the client state than for the patron state. For the latter, these risks are minimal, since the loss of a client results simply in a diminution of international influence; for the former, however, they are dramatic, since the loss of a patron means internal asphyxia and ostracism from the international community. In addition, the change of patron is more costly for the dominated state than a change of client is for the dominating state. For example, Ethiopia's change from American patronage to Soviet patronage intensified the dependence of the former empire of the Negus; and the release of Iran from clientelism after the Islamic revolution was such a profound setback for the former empire of the shah that Khomeini had to die before Iran's more "realistic" insertion into the international system, which favored the return to power of young westernized technocrats who agreed to make certain concessions to the powers that had educated them. Also, conforming to the traditional logic of clientelism, movement remains fundamentally asymmetrical, having a different meaning depending on whether it is initiated by the patron or the client. Entrenched in the center, the patrons not only master the language and rules of the international arena but also produce the norms that regulate all the actors.

This asymmetry works at the financial, economic, military, and technological levels, but it also functions symbolically. The patron state defines the symbols that the client state must adopt if it wishes to maintain the relationship. All verbal, musical, and sartorial expression, and all that contributes to the scene of power, develop in the center in order to organize the sociopolitical life of client states. Clientelist relations thus create their own inequality by the practice of forced resemblance: the portraits of Marx, Engels, and Lenin will "emigrate" from Mogadishu to Addis-Ababa with the inversion of clientelist relations from Somalia to Ethiopia;[28] the hammer and sickle of the Soviet flag will decorate the flags of states exchanging Western patronage for Soviet.

What is more, the asymmetry of these relations produces the phenomena of forced constitutional imitation. The client state must bring its own political structures into alignment with those of the patron state. This can be seen in the first wave of political parties devoted solely to mobilization set up by the "progressive" states of Africa, which were modeled on those found in the East; it can also be seen in the call by the Western patrons to their clients to conform to Western, democratic history. The influence of the patron state affects the client state's very identity, whereas the reverse influence is minor, bringing only marginal modifications to the sociopolitical balance in the dominating states. The decisive elements that turn clientelist relations into dependence relations can be found precisely in this asymmetry.

The *verticality* of relations clearly goes in the same direction. This verticality constitutes the logic of clientelism, since the client's behavior privileges relations linking it vertically to the patron over relations linking it to other clients. This process is reinforced during precarious times: when resources are limited, it is both more rational and more cynical to channel them toward the patron, without becoming allied to others who are also in need, in order not to have to share and in order to receive for oneself whatever allocations may exist. Clearly, on the international scale, dependence is largely fed by such calculations, which provide concrete obstacles to the construction of regional subgroups. Pan-Africanism, like Pan-Americanism, suffers directly from this logic; every regional ensemble, moreover, feels the repercussions of the individualism of its member states that aspire to privileged relations with a more powerful exterior state. This is the case, for example, with the Union of Arabic Maghreb, contained by Morocco's foreign policy of privileged partnership with West Europe. It is also the case with the European Community itself, whose integration is held in check by the hesitation of the United Kingdom, which seeks to optimize the benefits of its privileged relations with the United States. Thus, the force of clientelism for the world's states depends on the ability of their bilateral relations to supplant any effectiveness that associative logic might have or, at least, to justify their own durability in a policy of integration that they can only keep in check. From then on, the recomposition at all levels, from the richest to the poorest, of a pyramid of vertical relations helps not only to prevent horizontal alliances from thriving but also to make the relation of dependence functionally attractive, which appears clearly in the competition between the less endowed states.

The individual nature of the clientelist relation, on the other hand, makes it difficult to apply this model internationally. Clientelism highlights individuals only, not collective beings: patron and client are called upon to know each other, to establish personal, nonmediated relations that may even be characterized as emotional and affectionate. In light of the bilateral nature of such exchanges, the idea of this type of relation existing between states is untenable; such an analysis leads the internationalist to a metaphorical concept of clientelism, which implies, in effect, a minimum of conscious, individualized choice and clear-minded acceptance. Thus clientelist relations are totally comprehensible only when they specifically include individuals whose own interests depend on the continuation of clientelism. However, it cannot be denied that state clientelism tends to value personal mediation more than institutional mediation and to involve the leaders of the client states directly as individuals, all the more effectively in that the neopatrimonial nature of clientelized political systems willingly supports such involvement. This process supposes in particular that the favors furnished by the patron are separable and that the prince of the client state draws some material and symbolic advantage superior to what he could receive from either political independence or association. The argument is, certainly, a useful and, all things considered, rather popular way to explain the corruption of certain leaders in the Southern countries. As such, however, this argument is insufficient. Of course, it does have the advantage of closing an essential link in the chain of dependence that Galtung had already foreseen. The at least partial personalization of the allocation furnished by the patron state consolidates the loyalty of the dominated prince to the dominating prince; it also allows for the reproduction of a neopatrimonial order at the periphery of the international system that, as we have seen, fits right into a logic of dependence: the prince of the South becomes, in turn, the patron of his people, the principal dispenser of foreign goods. Consequently, he personally decides how changing international inflows of goods will affect his country, and thus becomes the attentive regulator for his nation of the relations of domination.

Such an analysis, however, is not very fruitful. Aside from being essentially cynical, too easily verifiable to be truly convincing, and totally controlled by the postulates of methodological individualism, it forgets that pure politics contains contradictory forces. The prince can play the card of a populist type of mobilization by relying on the contrary nationalist argument; he can go beyond that and establish his legitimacy as one who contests the international order, and thereby seek support beyond the borders of his own country, as has been done from Nasser to Saddam Hussein, from Sukarno to Nkrumah. Thus the clientelist relation is personalized in a more complex way than what seems to be the case with a strictly utilitarian approach. This relation must be seen in light of the changing strategies of leaders in the peripheral states; it must also include their condition of political socialization and cultural dependence, account for their perception of the international scene and their possibility of taking a part in it, and finally, consider their vision of the Western model of government and of the necessity to import it. As a result, the clientelist relation is built principally by client initiative and understood as the most favorable compromise against a series of contradictory requirements: to administer a Western-style state within the sociopolitical context of another culture; to safeguard skills linked essentially to the administration of the state and which are financially more successful internationally than within each of the dependent societies; and to derive from their role as importer of the model state the maximum protection and promotion of their own political careers. Thus clientelist logic is driven by individuals and simultaneously promoted as the constitutive principle of dependence relations among states.

This logic entails a series of consequences. First, it includes an effect of duration: as in any clientelist relation, the longer dependence lasts, the more effective it is. Loyalty thus becomes the first requirement from both patron and client and becomes a legitimate expectation around which the client organizes both its external and internal policies. Thus when the shah reviled the treachery of his American protector, he revealed that for decades his entire strategy had been developed in order to capitalize on the internal and external benefits of the absolute loyalty that linked him to the United States.[29] In this relation, the patron feels similar constraints. The privilege accorded to Morocco in France's Maghrebian policy transcended manifestly the orientation of parliamentary majorities just as much as it did the political options of the Elysée Palace. Relying on the principle that the sharifian kingdom is a pole of stability in a region subject to numerous upheavals, French policy had to sacrifice many advantages from other quarters because they might offend the sharif. Whether it concerns disputes between Algeria and Morocco, Western Sahara, or the preference given to Morocco in its conflict with Mauritania, or whether it concerns France's actions regarding opposition within Morocco, the idea has always been to anticipate the special favors that the patron can hope to gain from long-term loyalty. The American attitude during the Gulf crisis was the same. The investment represented by several decades of American protection of Kuwait limited drastically any maneuverability the White House could have, as much because a noninterventionist position risked annulling a posteriori the effects of favors already dispensed to the As-Sabah family as because it would ruin the credibility of its protection, also offered to Saudi Arabia and other clients in the region.

In this way, the clientelist relation leads logically to an accumulation of pledges, on both sides, according to the modalities and rhythm that, little by little, give it a real autonomy as far as the very will of the actors is concerned. With a diminution of choice, international relations grow somewhat rigid, to a much greater extent than the constrictive effects produced by the military alliances of the past. The logic of accumulation is, in effect, quite different: the characteristic of clientelism is to engage in continual and daily investments that increase the cost of a break in loyalty the longer the relation has been in effect. Even if the asymmetry of the relation protects the identity of the dependence relation, one cannot escape the fact that the protector's position relative to the client is not that of the free man relative to the slave. In fact, what the patron derives from this relation is essentially based on an international system in conformity, in both structure and distribution, with its own values and interests. In no way is this an absolute mastery either of events or of the daily elaboration of external policies.

Clientelism takes, of course, many forms. The dissimilarity of the situations in Chad, Saudi Arabia, Brazil, and Vanuatu is evident. It would be a mistake, though, to think that the clientelist relation functions only to unite the Northern countries to the least developed Southern ones. The oil boom, while enriching countries with abundant natural resources, has not only modified but perhaps even aggravated dependence situations, as can be seen in the notion of the rentier state. This notion applies to "any state that derives a substantial portion of its revenues from foreign sources in the form of rent."[30] This financial source provides from 70 to 98 percent of the revenues in states as different as Algeria, Libya, Iraq, and Iran are from

Saudi Arabia. The main effect is to increase very substantially the autonomy of the state relative to its social actors, since the quasi-totality of the revenues comes from sources external to the society. The effect of oil on the economies and the sociopolitical life of the producing countries can thus be compared to that of gold in sixteenth-century Spain. The economy of rents encourages passivity in the elites and facileness in the states.[31]

The passivity of the elite, which sets the tone for everyone else, is easily understandable. Rather than undertake the exertions of productivity, they find it much easier to buy large quantities of goods from abroad. Rather than adopt entrepreneurial behavior characteristic of Weberian asceticism, everyone else finds it better to enjoy the lucrative activities of a rentier bourgeoisie, dividing one's time between financial speculation and the acquisition of sinecures in the high-level state bureaucracy. The logic of dependence is here largely reconstituted. By distancing itself from the work of production, especially by abandoning the agricultural sector to buy from abroad, particularly Australia and New Zealand, the rentier bourgeoisie in Iran has noticeably increased its dependence on the exterior. By abandoning the basic functions of production to an immigrant elite in order to specialize in the financial management of rents, the Saudi elite has achieved the same result.[32]

By choosing the easy way, the rentier elites have only intensified the same logic. The abundance of foreign revenues makes taxation seem a most meager source of income. In fact, in a short-term rationale, taxation becomes counterproductive, a hindrance to neopatrimonial strategies that encourage the prince to profitably ally himself with potentially rival elites. The nationalization of oil industries, far from diminishing these effects, only intensifies them, since on one hand, it encourages a more direct and immediately available substitute for tax revenues and, on the other, it encourages the formation of an entire state bureaucracy whose best posts are held by the elite. In this light, the perverse consequences of nationalization appear manifest. While nationalization supports, albeit symbolically, the will to resist mechanisms of dependence, its realization and especially its subsequent implementation reinstitute the effects of dependence. The nationalization of Iranian oil by Mossadegh in 1950 falls more in the context of rivalries internal to the Iranian political system than that of international relations. By promoting symbols of nationalism, Mossadeghism sanctioned even more the will of a young, Western-educated technocratic elite to become cogs in the political machinery rather than to work for a genuine national independence. Nothing up to this point presented a fundamental challenge to the clientelist relations cemented with the Northern states. On the contrary, the enterprise augmented and diversified the network of potential clients by promoting their access to an entirely new state bourgeoisie.

The rentier state, for its part, is strengthened in its relation with others by policies of allocation and distribution. The augmentation of its resources allows it to increase its public expenditures, to improve its credit, to reduce its investments, and thus tangibly reinforce its legitimacy–or in any case its effectiveness–by establishing a genuine policy of well-being and, for the best-off among them, by providing numerous free services. Here too, however, the results are ambiguous. The rise of providence states in the shadows of oil derricks also reinforces dependence, and even the submission of society to the state, since the former is not strengthened along with the latter and has no means at its disposal to reclaim control. Thus constituted, the providence state, financed by external sources, depends on the exterior and finds in its policies of generosity the means to more effectively exercise its own clientelist and patrimonial control over all social spaces.

We must, however, be careful here. In relative terms, the rentier state is far from being the most effective condition of well-being. On the contrary, the differences are patent. If one compares their ranking in terms of GNP to that of the highest indicators of human development (IHD), most of the rentier states are seriously behind. For example, Saudi Arabia loses 37 points, Kuwait 30 points and the United Arab Emirates 43 points. This loss shows that most of the rent is not used in social expenditures but rather directed toward nonproductive sectors and those external to society. Even if in 1988 Kuwait did spend a record amount of $536 per capita on human development, this amount was only 4 percent of its GNP, whereas Zimbabwe spent 12.7 percent, Malaysia 6.4 percent, and Costa Rica 5.4 percent. Globally, in 1990 the IHD placed Kuwait in 48th position, behind Mauritius, Gabon in 50th position, behind Albania, and Saudi Arabia in 69th position, just after Guyana and Tunisia. Life expectancy in Saudi Arabia (64 years) is less than in Vanuatu (69.5 years), in Cape Verde (67 years), and in Algeria, Turkey, Tunisia, and Brazil (65 years).[33] All this just goes to show that a rentier economy, even a very successful one, does not necessarily lead to extraordinary levels of development and that, in any case, the results are not sufficient to draw the countries in question away from dependence relations. In fact, based on the foregoing data alone, one can conclude that rentier policies encourage and strengthen dependence more than diminish it.

Other indicators easily confirm this view. Demographically, most of the Gulf states have understood the conditions of their dependence, being more and more the recipients of support and a skilled workforce from abroad. Choosing primarily nonproductive employment, the Saudi elite abandoned the most important positions to engineers and technicians from elsewhere, in particular from the Arab world. Studies of these immigrant populations reveal that, with the exception of a minority, they do not identify principally with their status as citizens of the Arab world; rather, the most skilled and competent among them identify first of all with either their company or a value system dominated by moneymaking, technocracy, and secular cosmopolitanism.[34] In sum, the social logic of a rentier economy promotes a socialization of the elite toward Western cultural referents and precipitates their integration into social networks dominated notably by numerous clubs centered on loyalty to Western countries, where they, in fact, obtained their university education.

Economically, most of the indicators of dependence remain with the state: the commercialization of oil escapes the producer nations to remain essentially with the large corporations; Arab capital is for the most part managed by Western banks, most of which are American; most of the food is imported; technology, both in oil production and selected efforts at industrialization, is almost exclusively Western in origin.[35] In each of these domains, the forces of dependence control the strategies of the rentier and bureaucratic elites who profit from them.

All these elements extend into foreign policy, where they reconstitute the entirety of clientelist logic. The dependence of rentier states on military equipment produced in North America is practically total. Thus their sphere of activity, even in the very heart of their own region, is basically at zero. The Gulf crisis of 1990 and 1991 showed this very clearly; the ability of Saudi Arabia and its allies to react was directly a function of American engagement on their side. The clientelist relation is particularly evident here: the obligation is clearly reciprocal, since the technological and military dependence of the Gulf states reduces in turn the autonomy of the United States, who, if it refused to intervene, would inevitably jeopardize the soundness of its client as well as the credibility of its patronage. By emphasizing this reciprocity of obligation, clientelist logic is closer to reality than the simple dependentist hypothesis. At the same time, the patron's obligation can be stronger than the client's. Saudi Arabia could remain deaf to American injunctions during the October 1973 war or during the Camp David accords because it knew that diverging from political agreement on the foreign front was not sufficient to jeopardize the protectionist efforts that American diplomacy had for decades worked to establish. At the same time, American insensitivity to the Iraqi threat in the Gulf could have led the Arab states to consider American patronage of little consequence.

By neutralizing, within the limits indicated, the variable constituted by economic development, the example of the rentier states gives a clearer, more exact idea of the forces of clientelist dependence. For the client-dependent, such dependence presupposes access to an international system whose technical, cultural, and symbolic skills it has not mastered. Consequently, it implies loss of sovereignty and the incapacity to act autonomously both on the international scene and in the elaboration of internal policies of redistribution. For the patron, this dependence presupposes not only a vigorous policy of allocation to its client but also a tangible reduction in its choices in the sphere of foreign policy. Though it maintains its sovereignty over the nature of the values allocated, it loses these values by definition at the very moment and by the very intensity of its allocation. The exchange mechanism sets in motion a twofold consequence. The example of the rentier states shows first of all the importance of material and symbolic accouterments: the strategy of the Southern princes is to derive a maximum of gain from this relation in order to make it acceptable to public opinion. The productive countries can effectively help with this requirement. Setting in motion social policies, often more imaginary than real, supplying state-of-the-art technology, donating sophisticated but often unusable military equipment in the absence of an active patronage, are so many elements that obscure the reality of dependence and even allow for the socializing of a population, that would otherwise object, to a genuine feeling of national pride.

The second consequence needs to be more individualized, since it aims to motivate the leadership ranks to be part of the circuit of dependence. Efforts on the part of the patron are, from this point of view, far from negligible and extend to the university education of future elites through their preferential incorporation into the international system. More precisely, these groups receive from such a situation the possibility of attaining particularly lucrative social positions, either by profiting individually from a rentier economy or by integrating themselves into the sociopolitical system by obtaining remunerative and prestigious bureaucratic positions, but which are in fact devoid of any responsibility or real power. In Kuwait, no less than 55.3 percent of the working population are in the bureaucracy.[36]

More generally, the force of clientelist dependence is to engender within the subjected societies a category of leaders who have obtained from patronage positions of dominance that, as they quickly learn, could not be improved upon by promoting an alternative, nationalist strategy. Even more precisely, these leaders strengthen their position as client when they establish by experience that their own power is truly reinforced by exercising the role of "domesticators" of foreign aid. The conjunction of these negative and positive elements of appreciation tends to found the strategy of "client sovereignty" experienced by the former Ghanaian president Kwame Nkrumah.[37] Nevertheless, this conjunction accounts only for the purely utilitarian dimension of the actions of the Southern princes and their entourage; for this reason, it does not entirely explain their behavior.

Dependence Beyond States

A new dimension has recently been added to the sociology of international power, notably by Susan Strange, whose works go beyond the mere relational to reveal the substantive nature of the phenomena of global power.[38] Classical imperialism, based on coercion and on the relations of direct administration, has failed: the colonial empires counted on the mobilization of resources that have not only been devalued, but that many consider to have backfired against those who formerly used them. The dismantling of the French and British empires, then that of the Soviet empire, has shown that the very meaning of power and the means of obtaining it have changed profoundly. From a Weberian perspective, power designates the capacity to impose one's will on another. Integrated into the study of international relations, this conception privileges the idea that states acted coercively, with the goal of enlarging their spheres of influence. Colonial and imperialist logic remained linked to an age-old vision of conquest, where to dominate meant first of all to administer a vast territory. Neocolonialism differed from this construction in form only. It assumed that there would be a continuity from the administration of the dominating state to that of the dominated state, which could transcend the effects of a merely symbolic independence. Fundamentally, the presence of the dominating state remained territorial since it was felt precisely and exclusively through the intermediary of the client state on the client state's own territory.

The growth of transnational exchange has seriously shaken this model. More and more, the resources of power move from place to place, ignoring borders, confounding sovereignties, and bypassing states. From an interstate world, the contemporary international system has evolved toward the "multicentered world" mentioned by Rosenau.[39] In a certain light, it also occasionally resembles what Hedley Bull calls the anarchic society–the erosion that affects the sovereign omnicompetence of states and the actual reduction of centers of power, both of which are results of transnational inflows.[40] Whether these inflows are cultural, economic, religious, demographic, or in the realm of communications, the problem is fundamentally the same: these centers increasingly acquire powers that, by definition, escape the control of states and tend to exist outside any territorial support. From this point of view, the ability to control the diffusion of technical knowhow, to regulate the circulation of money, or to morally or politically influence a religion are not resources that can be investigated through a purely interstate approach to dependence.

American hegemony is largely made up of these bases. Having in the past suffered imperialism in its classical form, the United States has incontestably constructed its "neo-imperialist" power by seeking successfully to master these inflows. Beyond state patronage, the United States has based its power on its capacity to extend credit, to determine whether to encourage or fight inflation in the world economy, and also on its mastery of knowledge, of research, and education of the elite, on its mastery of communication, as well as on the worldwide use of the English language, on the generalization of marketing and management models developed in its own universities, and on technological and military means of assuring its security. These means allow for the exercise of authority over the populace much more than over governments and, eventually, to bypass states if their leaders hesitate to accept American diplomatic orientations. It is clear from this point of view that the range of nationalist and anti-American strategies deployed in the 1960s with the initiative of the great figures of nonalignment, such as Nasser, Sukarno, and Nehru, found its limits in the effectiveness of this approach to power exercised directly on the populace and the elite. Taking charge of the socialization of the latter is particularly important, for it explains, among other things, the fact that the intermediary technocratic elite tends to contain anti-Western pressure, as did the young executive class of the Islamic Republic of Iran, who were for the most part educated in American universities and thus spoke English and based their future careers principally on their American educations.

Of course, the mastery of cultural inflow is more difficult to understand and evaluate.[41] However, the domination of American press agencies, of television programs made in the United States, of trends in music, clothing, and cooking are far from being without effect, though one should not underestimate the importance of the selective and critical receptivity of communication inflow. Investigations have even shown the boomerang effects produced by the diffusion of certain American television programs, notably in the working-class suburbs of Santiago, Chile, during Allende's presidency. No matter how important these reactions and the resulting variations are, they do not diminish the importance of the inflow. At most they displace the locale of their impact to affect the middle classes more than the rest of the population, since the former look more to Western cultural models to assure their own social standing and particularly their integration into the state bureaucracy. This phenomenon has been observed particularly in the Middle East and sub-Saharan Africa.

The mastery of religious inflows is more difficult to integrate into this type of analysis. On one hand, they are by nature more autonomous than the others, both in the context of their production and in the control of their orientation. A neo-imperialist policy can more easily be built by a manipulation of inflows in finance or the media than by those of a religion. On the other hand, they are more likely to be endogenous and to function precisely as a protection against the diffusion of transnational influences coming from the North. From this point of view, the role of Muslim religious influence is particularly significant. However, the renewal among most all the Protestant sects is clearly part of this neo-imperial context. The archbishop of Guatemala, Monsignor Prospero Penados, himself stated in January of 1989 that the United States supported "non-Catholic groups . . . to consolidate [their] economic and political power in Latin America" because "the evangelists defend an individualist conception of eternal salvation that coincides fully with the position of liberalism and capitalism."[42] Without taking the conspiracy thesis too far, and especially without forgetting that most of these sects arise within the ambient cultural context, it must be acknowledged that they are in a line of development that, in its origins, blends with American cultural history and that they are trying to supplant a Roman Catholic Church from another culture's history and value system. It is difficult to establish the effects of this countersocialization; it is also just as difficult to deny that it can be integrated into the transnationally inspired neo-imperial model.

In any case, it is certain that the double disconnection between power and territory, and between power and interstate activity favors a new international order that privileges the United States in relation to Europe, and formerly in relation to the Soviet Union, and that easily complicates the problematic of dependence. This problematic designates a system more than relations among states or, more exactly, makes states and interstate relations only the components of this system; it also noticeably reevaluates the role of mediator played by all the other actors in the diffusion and reception of transnational influences that emerge as the principal components of a system of dependence.

The Deceptions of Sovereignty

Whatever may be the methods and mediations by which it functions, the dependence relation is first of all political and is part of the deceptions of sovereignty. Dispossessed directly or obliquely by a social network beyond its control, the dependent state must deal with three types of deception, each having to do with three sectors essential to its sovereignty: the diplomatic function, the coordination of socioeconomic functions, and the organization of public space.

The deception of the diplomatic function is probably the oldest and derives directly from traditional state logic and paradigms of power. The first manifestations of one state being taken control of by another lie most often in the dominating state's efforts to dismantle the dominated state's expression of sovereignty internationally. The treaty of 1814 between Britain and Persia thus had the principal function of sealing Britain's promise not to intervene in the *internal* affairs of Persia, in exchange for the shah's commitment to let no foreign power traverse its territory other than Britain and, especially, to fight its Muslim neighbors in the case of an Anglo-Afghan conflict.[43] Similarly, from the beginning of the nineteenth century, the goal of the region's great powers was to establish direct relations with the leaders and tribal chiefs in order to break up monopolies and disrupt the diplomatic functions of which the shah of Persia or the khedive of Egypt took advantage. Inversely, but by the same logic, diplomacy was frequently used to encourage a direct intervention of the Western powers in the internal sociopolitical lives of the dominated states. Diplomacy was freely utilized to obtain precise and concrete engagements from the Muslim sovereign that would benefit the foreigners and Christian minorities who were his responsibility. In a treaty between Süleyman the Magnificent and Francis I in 1535, the sultan exempted from taxation the French people residing in the Ottoman empire; at the same time, bilateral engagements with each of the Western states established the right of international protection that thereafter benefited the diverse Christian communities, the interdiction against condemning to death Muslims who converted to Christianity, and the alleviation, even the disappearance, of legal inequalities that differentiated the Muslims and Christians within the empire. Similarly, the installation by international treaty of the capitulation system recognized, in 1569 for France and 1601 for England, the right to remove their own nationals from Ottoman jurisdiction and consign them to the judicial authority of their own consuls.[44] The progressive extension of this practice to protected minorities, even to those Muslims who requested it, quickly led to the constitution of a foreign state within the Ottoman state, as in the Persian state and many others as well, and to effectively dismantling the logic of sovereignty.

The deception of diplomacy is thus at the very center of the logic of dependence. Very ancient in its achievements and very clearly preceding even the practice of colonization, it constitutes one of the most evident basic elements, since on one hand, it follows from the imbalance of power and, on the other, it leads to a progressive increase in the dismantling of the dominated state's sovereignty. In the evolution of capitulations, there is notably no clear limit between the recognition of exorbitant rights accorded to foreign communities and the establishing of consulary control over the principal political functions of the dominated state. For this reason, the deception of diplomacy quickly becomes an instrument for other ends, laying the groundwork, in particular, for colonial domination.

In the postcolonial era, the same ambiguity remains, even if the unanimously proclaimed will to go beyond and castigate outdated practices leads to even more subtle distinctions. The diplomatic function is used more informally, in such a way as to maintain a facade of sovereignty for the dominated state. It is distinguished from intervention more clearly in the internal workings of the sociopolitical order, which freely takes other paths to its ends. As a judicial mark par excellence of state sovereignty, the diplomacy of the weak state is no longer taken over by the strong state through unequal treaties or the practice of capitulations, but by the common application of clientelist logic: the dominating state becomes the patron state through an image of itself as the bestower of a rare resource that allows it to obtain, in turn, the dominated state's participation in or support of its diplomatic goals, particularly within international institutions or in the context of regional military conflicts.

This logic can also allow for a similarly unequal process of exchange, but in contrast to the clientelist relation, it is not *durable* and does not constitute *loyalty*. The evolution of China's attitude in the Gulf crisis resembles the use of Chinese diplomacy by the United States, based on an inequality that created a de facto dependence. The People's Republic did not initially hide its hostility to all military intervention against Iraq, and several official delegations went from Beijing to Baghdad to communicate this position. Even so, China did not veto Resolution 678 of the Security Council, which expressly authorized force. However, on the eve of this debate, President Bush announced his intention to receive the Chinese minister of foreign affairs, Quian Quichen, to whom he accorded an audience a few days later. At the same time, the United States decided to no longer oppose a loan of $114,300,000 by the World Bank to China to stimulate its economy, particularly in the areas of technology and rural industry. Also, it is well known that annual loans of about two million dollars had been granted to China before the repression following the "Beijing Spring" and that the international community, led by the United States, had decided to end these loans to punish the Chinese government for its policies.[45]

The logic of dependence appears here in three aspects. China, which cannot finance its development alone, needs foreign aid and thus needs to integrate itself into the international community, for which it must make concessions either by changing its internal policies or by reorienting its foreign policies. To choose the first of these options, including the turn taken by the events of Tiananmen, would require its current leaders to step down, whereas the second option would obviously require less drastic action. As important as it is, a concession made in foreign policy was thus more acceptable and more rational: it would require in any case that the Chinese government abdicate part of its diplomatic sovereignty, in exchange for a minor accommodation on the part of the United States, by which, on the material level, it would pay its share of a collective financing and, symbolically, by justifying that the moment had arrived to lift sanctions. Sino-American relations reveal the same inequality of obligation that one finds in clientelist relations, and thus here one finds the essential characteristic of all dependence relations.

Yet dependence does not stop at a simple claiming of diplomatic sovereignty. China's vote on Resolution 678 does not indicate only the reorientation of China's diplomacy and of its declared principles and policies. It inevitably implies a loss of credibility with its privileged partners, particularly in the context of an attempted reopening to the third world. For that, this reorientation involves the risk of dissolution or at least the weakening of its own sphere of influence and its clientele. Even if China had never been a protector of Iraq, its public determination not to stand for a policy of force strongly discredited the value of its patronage in light of its vote on

Resolution 678. So beyond a timely deceptiveness in its own diplomacy, China passively witnessed a situation of dependence that led to a loss of the power capital that would allow it to accede to the role of patron state.

Finally, the vote on Resolution 678 was not an ordinary political act, since it created precedence and pronounced on the meaning of international morals. By associating with it, China played a role in both the definition of the right of intervention and in the construction of what is explicitly seen as the beginning of a new normative international order. Its vote thus helped obscure, even to abolish, and in any case to eliminate the conflictual nature of international relations on which it had based one of the fundamental principles of its foreign policy. By thus joining the international community and its order, China clearly proclaimed that the abandonment of diplomatic sovereignty is the price to pay for receiving material support from an international integration in which it plays a role in name only.

This deception in the diplomatic function's normative dimension is one of the more important, and one of the most stable, marks of the dependence relation. Diplomatic conformity clearly constitutes one of the surest methods a weak state can use to protect itself and is a more rational choice than recourse to speeches and protest. Consequently, inter-African organizations and each of the African states individually have made a special effort to develop procedures for the transition of power, to invoke territorial heritage based on the colonial era, to proclaim the inviolability of borders, and to claim the right of independence and national sovereignty.[46] In the vulnerable situation in which the dominated state invariably finds itself, the minimal guarantee of the right to the status quo seems the best strategy against temptations to restructure the international order according to criteria external to the Western conception of the state and the political geography that results from it. That is how it has been with the numerous failed attempts to reconstitute the *Umma* or to form a federation among several African states. The logic of dependence causes conformity and conservatism to predominate over protest and challenge, thus promoting the continuation of an international order whose active denunciation would be too risky for any state acting alone. It is in this perspective that the Southern states appear as the most active and assiduous supporters of international institutions and that one finds in Africa, for example, the greatest number and the greatest density of international governmental organizations, each fastidiously reproducing the logic of the state as well as international law as it is currently constituted.

*

The deception of socioeconomic functions of states is an initially more discreet mark, but one that increasingly entrenches the logic of dependence. In postcolonial situations, its role is crucial. While overcoming or circumventing formal independence, it leads the dominating states to successfully incite the dominated states to manage their socioeconomic environments in accordance with the rules of a market economy and those of neoliberalism. We know from Polanyi that both have their own histories and cultural foundations. We also know that most non-Western societies are characterized by a complex network of informal and community-based economies that are not easily reducible to market logic. We know too that the importance of the public economic sector derives in part from the neopatrimonial strategy of the princes, but also in part from the need to eliminate underemployment among the newly elite. Finally, we know that the policies of government funding for basic necessities, though representing a significant financial burden, contributes significantly to maintaining social peace. However, the evolution of aid policies in developing countries has tended to upset these givens by ignoring, for the most part, the social and cultural parameters at work in these countries. The failure of economic policies of bilateral cooperation sanctioned in the early 1980s the rise of multilateralism, which gave the International Bank for Reconstruction and Development (IBRD) and the International Monetary Fund (IMF) basic economic supervision of the dominated nations. This transfer of jurisdiction led these two international institutions to impose, in exchange, certain accommodations with a strongly neoclassical orientation. From the essentially political negotiations that reflected their interstate nature, dependence was changed henceforth into an economic type of interaction. Aid depended on the dominated nation's agreeing to structure its economic landscape in conformity with the views and options of the most developed Western countries. The resulting type of dependence has two aspects: the procedure tends to give the South the heaviest burden of accommodation to a world economy in a generalized crisis; it also leads the Northern countries to influence national choices of the South and to transfer to them their models of economic development at a pace all the more rapid and dramatic the less developed a given country is considered to be. Exportation toward the South of models forged in the North tends to accelerate the more inappropriate these models are, thus creating a vicious circle.[47]

This vicious circle is, it seems, easily activated, since the combination of multilateralism and drastic readjustment appears to reassure and to interest each of the patron states individually. For example, the budgetary costs of bilateral aid and its relative ineffectiveness have led the European countries to accept this new practice, though seeking to amend it in a manner more formal than real. The Brussels Commission thus had the Council of Ministers adopt a resolution, dated May 31, 1988, that supported a harmony between development and accommodation, though the concrete conditions of such a unity were never established.[48] Britain seemed committed to encouraging those states in its sphere of influence that have most clearly opted in favor of accommodation policies; whereas France, initially somewhat critical, seemed to go along with the resolution all the more because, since the multilateral institutions took charge of such drastic effects, its budgetary constraints seemed to have lightened and thereby revived its own bilateral aid on more effective and profitable bases.[49] Far from being perceived as incompatible with state patronage, adjustment policies set in place at the multilateral level have been experienced as a functional complement that partially relieves the patron state from the heaviest share of the financial burden while ultimately allowing it to profit most fully from its function as patron.

For these reasons, the "IMF policy" reflects the shape of a new type of dependence that completes, rather than surpassing or negating, the clientelist type of dependence, and introduces a sharing of the tasks. Multilateralism promotes an increasing intervention by the Northern countries into the socioeconomic lives of the dependent states, the diffusion of models of development, and a greater, more vigorous interference in their economies because of the greater possibilities for anonymity multilateral action offers. In addition, the maintenance and reorientation of bilateralism permits a consolidation of the advantages of political dependence "on more solid grounds."[50] Thus leaders in the Northern nations seldom pay attention to informed criticism of accommodation policies. These policies are criticized for being recessionist; for causing enormous social costs, among others in the areas of health and education; for worsening poverty in the most disadvantaged classes; for disrupting production destined for local consumption, notably traditional agriculture; and for increasing unemployment in conjunction with the reestablishing of public services.

The solidarity of these perspectives and the internalization of this complementarity appear, moreover, quite clearly in the policies of cooperation set up by the patron states. In its aid policy to Latin America, the American government insists explicitly on the condition of debt renegotiation, linked directly to a restructuring of the economy and the deepening of diplomatic loyalties. Thus, in December of 1990, George Bush was able to assure President Menem that Argentina would profit from the Brady plan and that its foreign debt would be reduced; he also praised the reorientation of Argentinean economic policies in the direction of free exchange, of privatization, of an opening to foreign investment, and also the positive results for American diplomacy by two warships sent to the Gulf. The orientation toward Brazil is comparable, as can be seen in American support for the Collor plan, which also supported privatization; the new Brazilian head of state opted simultaneously for a much more conformist diplomacy than that of his predecessor, José Sarney, who for the first time in Brazil's history paid an official visit to the Soviet Union.[51]

The combination of bilateralism and multilateralism maximizes the possibilities of the deception in the socioeconomic functions of states while being compatible with the survival and deepening of clientelist relations. In sum, this combination prolongs dependence through images: policies of restructuration and policies of accommodation have not only organized a certain type of regulation of the international economic system and certainly of maintaining economic dependence in the Southern nations by subjecting them to inequalities in the treatment they receive as a response to the international crisis, but also and especially of promoting the universalization of the liberal model and presenting market economy as the only economy possible. Behind this triumphant neoliberalist victory lie all sorts of rhetorical variations about the end of History: the extinction of the competing economic models at a moment when those African nations with socialist leanings appeal to the IMF; the convergence of economies toward a single model; the legitimation of dependence, henceforth perceived as the normal expression of an obligatory reference by all the developing nations to the economic order conceived and practiced by the most developed Northern nations. Diplomatically, this orientation constitutes the surest defense against offers of patronage by other nations, whether they be from China or the former Soviet Union.

The evolution of the Maghrebian countries, Tunisia and especially Algeria, exemplify the movement from an interventionist and even socialist economy toward a progressively liberal model that would seemingly bring about political and diplomatic changes as well. With its Sixth Plan of 1981, Tunisia called for a "liberalization of its economy, a loosening of strict controls, and a strengthening of the mechanisms of liberalization." With the following plan, private savings were encouraged, particularly for starting small and medium-sized businesses, which, for the first time, accounted for 50 percent of investments. Thus the state began a reform of the tax system, moving toward the decentralization of economic decision making. In July 1985, legislation of public enterprises was effected that increased their number from 307 to 500. Similarly, the state ceded numerous assets in order to hasten its withdrawal from economic activities. Finally, as a final end to the incentives instituted by the IMF, President Ben Ali decided on August 12, 1989, to raise the prices of certain products by 10 to 15 percent, notably the price of bread by 14 percent, in order to move toward true market values.[52]

Thus the "global model of socialist development" that Habib Bourguiba had ordered Ahmed Ben Salah, in 1962, to set up with the purpose of better marking Tunisia's independence from France, had clearly come to an end.[53] At the time, this change was important and was considerably orchestrated, notably by the subsequent transformation of the Neo-Destour into the DSP (Destourian Socialist Party), a move that clearly marked its anti-imperialist, anticapitalist, and leftist orientations, while the Zain (President Zain Al Abidin) confiscated land owned by former colonists. In the 1980s, the logic of dependence clearly favored a reversal: entering the ranks of a neoliberal economy, Tunisia found itself deprived of one of its marks of independence, whereas the state recomposed its economic functions in a way that at last clearly affirmed its conformity to the international economic system.

The parallel transformations experienced by Algeria are even more significant. There, the reference to socialism was even more marked, and Algeria's role in the affirmation of national identity and in the construction of its diplomacy was much more clearly defined. The visit by the president of the World Bank to Algiers in July 1989 was the culmination of an extremely significant process. With the five-year plan begun in 1985, the state was required to withdraw from the economic machinery, leaving it to other agents, enterprises, and households. Private savings were openly encouraged. The private sector was recognized and even given crucial functions, since it had to meet the "essential needs of citizens, of exportation, of contributions to the creation of jobs, and regional development."[54] At the same time, state farms were ended and a new economic policy was put into place that, without espousing the radical characteristic of the Tunisian model, tended to valorize the same neoliberal orientations. The political implications of this evolution were evident: Algeria had to accept the recommendations of an international institution that it had previously denounced as imperialist; as a result, it had to modify its economic landscape, adopt a Western model of development, and renounce the socialist symbolism that was the sole doctrinal mark of its identity as a nation and of the NLF. As a result, the NLF found itself adrift, which left the field free to Islamic protest. Yet this reorientation was accepted and even desired and effected by a new technocratic generation, who found in the shift toward liberalism a means to deny its responsibility for a failing economy and to open itself to the exterior in order to gain new advantages. Thus the deception of the socioeconomic function of the Algerian state resulted from both external pressure and expectations from within. The evolution toward economic conformity was supported by common interests, which increased its chances for durability.

This logic resulted in a convergence of Maghrebian economies, which was immediately echoed on the political front. The homogenization of socioeconomic structures promoted the construction of the Union of the Arabic Maghreb, officially founded at the February 1989 summit in Marrakech, precisely in the context of economic restructuring. Each partner followed the same process. Having already set up a liberal economy, Morocco increased privatization and the withdrawal of the state while reactivating its stock exchange. Mauritania, under the injunction of the IMF, abandoned its shares in the banking and industrial sectors. Even Libya did not escape this logic, since in March 1987 the government turned away from its former policy, putting an end to state monopoly of industrial properties; concurrently, small businesses liberalized and a small sector of PME (Petites et Moyennes Enterprises) appeared. In their use of models and solutions that became commonplace and increasingly similar, the governments of the region revealed their awareness of the dominant orientations of world economy, which resulted in a parallel restriction of the breadth and significance of their own political identities and a renunciation of intent to create their own particular distinctions and political visions. This dynamic of conformity, which engendered one of convergence, promoted the establishment of negotiations with the actors on whom the future of new economic policies depended: the IMF, the World Bank, the United States, or the European Union, whose unification constituted another element of constraint for the Maghreb.

The deception of the functions of institutional innovation preceded the other deceptions and covers, by extension, the entirety of dependence logics. European aid to Egypt had thus been subordinated during the financial crisis of 1876 to constitutional reforms that instituted notably the principle of a taxation vote by the Egyptian parliament, which conformed to a model initiated by Western constitutional history. Almost one century later, Anwar Sadat abandoned Soviet patronage and turned to the West in order to deal with the aftermath of the October 1973 war. He thus set up the conditions of a multiparty system that succeeded the single-party system and adopted the Western pluralist model.

These more or less forced alliances can be analyzed for their symbolic function, since they appear immediately as the mark of patronage, an essential element in the enunciation of the exchange at work between the patron and its client. For this reason, institutional conformity appears to be formal before it is real: the client states of the Soviet Union quickly set up a single-party socialist system and incorporated Marxist symbols; the client states of the Western democracies took on parliamentary institutions that were most often artificial and integrated into their representative system principles that established the separation of powers and cultivated symbolic references to their tutelary state.

Beyond this gesture, which is a privileged element of the logic of dependence and probably even its manifesto, the dynamic of political imitation merits consideration at two other, more serious and more crucial levels of analysis: as a sign of the cultural attraction exerted by the institutional models of the Northern countries, as if revealing the strategies of an actor, and the strategies of the dominated society's elite who reap benefits and resources from their function as importers of symbolic and institutional goods from the dominating states. These two properties are united: the universalist claim of the Western model of government would remain merely formal if it did not develop a particular meaning or were not noticeably echoed within the elite of the South. For the strategy of importation employed by the Southern elite would attain neither the same level of performance nor the same meaning if it were not reinforced by the very content of the institutional products imported: actor and culture are two indissociable elements of sociological analysis.

For these reasons, forming the political-institutional system has a separate status. By acquiring the diplomatic function, the dominant state proceeds by instrumentalization; by acquiring the socioeconomic function, it constrains its clients to enter into an international economic system in which it derives maximum material advantages; on the other hand, by acquiring the function of political and institutional design, the dominant state acquires no immediate resources, but is content to activate an international conformity that aligns a multicultural world along the lines of its own model. The inequality resulting from dependence can be appreciated in two ways: in terms of the unequal chances of each culture to inspire and control social action and innovation within a particular collectivity, and in terms of the unequal performance of social collectivities more or less hampered by the obligation to fashion themselves according to external cultural models.

This double paradox, which is probably the basis of the logic of dependence, illustrates its essentially political character and separates the effects of structure and the effects of manipulation that make it possible, and finally and especially, determines what constitutes the clientelist relation between dominant states and dominated states. The paradox thus brings to light the essential elements of a problematic of dependence: What is the foundation of both the universalist claim and the impulse to export the Western model? What principle drives the importation strategies practiced by the leading actors of dependent societies?

2. The Universalist Claim of the State

What sociology says about power can also be said of dependence: the less it operates by coercion and constraint the more effective and dynamic it is. As with any relation of domination, dependence finds its surest support in the fact that no one actively promotes it, either intellectually or politically. In reality, it is tautological to argue that Western models of government are universal, since of all political orders, only the state proclaims itself universal, and it does so with a postulate it cannot divest itself of since that postulate is perceived by everyone as constitutive of its definition.

The Invention of the Universal City

As any typological exercise will show, the state is the only form of government that systematically impugns all particularist identities. The Greek city grew out of individual groups that created its identity, which it intended to perpetuate.[1] Patrimonial monarchies constitute themselves on the particularity of their dynastic center. Empires construct themselves around a specific culture that they intend to defend, promote, or possibly expand. But the universal is nothing more than a fictional and uncertain finality, realized precisely by negating the culture of the other. Finally, segmentary systems constitute the simple, nonmediated realization of a communal social order, and thus they are built essentially on the particular.

The state works completely differently. It is constructed in direct reference to reason and can claim nothing short of universality, nor can its functioning principles aim at anything other than reducing the variety of political orders that make up the international system. Since, in contrast to all other entities, it implies an autonomy in its political sphere and the formation of a public space different from civil society, the state becomes complete only by distinguishing itself from the singular, whether that be private interests, specific religious groups, or community groups. This position is not only intellectual, for its truth is borne out in the daily activities of the state and through its functioning within an international system that reflects its own image.

In terms of legitimacy, the reference to reason constitutes a threefold rupture from the past. First, it constitutes a hierarchy that places the state at the summit of all categories. Corresponding to the origin of the state as a model, rational-legal legitimacy is in essence superior to other formulas of legitimacy and has led diverse sociological traditions to associate the state with modernity. Moreover, the use of reason introduces the formidable arguments of convergence and the end of History. As the only governmental formula to conceive of itself explicitly as outside the singular, the state can only be a generalized entity among the entirety of cultural entities by representing "progress" and by entering the Comtian positivist stage. Daniel Bell had already enunciated this thesis in the 1960s; it reappeared thirty years later in the writings of Fukuyama.[2] Reason inevitably triumphs over history, commanding the field, setting to flight all other types of social construct. Finally, science and the state inevitably fit into a transitive relation: the state does not defend itself as being a good political system, but rather as being the logical choice for all efforts to diffuse knowledge.

Reference to public space carries the same dynamic. The state derives part of its identity from its ability to abstract politics from society, to construct itself apart from society, in its own space. This is the reverse of the imperial order, which supposes a total fusion of politics and society. This work of differentiation is also an attempt to emancipate traditional and particularist allegiances; and based on that emancipation, it inevitably considers itself the source of progress, of new rights, and especially, because of the allegiances that characterize citizenship, the producer of an egalitarian and universalist conception of political relations. Human rights thereby become rights of humans and of citizens and are presented as universal rights. Since it effaces singularity within societies, the construction of public spaces seeks to efface differences among societies: by presenting itself as both emancipatory and individualizing, it becomes a universal way to recompose social bonds. In these conditions, all community resistance, all expressions of allegiance other than that of citizen inevitably become a regressive resurgence of the past. Culture itself is displaced: from an expression of identity or collective consciousness, it is reduced either to a formula of legitimation of the political system under the term "political culture," or simply to a residual principle abandoned to anthropological curiosity.

Western political science is a valuable tool for verifying these hypotheses. The culturalist adventure has significantly oscillated from the desperate attempt to resuscitate the ideas of the founding fathers of this discipline and the militant will to envisage culture as a means of reproducing a model of civic integration, found notably in the Anglo-Saxon behaviorist trend. The influence of Durkheim and Weber resulted in culture being relegated to premodern forms of government. Following the French thinker, sociology in effect assimilated culture and religion to valorize the sacred as a "shorthand expression of all collective life,"[3] but also to accept that the modern state indicates the "retreat of the Olympian gods" and the substitution of a new form of integration in place of integration by means of culture.[4] Sociologists who followed the German thinker distinguished the blueprint of *The Protestant Ethic*, which noted the production of thought dominated by reason, from religious categories, which, according to Talcott Parsons, constituted "culture-niches," genuine impasses of social modernization.[5] In such constructions, cultural analysis is strangely confused with the analysis of distant "cultural spheres," since, but for rare exceptions, cultures proper to Western societies were neglected other than to study phenomena of resistance among minorities or subcultures. Strangely, Weber and Durkheim present the same enigma to their commentators. Weber fully developed the logic of his argument in *The Protestant Ethic* with his assertion that "only the west had at its disposal a judicial system and an administration of such a high degree of legal and formal perfection,"[6] thereby leading his followers to present not only Protestant culture but, in fact, Western culture as the chosen culture that draws its exceptional status from its exclusive capacity to attain the level of reason. With this assertion, Weber discounted the validity of comparing political systems based on the concept of culture, because he considered the state an order of domination founded on both culture and reason, with culture being able only to explain why, in other histories, the state did not form. Culture thus became a residual way to explain events that could not be based on revivalist propositions, and which could conceive a modernity proper to Islam or to Indian culture. Similarly, Durkheim detects an even more evident dilemma. In *Division of Labor in Society*, he analyzes the retreat of religion and the progressive triumph of a secularized state as well as an individual morality, whereas in *Formes élémentaires*, where he proposes that "almost all social institutions are born in religion," the cultural explanation prevails.[7] Again, the acceptance of Western modernity is, at least implicitly, confirmed; the force of the cultural explanation fades before an analysis in terms of the universal.

The reversal affecting cultural analysis since the 1960s has been very significant. While the Africanists and the Orientalists have conducted their research in terms of identity, the political scientists in the West have taken an opposite direction. For them, to study a culture consists in researching the system of attitudes that could be universalized and, thus, assure the model of modern government a maximum of stability and integration. For example, Almond and Verba defined the contours of a civic culture, which saw the allegiance of citizens as very concrete, and also allowed for a classification of different societies in terms of performance, in which Britain held first place and Mexico practically the last.[8] Similarly, studying Norway, Harry Eckstein did not try to grasp the cultural foundations of the Norwegian political system as much as he tried to establish the outlines of a system of attitudes with the greatest potential to support the stability of democratic institutions.[9]

Beyond even the idea of culture, all aspects of political science attempt to validate the progression of the Western models of government toward universalization. Long the dominant approach, the systematist tradition employed a transcultural representation of political relations that included typologies only to classify types of systems in terms of their political capacity. Technically, modern political interaction is all the more effective because it is neutral and because it makes ideological references abstract, whereas culture in this type of construction can function only when it reinforces the capacities of the system. This is precisely why such authors as Lucian Pye and Gabriel Almond consider secularized political orders as developed, that is, as those in which the sacred gave way to reason and a political technology deriving from the state.

It is definitely because of such a postulate that the concept of political development came about. This concept was meant to describe how the universal was realized within non-Western societies, but it also interpreted as inevitably transitory–and thus functional–the manifestations of authoritarianism that structured the political life of developing societies. Though severely criticized and less and less accepted by the scientific community, developmentalism nevertheless had definite political influence because of beneficial exchanges between the leaders of the Western world and those identified as "non-Western" or "developing."

Developmentalist political science presents a double advantage for the Western prince, that of super-legitimizing his order and justifying the constitution of an international system based on his legal system and its institutions. For the prince of other societies, it opens considerable strategic perspectives.[10] First, it legitimizes his recourse to authoritarianism, a sacrifice as functional as it is inevitable, in order to arrive at democracy. In effect, it allows for variations in participation caused by varying levels of capacity attained by the political systems. Furthermore, developmentalist political science offers the possibility of attaining legitimacy by being a bearer of modernity, as a means of support against representatives of traditional resources of power. Though traditional authority is difficult to delegitimize, it can be weakened or limited by the active mobilization of an entire arsenal of modernizing symbols that disqualify any power seeking to exist on the periphery. Finally, and paradoxically, developmentalist logic allows the leader to point at the constricting effects of the gap between modern and developing societies in order to denounce publicly the practices of dependence and the socioeconomic failures it brings. This skillful combination of an apologetic developmentalism internally and a denunciatory developmentalism externally is found frequently in African and Asian societies. It can be detected in Nasser's 1955 discourse conjointly denouncing feudalism and imperialism, in that of Félix Houphouët-Boigny when he sought to legitimize his power by ideas from the modern state that disqualified the representatives of traditional authority, and also by the explicit challenge from the Western states and their inability or their refusal to support the trading price of raw materials.[11]

The tangible effect of this strategic convergence was to export the state model as a form of government, but also and especially to reconstruct the international scene as the exact image of state logic. The discourse of *Leviathan* combines precisely the elements of a sociological hypothesis that takes account of the process by which the state is invented as well as that of the philosophical discourse that legitimizes universal reason.[12]

The *sociological* hypothesis shows through clearly in Hobbes's famous chapter 17 of *Leviathan*, "Of the Causes, Generation, and Definition of a Commonwealth," when he affirms that "the final cause, end, or design of men, who naturally love liberty, and dominion over others, in the introduction of that restraint upon themselves, in which we see them live in commonwealths, is the foresight of their own preservation, and of a more contented life thereby."[13] This functional requirement is satisfied by the "covenant of every man with every man, in such manner, as if every man should say to every man, *I authorize and give up my right of governing myself, to this man, or to this assembly of men, on this condition, that thou give up thy right to him, and authorize all his actions in like manner.*"[14] Thus Hobbes's response to the functional requirement that he had posed takes up the proxy formula, which clearly includes all the characteristics that sociology generally ascribes to the state. First, the differentiation of the political sphere, which is based on the very specificity of its functions and on its existence as a site of remission. Second, the individualization of social relations having the *individually* rational character of this remission. That character is the precedence of citizen allegiance, which is almost a tautology, since this allegiance is guaranteed by the exchange of advantages that occur between the individual and the republic, known, therefore, as "mortal God."[15]

Moreover, this sociological hypothesis can be verified twice over. Empirically, works by late medieval and Renaissance historians in Europe show that the hypothesis describes rigorously the very process of construction of the state, the context of endangering the security of both goods and people, the practice of abdication formally approved by the social actors, weakened nobles, bourgeois concerned with the security of the marketplace, and peasants affected by the uncertainties of nascent rural migration. In particular, this hypothesis corresponds manifestly to changes in the social structure, when one establishes how the Western state was born from the impoverishment of communal structures, notably village communities and familial communities, and from the inability of civil societies to give full measure to their associative structures.[16]

Philosophically, Hobbes's hypothesis supposes that recourse to a proxy is the only formula able to satisfy the protection requirement. However, sociological analysis concludes otherwise: community constructs of the social were durable and presented an obstacle to any conclusion of the Hobbesian pact, while supplying other possible ways to provide security. Thus the community is perhaps conceived as the prime place for the protection of the individual, since history at the end of the Middle Ages shows that the state imposed itself precisely because of the inadequacy of village and familial communities.[17] Hobbes seems to reject this hypothesis when he specifies that "[n]or is it the joining together of a small number of men, that gives them this security; because in small numbers, small additions on the one side or the other, make the advantage of strength so great, as is sufficient to carry the victory; and therefore gives encouragement to an invasion."[18] By establishing this point, the British philosopher falls incontestably into universalist logic, whose traces can be found in a number of traditions: Ibn Khaldūn, for example, shows the devastating effects of cohesive communal groups when they lead tribes to attack and conquest. On the other hand, conclusions offered and the solutions practiced do not seem universally shared, since this same Ibn Khaldūn considered that the principles of the state's reconstruction lay in cohesive communal groups.[19] By stipulating that the organizing principles of social bonds had a greater chance of guaranteeing social order than completely altering them and replacing them with other bonds, the Maghrebian writer acted as a sociologist, opening a debate that would long remain compelling. Echoed by contemporary anthropologists, he saw paradigms that receive considerable interest even today: in the work of Clifford Geertz, in his reference to tribal identity in Arab towns, or in that of Gellner with his idea that the loss of communal identity in cities implies the establishment of substitutes that he describes as clientelism or, in Morocco, as sharifism.[20]

Sinologists too have noted that the current vision of the Chinese imperial, bureaucratic, centralized state gives only a partial idea of sociopolitical reality, and probably even the least relevant part. After the third-century B.C. experience with legism, the Chinese imperial order initially took the form of a communal and antibureaucratic (*fengtian*) government in which politics was not built on an abdication of communities, but rather by establishing a correspondence of communal, familial, and peasant life with the imperial center.[21] Each dynasty could install its power after a more or less explicit pact between the new political center and the reconstruction of rural familial communities. The Tang dynasty elaborated an agrarian ordinance that redistributed land so that each familial unit had not only the resources it needed but also the necessary surplus to enable the payment of taxes, which in turn supported the empire. There was nothing Hobbesian about this agreement. It did not sanction an exchange of liberty for security, nor did it produce sovereignty, but it did assure social harmony, whose maintenance alone guarantees that the imperial dynastic center will endure. Moreover, in such a model, the political function is almost entirely submerged in the social order. Far from having its own resources, the imperial center has value only through its capacity to benefit from the mobilization of communal structures; far from commanding priority in citizen allegiance, it must incorporate agrarian communities within itself; far from constructing itself on a remission of individual liberty, it must protect the equilibrium between its own intentions and those of social communities. To have power in this context does not mean to intervene, to act, to transform, but rather to be the one exempt from deciding.

This model, seriously shaken by both its own decay and the increase in westernization, was gradually replaced by a centralized state bureaucracy (*junxian*) separate from society and dissociated from economic life. Since this model contains certain elements of traditional legism that had predominated in the early period of imperial China, but since it is also related much more obviously to the Western state tradition, this model recombines several givens of the Hobbesian pact: the construction of a differentiated and sovereign political space and the individual's direct allegiance to the political center, thereby forming a complex bureaucracy. But Yves Chevrier has shown that this model did not definitively succeed.[22] For its part, the Maoist system tried to reconnect with the old *fengtian* tradition by basing itself on peasant mobilization, on the dissolution of political functions in social spaces, and on the reconstitution of an economic and political differentiation from the system implemented by Deng Xiaoping, which seemed, in contrast, to be aligned with the *junxian* model. Deng clearly relied on the state, economic decentralization, and the rebirth of a market distinct from a bureaucratic power, which relies on citizenship. Better still, he sought to correct the results of crumbling social control by turning to nationalism, relying on the regression of both Marxism and traditional cultures. Importing a key element of the Western grammar of modernization allowed for the reconstitution and completion of a model resembling Hobbesian universalism.

Sociological analysis, therefore, does not confirm the universality of the Hobbesian pact. More precisely, it shows the variety of social pacts, including as many individualist formulas as communal ones. Far from disappearing, the latter are recomposing and redeploying, whereas actors seeking political effectiveness must seek to integrate rather than efface them. More precisely, non-Western models, and in particular the example of China, suggest that individualism and communitarianism can either complement each other or alternate with each other according to different political regimes, as in communist China. Unless one considers these manifestations as residues of tradition that, as such, should be dismantled by modernization, one has to admit that they form a competing model of allegiances not integrated into the Hobbesian construct and whose deficiency constitutes a direct attack on the legitimacy of the political system.

Thus, Hobbes the sociologist shed light on the context in which the state could be invented. As a philosopher, he placed this perspective firmly in a normative theology that added another aspect to his pact: the invention of the state does not occur relative to a context, but through an operation of reason. In Hobbes such an operation appears beyond human nature, which borders on the predatory, and at the same time, beyond religion, which entails another type of obedience. Hobbes defines reason as the order of addition, of calculation, of researching the consequences—as leading to the domain of science. Moreover, the domain of science is precisely where Hobbes places the social pact, established specifically as a calculation by man to neutralize the harmful consequences of his passions. Hence the scientific identity of not only the state but of all mechanisms of obedience that Hobbes attributes to it. Not only has rationality been confirmed by the Enlightenment and then embraced, as we have seen, by the sociological tradition, but since the end of the eighteenth century it has been identified as such by intellectuals and political actors of the non-Western world. Because of its technological successes, the West has been able to prevail as the "civilized world" and has made itself accepted as the agent of positivist knowledge and the disseminator of science. We can note that the first exporters belonged to different rationalist and positivist currents in nineteenth-century Europe. Other currents were also instrumental: Freemasonry spread pretty much everywhere, first in Persia and the Middle East; Saint-Simonism was a strong presence in Egypt as of 1830; and positivism enjoyed considerable currency among the Young Turks.[23] Similarly, in China Western science appeared well before other concurrent philosophical traditions. As of the second half of the nineteenth century, the creation of the first foreign language institutes in Beijing, Shanghai, and Canton accompanied the formation of technical schools attached initially to naval shipyards. Likewise, missionaries accomplished the same diffusion of scientific knowledge, while the first Chinese students were sent to Europe and the United States for training in industry and medicine. At the same time, the integration of Western and Chinese mathematics was begun.[24] This scientific vector was all the more effective in China because it led to the diffusion of a remarkable evolutionist thought through the work of Yan Fu (1852–1921), who had been educated by one of these schools, the Arsenal of Fuzhou, and trained in the British Royal Navy. There he read Darwin and Spencer, studied British law and administration, and translated into Chinese the works of evolutionist philosophers, as well as John Stuart Mill and Montesquieu. It was specifically in this scientific context that Western political ideas and the first institutional models penetrated into China. Similarly, the *Appeal to Youth* of Chen Duxiu (1880-1942), who was educated in France and later headed the Chinese communist party, draws on the Western spirit of enterprise.[25]

Scientific justification for the invention of the Western state and Western technological hegemony combined to support this vast movement abroad. This explains why the nineteenth century was a turning point in this process and the very moment when the universalist claim of this entire production had the greatest chance of being accepted. But the essential is still missing: in these few examples, the Western model of government had already been imported, by the new elite governing non-Western societies, both those in power and their intermediaries. As important as it may be, in practice the sociology of proselytism explains only a small part of this diffusion; some background is required to understand this issue. Rather than a concerted effort of the Western states, this diffusion reflected the demands and strategies of the elite, who were often educated in Western values, but who generally acted not to further Western interests, but rather to realize their own objectives, which usually involved emancipation. These actors worked in concert less than could be supposed a priori. Their non-governmental, humanitarian, or religious organizations, their Protestant or Catholic missions, their scientific, Saint-Simonian, or Masonic organizations—each one acted autonomously and in its own interests. Given the nature of the diffusion from the mother country by its university and cultural institutions, official joint organizations played only a minor role.

The Westernization of the International Scene

Westernization occurred systematically as the Western states transformed the international scene in their own image. Contrary to certain hypotheses, the Western state is not the product of a new international system. We now commonly acknowledge that it originated in the workings of late medieval rural societies, and this has replaced the idea that it originated in the international system produced by market capitalism in the Renaissance. On the other hand, the state profoundly influenced international relations, all the more decisively as the nation-state emerged more and more within the context of the globalization of international life. At least three axes of this process can be counted: the diffusion of the principle of territoriality, the diffusion of a normative system strongly marked by the Western conception of law, and, finally, the diffusion of international rules of conduct.

Territorializing the World

The principle of territoriality often eludes critics because it seems so obviously universal. It is a decisive component in the actions of the state, but it is, nevertheless, linked to a historical development. As an essential element of the contemporary international system, it collides head-on with several other histories and a number of other cultures. Though present-day international relations conform more or less with the interstate model elucidated by Raymond Aron, they were initially constituted by the forced universalization of the idea of territory.[26] But throughout history, the distinctive features of this idea were based on several characteristics. First of all, it assumes that the community's social logic becomes secondary. In the state order, territory becomes a functional category of political regrouping, for such a regrouping implies that individuals will submerge their identity based on their allegiance to a center that seeks to monopolize authority. In that, the logic of territoriality contradicts the communal construction of the social; when the latter is valorized, membership in a tribe, clan, or extended family makes territorial identification ambiguous or debatable. Inversely, such an identification becomes operative when all intermediaries between the state and the individual disappear, that is, when territory becomes the geographical unit of the notion of public space. Anthropology and historical sociology understood this process of individualization only when it began to affect Europe in the eleventh and twelfth centuries, precisely at the moment feudal logic weakened and the Western idea of a defined territory took form.[27]

Territory, then, represents the superseding of feudal logic. In feudal logic, territory does not have the same meaning, for it represents neither identification nor primary allegiances, and it never had the finite and institutional character that statehood could confer. It has also been shown, notably by Norbert Elias, that feudalism played an essential role in the progressive construction of the idea of territory and, especially, in its conversion from being an individual resource guaranteeing the protection of the feudal lord, into an institutional resource favoring state domination.[28] German sociologists have, in effect, explained how competition between feudal lords unequally endowed with territory led to armed conflict and encouraged the victor to claim monopoly and dominion over the conquered lands. To this extent, the feudal structure institutionalized territory politically for the first time by making it both the essential condition of domination and of political identification and the exclusive indicator of sovereignty exercised by each ruler. The state moved beyond a hierarchical system that invested territory with a relative political significance to a construct that made territory an absolute, which became the only means of assuring its authority. In this sense, the invention of territory in its present configuration is linked to the Western feudal past.

Similarly, territory surpasses imperial logic, which itself is based on the notion of a nondefined territory. The empire exerts a strong tension between the particular and the universal, between reference to a specific culture and the will to extend that culture; so by definition, it unfolds onto a noninstitutionalized territory without fixed limits. The Omeyyad and Abbasid empires derived from a *dar al islam*, that is, from a part of Islam not totally reducible to a geographical category. In Christendom, the emperor's renown extended beyond the limits of his territory proper, into the entire Christian world, strengthening the legitimacy conferred upon him by his possessions. In the Chinese empire, the border meant merely the fringes beyond which lay wilderness, and these fringes, by nature unstable, could not constitute a defined space. Within empires, however, lived different cultures and peoples whose identity included not reference to territory but rather to religion (cf. the *millet* in the Ottoman empire), to language (in the Chinese empire), or to political status; and citizenship in the Roman empire referred neither to place nor space, but to a political act. Until the Edict of Caracalla in the third century linked citizen and land for the first time, the imperial order dissociated territoriality and civil status.

Territorialization also surpassed Western rural society. Without falling into too simplistic an evolutionism, one can, in fact, make use of the conjunction of national territory and progress in market economy. The latter supposes a modification of political spaces. If too vast, empires risked stifling merchant circuits and damaging the autonomy of civil societies and the market; if too small or if fragmented, city-states or groups of cities risked hindering commercial trade and fitting poorly into the nascent economic system. This developing system powerfully transformed Europe, so much that the level of nationhood achieved became the universal measure of political systems. Thus in the processes of its own constitution, civil society upholds the principle of territoriality. The undifferentiated economy of communal structures was clearly unable to support the construction and legitimation of territory. Economies based on affinities, to which Goran Hyden refers in his analysis of East African societies, limit social exchanges, enclose economic functions in communal structures, and devalue the role of the local administration—all of which deprive the territory of potential to evolve into a genuine political entity.[29]

Incontestably, only state logic can confer on a territory its clearest political identity. The completely constructed state tends to institutionalize, even to make sacred, the idea of a defined territory. The state is complete only by appropriating all intermediary allegiances, by defining citizenship as the direct subjection of the individual to the political center. Only here can territory remain a legitimate indication of this relation, which must be unambiguous. Furthermore, it must give rise to a *jus loci* that, little by little, supersedes the *jus sanguinis*, and it must establish juridically intangible borders. Such was the case with the entities that grew out of the Peace of Westphalia; the same occurred throughout the mutations affecting the European kingdoms at the end of the Renaissance, when the very notion of markets had disappeared. The vagueness characterizing territorial identity in Lorraine until 1766 faded with the principle of a henceforth closed territory.

This construction of territory claims to be universal and has, in fact, made itself universal. The contemporary international system is thought of and conceived as a function of this principle, which requires that every actor within it belong to a defined territory. It is precisely because of the fiction of territory that the Catholic Church claimed membership as a legitimate actor on a level with nations; it is by claiming a territory as their own that dominated collectivities, whoever and wherever they are, can universally claim legitimacy for their cause. This alignment forced on Western history created uncertainties and tensions that clearly reveal the limits of such an exportation.

The contemporary uncertainty surrounding the territorial system is due to two series of factors: first, the persistence of communal cultures that continuously challenge or alter the system; second, conceptual differences at work within various cultures that assign a meaning to the idea of territory that contrasts sharply with the idea developed and exported by Western culture. The hypothesis of a communal culture has often been proposed, and is based on the postulate that, beyond their diversity, communal social structures share a common network of meanings that distinguish them from others. These principles are in fact numerous: community is the principal provider of identity, allegiance, territorial landmarks, and significance given to land.

As the primary, even exclusive, provider of identity, the *community* does not easily lend itself to territorial constraints. The Tamil conceive their identity in terms of community, either by reference or by recourse to religious or linguistic markers: with its Sri Lankan citizenship directly challenged, Tamil identity has to be expressed in a territorial language that simultaneously betrays it and radicalizes it even more. In fact, territory and communal identity have never harmonized in the island's history, a situation that affected dramatically the conditions of an eventual partition. Hindu Tamils and Sinhalese Buddhists used to coexist on distinct geographical bases, with the Tamils staying in the north and east, and the Buddhists in the center and the southwest. Immigrants from either group could integrate into the other through a caste system. Such is essentially the process of territorial design contrived by British colonialism, and communal duality set the stage for future conflicts. In the twentieth century, territorial unification carried out by the colonizers stimulated mobility among certain minorities, whereupon the Jaffna Tamils moved to the south and the British farmers hired Tamil coolies to work in the island's center. This heightened competition between groups, as well as the competition pitting them against Christian proselytism, only heightened the communal stakes according to a rationale of division that helped the colonial powers manage the whole of the territory. At the same time, the imported model of majority rule and representative government, effected by Home Rule, led the Sinhalese nationalist leaders to encourage antiminority sentiments.[30] This logic became common after independence and radicalized the Tamil parties, which moved from federal demands to separatist ones. Hence at the end of the 1960s, the Federal party became the Tamil United Liberation Front. At the same time, the rise of a liberal politics marked the decline of the welfare state, which was at least in communication with all Sri Lankan citizens.[31] The resulting discomfort led to increased emigration by the young Tamil elite, complicating even more the territorialization of the communal problem by extending it to the Tamil Nadu in India.

The territorial nature of the problem thus became unworkable and contradictory. Since the Tamils were considerably in the majority in the north, they acquired a de facto autonomy. On the other hand, in the east, where they were mixed with other communities, their mobilization evolved into an unresolvable civil war over a dispute that had no territorial solution. Clearly in the minority in the center, they became embroiled in communalist fights orchestrated by the Sinhalese. This impossible territorializing of the Tamil question totally undermined projects of autonomy or spatial arrangements, thus radicalizing the situation and sanctioning the creation of separatist movements that resorted to violence.

The same tensions between identity logic and territorial logic can be found in the Kurdish problem. Until the end of the eighteenth century, this tension did not exist, since Kurdish identity was wholly integrated into a communal tribal order. At that time the Kurdish tribes were grouped into confederations or emirates, such as those in Bitlis, Jazira, or Rawandaz, and led by men chosen from noble lineages and assisted by councils composed of tribal chiefs, a small bureaucracy, and a light army. This arrangement could be relaxed because certain tribes existed outside a confederation, composing tactically beneficial alliances whenever needed. Political integration was not strongly based on territory because the collectivity was nomadic and, during seasonal migrations, it let Armenian and Nestorian peasants cultivate its pastures. The absence of territorial identification was compensated for by communal integration and by easy negotiations between the emirs and the Ottoman and Persian governors. It was also compensated for by identification with the Sufi sects, notably the Naqshbandi order, which united the groups in a common bond.[32]

The construction of a state from the Ottoman empire, begun by the sultans at the end of the eighteenth century, combined with the already perceptible effect of the presence of states on the international level, undid all these facts precisely by promoting an unmanageable territorializing of Kurdish identity. In his capacity as head of state, the sultan could no longer tolerate either the authority of the Kurdish emirs or the continuation of communal allegiances that might prevail over subjection to the imperial center. As a result, the *vali*(s), governors, tried to forcibly integrate these emirates into the Ottoman territory. And in particular, since it had taken up practices that were henceforth territorial, the Ottoman administration tried to settle the Kurdish population, thereby inciting intense competition between sedentary cultivators and the former nomads, between Armenians and Kurds, in which the latter engaged in raids against Armenian villages. In the context of confrontation between communities, Kurdish identity became a source of conflict, making territory both an object of discord and a mode of identification burdened with intercommunity tensions.

At the same time, the Treaty of Erzerum (1847), which ended the war between Persia and the Ottoman empire, supported the insertion of the region into an international system codified by the rules in effect among states. As the first treaty that genuinely conformed to public international law, it established a delineation and institutionalization of borders that from then on prevented Kurdish tribes from benefiting from the impreciseness of territorial structures. Similarly, Russian-Ottoman rivalries reactivated Armenian claims of autonomy as well as the hope of promoting their identity by a confrontation among states.

The demand for a free Kurdistan also resulted directly from the universalization of the Western conception of territory as supporting a political order. This demand was to become an insoluble problem. Raised after the Treaty of Sèvres, it encountered several obstacles that remain today. The very idea of a Kurdish territory was contradicted by the overlapping of different communities on the same land; moreover, the Kurdish peoples were unable even to agree on a choice of representatives at the negotiating table. Such contradictions between tribal order and state order account for the recurrent and almost consensual process of elimination or marginalization of the Kurdish issue internationally by actors in other countries. The territorial solution to the problem progressed only when it became embroiled in political interactions internationally: after World War I, when the Ottoman empire was divided into different countries; and in 1946, with the creation of the ephemeral Republic of Mahabad, which the Soviet Union hoped would give them access into Iran. With the Kurds or the Tamils, territory limits rather than supports the expression of identity; it complicates the realization of identity rather than providing a solution to the problem.

For similar reasons, communal culture has equally hindered the move toward territorial affiliation. The example of the Kurdish political organization reveals a subservience system that bears no relation to territory. Even more clearly, the example of the people living in former Spanish lands of the Sahara reveals the uncertainties and other effects of blockages deriving from the reference to territory. Initially, at the time of decolonization, the Spanish government intended to concede autonomy to Western Sahara; but this provoked an immediate reaction by Morocco, who also claimed sovereignty over this territory. Understood this way, the International Court of Justice distinguishes with absolute clarity between the ideal of allegiance and that of territory. While it accepts that bonds of allegiance exist between the sultan of Morocco and the Saharan tribes, the ICJ rejects that these constitute bonds of sovereignty between the territories of Morocco and Western Sahara. The reason for this lack of correspondence is clear: before colonization, Morocco was not the only political entity existing in the region, and the Sahrawi tribes belonged to a "Chinguiti group," that is, the communal tribal structure localizable in the environs of the Chinguiti oasis, currently situated in Mauritania.[33]

Such a decision derives from the importance given to the Saharan problem. Certainly, in practice, it reflects a refusal to become involved in the dispute between Morocco and Mauritania, and prevents efforts to find a legal solution to the problem of succession to Spanish rule. Thus the decision sanctions the inability of international law to decide a dispute that weighs seriously on contemporary Maghreb, and thus to enact universal rules. Yet the essence of the problem does not lie here: by agreeing to the hypothesis of a "Chinguiti group," the court broke with a problematic founded on the universality of the state. Past or present, such an entity carries consequences that directly affect the contemporary international order; by distancing itself from rationality based on the state, it generates irresolvable tensions because they cannot be categorized in the grammar that currently governs international relations. In particular, this recognition proclaims the normative value of the dissociation between territory and allegiance. Not only does the latter constitute an autonomous reality, produced exclusively by the interactions of the communal solidarities and affiliation networks to which it gives rise, but especially, it cannot lead to the recognition of any territorial sovereignty. Thus allegiance to the prince does not imply his sovereignty over the land in question, just as political obligation can affect a population though it may lack its own territory. Therefore, to conceive a Sahrawi identity in terms of a national territory becomes impossible and raises an endless debate in which each of the countries involved can support the same claim. To dissociate oneself from identity in terms of territory would certainly allow a more precise definition of one's identity, but that makes impossible one's integration into the international sphere as it is today.

A comparable, though exacerbated dilemma confronts nomadic populations that find in their communal culture the only elements that can establish their territorial markers. In this case, Western territorial logic is exactly inverted: only by controlling territory can one control men, as the example of the Tuaregs clearly indicates. The Tuaregs have more than once been displaced by the importation of the principle of territoriality. First, by the colonial government, which not only disrupted the constants of the traditional economy but also organized the entire Saharan region, drawing borders and regulating the movements of nomads. However, these had a limited effect because colonization allowed caravans a relative freedom of movement in disputed areas. In particular, the construction of the postcolonial nation-state profoundly upset traditional equilibria and fixed, institutionalized, and in reality worsened the borders drawn by the colonizers. The area traversed by the Tuareg was divided into five countries: Mali, Niger, Burkina Faso, Libya, and Algeria. These territorial divisions reduced the number of basic regimes of which individuals were subjects. Farmers were no longer allowed to move with their families for the seasonal migrations; they were disarmed and brought under several authorities. Above all, territorialization set up border checkpoints that were reinforced each time the ministers of the interior met. Similarly, signs of rejection of citizenship within these populations were reduced, namely, disdain for the symbols of state sovereignty, change of nationality, and unpredictability of political behavior, which provoked mistrust of civil servants and political leaders.[34]

The failure of territorial logic could only exacerbate tensions. First, a recurrence of armed conflicts, beginning in 1962, pitted Mali against the Kel Adar Tuaregs. These conflicts progressively mobilized other nomadic peoples, notably the Tubus of Chad, who fostered an endemic source of guerrilla activity that gradually became the very symbol of the fight for power within the former French colony. As the ethnologist André Bourgeot noted, "The impossibility of nomadic movements" tends to transform these populations into a "lumpen-nomadic" collectivity that regenerates its identity by a migratory flow of the young generation into Algeria and especially Libya where they learn techniques of modern warfare and acquire the skills and reputation of fighters.[35] A twofold dynamic here affects the functioning of political systems and can go so far as to turn armed clashes into political rivalries that influence international relations in the region. From this last point of view, territoriality is the more troublesome because it is a source of indefinite blockage. By making the autonomy of Malian Adrar its principal demand, the Azawed Liberation Front spoke the language of international law and effectively influenced decisions, as was the case with the peace accord signed in Tamanrasset in January 1991. It failed, however, to address the essential aspect of the incompatibility between the notion of territory and the Tuareg conception–in nomadic terms–of the political order, which gave force to the Libyan myth of the "Saharan State," even though this force had more of a utopian nature than a real, institutionalized one, and even though, in the final analysis, it derived from the same territorial vision of political structure. Criticism of this vision gave rise, therefore, to more conflict rather than to a more politically modern alternative.

The difficulty could seem insurmountable: communal cultures confer on land a fundamentally different meaning from that found in Western cultures. Whereas the former see land as concrete and sacred, the latter conceive it as more pragmatic and institutional. In the areas where the communal bond predominates, ideas of land and territory merge to designate first of all the possession of the ancestors and then the source and spiritual foundation of the community. Social entities and other political relations are necessarily excluded. Taken to its extreme, this lack of differentiation is expressed, notably in African and Native American communalism, by a conception of nature as enchantment, where land and divinity merge. The tendency to sacralize the earth makes its conversion into an institutional support of anonymous and individualized political relations based on citizenship all the more delicate. As a source of allegiance in the communal model or instrument to formalize allegiances in the model based on citizenship, territory reflects two entirely antinomic meanings. The nationalist discourse of the sacralization of land that acquired currency in the West in the nineteenth century could reduce this gap only in metaphor: the themes of rootedness or mythical references to the "French land" sacralize the nation more than the land itself, whereas themes of natural borders found no juridical or sociological bases.

Discredited by the workings of communal cultures, the principle of territoriality was also reconstructed by the *system of meanings* characterizing each of the non-Western cultures. Islam supports the communal conception of territory. As the only legitimate collectivity, the *Umma* assembles the faithful and constitutes the perfect place for carrying out political functions and expressing allegiance relations. As such, its territorialization is obviously impossible, but it also maintains an entire conception of political mobilization attached to the principle of territoriality. The Muslim's allegiance to an order that requires his faith or his communal solidarity transcends the law of territory; Islamic movements have often expressed Islam's claim of sovereignty over the Muslim communities in Europe, hence they reject the sovereignty of European states over these communities. The Ayatollah Khomeini did not consider it interference to become involved in the Libyan conflict, or even in the political life of the Arab world in general, since he considered that he was acting within an area under his guidance, no matter what judicial considerations were at stake in the countries in question.

From this point of view, the notion of *dar al islam* that designates the domain of Islam, that is, the area in which the community is ruled by an Islamic administration, constitutes a first restriction, since it imposes an initial division within a legitimately indivisible *Umma*. In terms of international relations, this notion is in opposition to the *dar al harb* ("the realm of war"), the exterior space of Islam, in conformity to a dichotomy that acquired meaning when the *dar al islam* was unified within the imperial Abbasid. On this scale, all internal division could only be accidental or conjectural, based on some necessity. This is the diametric opposite of the Western principle of territoriality, which endows borders with institutional value and intangible quality. Here also stand in opposition two conceptions of the universal: with the Western model, the universal affirmation of the concept of territory and its divisions; with the Islamic model, the implicit affirmation of Islam's universalist orientation that relativizes the very meaning of border. Any territorial division represents nothing more than a convention, even more so since it derives most often from diplomatic and military interactions among the great powers. Far from being whims, periodic announcements of the total fusion of the states of the Arab world express symbolically a weak adaptation to nation-state status. Similarly, the organization of such parties as the Ba'ath derive from a more or less fictional national, that is, inter-Arab leadership. Finally, these announcements reveal how matters concerning borders have been overshadowed by clashes between regimes and modes for legitimizing power and by rivalries among national leaders.

However, the problem is not clear-cut. Though the highest-ranking leaders of the Muslim world resist the Western idea of territory, they must contend with it. As ambiguous as it is, universalization of the principle makes an impact, as much by exigencies within the international world as by the benefits that leaders receive from it, notably that of promoting or protecting their own hold on power. Prime Minister Mahatir has been sensitive to the specific nature of eastern Islam and careful to build a Malaysian nationalism that can unite the country's Muslim and Chinese citizens. In the *Umma* he referred to the existence of several peoples, thus giving some idea of territorial divisions. This idea was taken up by Mahamed Fadel Djamali, former prime minister of Iraq, who confirmed the existence of a plurality of cultures within the world of Islam, while the Moroccan nationalist leader Allal al-Fassi did not fail to note, in the context of the struggle for independence, the compatibility of nation and *Umma*. In fact, the plurality of allegiance networks protects against the risks of an all-encompassing single allegiance.[36] This is how territory becomes a sort of check against the domination potential of integrated cultural groups. Even more, it becomes the necessary stage through which an entire group of political practices must pass: the practice of emancipation from the colonial power, which is the basis of glorification of "national territory," and the practice of the exercise of power, which make the context of territory the site where domination comes to an end.

At the same time, the Oxford-educated Sudanese Islamic leader Sadik al-Mahdi observed that the territorialized state represented a lucky chance seized by the Westernized elite to catapult themselves to power and to create a political community loyal to them.[37] Clearly, the promotion of the territorial framework amply remunerates this type of elite. It promotes the reproduction of an imported state model that corresponds to their acquired skills; it subsequently protects the political figures currently in power, thanks to the valorization of its own abilities; finally, it gives the prince the supplementary means of legitimizing himself in the eyes of his people, allowing him to be the guarantor of national territory or the conqueror of new territories. Hassan II with the Green March, Nasser with the Suez Canal, Sadat with the Sinai Peninsula, and Saddam Hussein with Kuwait–all played the same card with the same conviction, in spite of unequal chances of success.

Arguments supporting the universalization of the notion of territory are obviously not negligible; they find a genuine echo within the very heart of political systems. The resulting hybrid order is not, however, without danger. The reality and multiplicity of the ways culture and society negate the principle of territoriality provoke tensions that at the same time weaken the legitimacy of those who use them. Still worse, they engender countermobilization strategies that, in the Muslim world, fuel as many Islamic movements as they do nationalist and populist ones. Thus during the Gulf crisis, Saddam Hussein tried to combine a strategy of territorial expansion with the call for a transnational popular mobilization, and to combine the effects of a war between states with those of a war effort to incite populations against the state. In this way he revived the inexhaustible potential, in the Muslim world, of the superimposition of two worlds, that of territorial governments undergoing the attraction of universalist principles and that of a deterritorialized political arena obeying endogenous cultural constructs.

Like Islam, Indian culture does not adapt easily to the notion of territory. The somewhat indistinct idea of a Hindu nationalism developed in opposition to those who refused integration into a Hindu culture that conceived of itself as a cosmogony. Such was not the case with the first invaders; it was, however, the case with the Muslim conquerors and then later the Western ones. The binary relation between us and other does not necessarily lead to a territorial sense other than negatively. Beyond these difficulties, the Hindu world never really developed as a single large group. As a world of castes and sects, identity developed at the microsocial level. As a world of *raj*, it has for a long time thought of its relation to the political only in terms of territorial micro-entities. Since historically it knew only episodic imperial periods, the only way it could serve its rulers was through cultural models that generally were not Hindu, but rather Buddhist (the Mauryan empire), Muslim (the Moghul empire), or Christian (the British Raj). Beyond these expressions, Indian culture appeared in a "galactic" political order, made up of the juxtaposition of innumerable religious, social, and political entities that, all together, created more of a world than a territory, in which diversity found value in its relation to the unified whole.[38]

This unity developed in the context of a nationalism that was for the most part imported whole cloth, syncretically, which allowed a Hindu identity, then an Indian one, to come about in terms of a Western grammar. This "strategic syncretism" allowed the success of reformist sects such as Brahmo Samaj and especially Arya Samaj, which altered Hinduism by conferring upon it a sense of unity that provided the basis for an Indian nationalism: reference to the Vedas as the unique book, attenuation of the caste system, rediscovery in Hinduism of principles founding its own modernity, valorization of the aryas, and a call for a golden age.[39] At the same time, Western borrowings were considerable. The founder of the sect, the British-educated Dayananda Serasvati, was firmly attached to monotheism; and from the very beginning, nationalist intellectual movements drew from the Enlightenment philosophers and claimed as their own the idea of a scientific state. Such was the case with Henry Louis Vivian Derozio (1809-31), an Indo-Portuguese philosopher and founder of the Young Bengal movement; and such was especially the case with Ram Mohan Roy (1772-1833), founder of the Brahmo-Samaj sect. He served in the administration of the East India Company and subsequently represented the Emperor Akbar III in London. In addition, he frequently visited France and was a thoroughly convinced disciple of Enlightenment rationalism, which he hoped to disseminate in India through the educational system.[40] Thus the passage from a cosmogony that considered alterity merely a poorly constructed identity, to a view of it in terms of a defined space, resulted from the discovery of Western rationalism and its claim to universality. Sites where this discovery took hold are clearly identified: ideas of unity and monotheism, reference to a unifying book, receptivity to a science imported from elsewhere, reunification of the social structure, but also the beginning of a revivalist dynamic that nourished the themes of a chosen people or, at least, valorized themes of the golden age and an alternative modernity in embryonic form. Exposed to Western modernity, Hindu revivalism, just like Islamic revivalism, turned to a differentiated knowledge based on the distinction between the universal and the particular. Hence, differentiated from a simple cosmogony, Indian identity became particularist. Opened to Western rationalism, it accepted a universalism that was historically external to it. Because of this particularity, it was henceforth identifiable and territorializable; because of this universality, the process of identification could take such shape as would have meaning in other cultures. However, for that very reason, Indian identity requires a cultural reinvestment that is simultaneously a source of mobilization against the other and which can, in turn, challenge the universal order. The radical Hindu revivalist movements, for example, illustrate this process in that, for these movements, state and territory appeared progressively as foreign imports and hence objects to delegitimize. Accordingly, marks of identity become, as in the Muslim world, indirect stakes in the process of mobilization. If, for example, the Arya Samaj could mobilize in the name of identity and a prenationalist doctrine, and merchants find a more advantageous position than that offered by their caste, the Rashtriya movement, based on Hindu radicalism, could integrate into its network of clandestine cells numerous groups of individuals socially frustrated by modernization who were willing to denounce the very fact of a national state.

The territorial conception of Indian identity is thus marked by a double tension: that which opposes the resistance of a cultural system to the universalizing efforts of another cultural system and that which creates a contradiction in the strategies of the actors, depending on whether they benefit or not from the cultural innovations resulting from contact with the West. The daily practices of political life are necessarily affected by the resulting instability. India's international reputation has been notably marked by ambiguity. The Republic of India finds its legitimacy only as a totality enclosing the world of all Indians. This has been demonstrated by the concept of limited sovereignty India has adopted regarding Bhutan, and even more remarkably, Nepal; it has also been demonstrated by India's involvement in the defense of the Tamil cause or the impossibility of finding a compromise to solve the Kashmir problem. Certain observers of the conflicts that have torn Southeast Asia see the conflict between the territorial cultures of Vietnam and Cambodia as critical, since the first has insisted on a defined territory and borders, while the latter was marked specifically by an Indian cultural heritage that considers territorial delimitations as "porous and mutable."[41]

Unification by Law

The normative system has the same universalist orientation as the principle of territoriality. International law was conceived in Renaissance Europe and has clearly undergone various vicissitudes and criticisms; no less significant are the discords and tensions experienced by its history and the contemporary, somewhat forced, efforts to revive it. The birth of international law is in itself significant. At the same time, the Renaissance felt the weight of the Protestant Reformation, which contested the legitimacy of the nascent state; of the resulting map of Europe where a juxtaposition of states definitively prevailed over the hypothesis of a unified Christian world; and of the opening onto the world, which supported the conquest of the seas and distant lands already inhabited by other established cultures with which Europe had to coexist, but which it also had to christianize. The task, then, was to attempt a self-definition relative to the other, to seek in this opposition another self, and to both discover alterity and reconcile it with a universal order.[42]

The simultaneity of these tasks characterizes the orientations of a law that would at the same time confirm the status of states and be the apologist for nature and reason. International law is the law of sovereign nations at the service of natural principles and, therefore, universal ones. Such a school of thought could only be Neo-Thomist, in which the Dominican Vitoria, as well as the Jesuits Suarez and Vasquez, found in the theological construct of the angelic Doctor all the postulates needed to reconcile nation and reason, law of nature and universal law, state, natural law, and Christianity.

The elements of the debate reveal, in fact, a grammar far from outmoded. A missionary among the Indians, Bartolomé de Las Casas demanded that a social law be recognized from which even a non-Christian could benefit. Thus the first clash among different civilizations that confronted international law also illustrated the functional orientations of the new law: they defined a unique normative system that could merge cultural differences and reconcile the right to be oneself and the right to spread the teachings of the Gospel. Here, natural law is the keystone: since natural law blurred differences—which necessarily were unique—because it is an attribute of human nature, it is superior to positivistic law, whose function is to manage human nature in whatever form it may take at any given moment.

Vitoria's work provided the basis for an international law that was in essence universalizable. If each people constitutes an irreducible entity, what can dictate the law among different peoples if not a natural law, uniquely expressive of the truth? If liberty is a natural law, then in situations where liberty is clearly inferior, it is effaced by the right to truth and, thus, the right to read and to receive the Gospel: the specificity of the Indians is a fact before it is a right; therefore, their natural aspiration for the truth prevails legally over their hypothetical will to protect their differentness. Similarly, colonial conquest poses the problem of safeguarding peaceful relations, but it cannot mask the right to well-being and development that the right to truth assumes.

There is, then, an international order subject first of all to a truth that represents a law of human nature. Moreover, this law does not negate the separation into sovereign states, since Vitoria sees the state as a necessity of natural law that succeeds a condition detrimental to individualization. There is an evident progression from a natural order, an order of truth and an order of the state, which assigns to the most advanced states the function of completing the structuring of the international order.

The evolution of this juridical construction is significant. The difficulty of defining the content of this law and especially of reconciling it with the principle of state sovereignty has led to the erection of the state into a first principle of natural law. This is confirmed notably in the work of Vattel, who postulated that man's happiness depended first of all on the well-being of his country and thus on the affirmation of the state. Here, the individual exists only as a subject of the state, with the latter the sole actor in international relations. This position restores a positivist coloring to international law, since obligation in international law exists only because it is consented to and recognized by states. The slide toward positivism is, however, deceiving, first because the declared principle of state sovereignty derives neither from a natural principle nor from a positivist construction. As we have seen, the state derives neither from a universal category nor from a political order empirically observed in all times and in all cultures. Next, and especially, it is deceiving because, taken in its entirety, positivism renders ineffective the very idea of an international law deprived of every obligation and every sanction.

Such absolute volunteerism has proved suitable. In certain contexts, the conception of a nonstructured international society deprived of obligations corresponds with the interests of certain states that seek to preserve their sovereignty and which have at their disposal sufficient coercive capacities to do so. In this spirit the Soviet Union, during the cold war and when the Soviet Union itself was surrounded, could adhere fully to such a construction. Also in the name of the principle of sovereignty, the Soviet Union denounced the free circulation of people and ideas between Eastern and Western Europe, and it rejected the right of "free radio stations" to broadcast into its territory. From the point of view of a strict juridical positivism, the argument was solid. It demonstrated that the principle of state sovereignty could be taken to an absurd extreme and that an international system includes the definition of a system of obligations that transcend somewhat the sovereignty of nations. The consciousness of this requirement, certainly not of recent date, helped relaunch the work of establishing an international law. Kelsenian normativism* played a considerable role in that it identified those very principles that form the basis of international obligation.

The end of the cold war and the completion of decolonization gave new life to the idea of natural law. The decline of East European ideologies, the abandonment of the priority given to military force in East-West relations, and the decrease in the number of sovereign nations have given cause to recast international relations in universalist terms. The further strengthening of the United Nations, and the treatment of the Gulf crisis as an "international police" operation led by "soldiers of law," resulted in the rediscovery of a natural law destined to organize international relations from which no one would be exempt. Of course, the idea of state sovereignty must still be cultivated; a "police operation" is legitimate only when it fights a state that has ventured outside its own territory. Of course, the means of imposing sanctions remains uncertain, but one must allow that discourse and practice have come together to reinvest the idea of a natural law with its original value as a principle that, of necessity, justifies a state's every international initiative. Use of this universal law served not only to legitimize action internationally but also to establish the idea of a unified international stage, consensually organized around common values. The ability of Western societies to produce these values, to present them as universal, and to disseminate them or impose them is the most salient feature of the Western model's propensity toward universalization.

This process constitutes one of the major stakes in contemporary international relations. Its feasibility is a matter of debate among two camps: those who desire to attenuate conflicts, and who thus consider juridicizing the international stage as eminently possible; and conversely, those who see the activation of the North-South conflict as indicating that cultural norms differ sufficiently to make improbable the constitution of an international law that all actors perceive as universal.[43]

Analysis of the conditions in which a transcultural international law has been constituted shows the complexity of the issue and the difficulty in deciding between these two positions. On one hand, it is certain that well before the Renaissance and the explicit formation of an international law, people in different cultures employed practices of negotiation and interac-

---

*Translator's Note: Hans Kelsen, 1881–1973, political and legal philosopher.

tion that supported an empirical and utilitarian normative system that was already quite complex. But it is equally true that with the modern and contemporary period, the extension of an international law claiming universality, that came from the West, and was extended essentially through relations of domination helped pile up ambiguities and root this law in an identity constructed as monocultural.

The formation and extension of the Muslim empires instituted numerous practices that were precursors of international law: the Prophet Muhammad had already concluded treaties with the Jews of Medina and the Christians of Aqaba; the Caliph Abol el-Malik had already engaged in negotiations with Byzantium; embassies had been opened in Constantinople as well as in Persia and with Charlemagne. Whatever the empire's claim to universality, its insertion into a world where it confronted the *dar al harb*, that is, the Christian world, brought it to consider itself as a territory: non-Muslim warriors were issued safe conducts, and foreign merchants were taxed upon entry into the empire.

In the same way, the third-century Chinese Han empire sent ambassadors to the kingdom of Funan (Cambodia) in order to establish ties with the empire of the Kushans. In the following century, Nanking housed numerous embassies from India and Ceylon. In addition, the Cao-Wei region had established diplomatic relations with Japan that grew stronger during the subsequent two centuries; the Sassanid Persians sent ambassadors to the Tang dynasty. Also, an alliance was formalized at the end of the eighth century between the Tang and the Abbasids for protection against the Tibetans.[44] Later, in the sixteenth century, tumultuous relations between China and Japan, exacerbated by the increase in piracy, were calmed and regulated by subtle diplomatic moves and a succession of embassies.

Of course, within these constructions no defined international law can be located. The very idea of a treaty reveals many ambiguities; for example, for Muslim jurists the treaties concluded were measures of expediency and established only a provisional agreement that, apparently, could last no longer than ten years. Furthermore, these treaties of necessity prevented even hypothetical sanctions and possessed no real value in the larger international order. In reality, what occurred was an international practice from which was excluded the principle of *pacta sunt servanda*. Regarding integration into the international system, the actors relied on their absolute sovereignty as a basis for an order or juxtaposition of entities in which the only essential element was the ability to enter into contact with each other.

The apprenticeship of an international system that one could join and even integrate with came later, as soon as relations of domination appeared. The first alliance treaty concluded by the Ottoman empire linked Süleyman the Magnificent and Francis I on an explicitly interstate basis, since the Ottoman sultan considered the king of France as his equal and made the treaty for an extended period, and thus not based on a temporary necessity. Soon after, however, the right to contract treaties served to establish policies of capitulation, in favor of France in 1569 and England in 1601. The principle of the natural right to sovereignty of nations and equality among them was shaken by the logic of domination as soon as the first movements toward constructing an international order had borne fruit. Thus the first peace treaty in conformity with the model of international law was imposed on the Ottoman sultan in the context of a defeat. The Zsitva Torok Treaty of 1606, the first to effectively correspond to the formal requirements of a document between states, carried no pretense of the sultan ordering his governors to act in conformity with international accords to which he had personally subscribed. At the same time, the Western powers continued throughout the nineteenth century to reach agreements with certain governors of the empire and successfully convinced the Sublime Gate to deal with non-Muslim representatives through its own minister of foreign affairs.[45] Similar events occurred in Persia, where a succession of treaties with Britain during the nineteenth century brought about a capitulatory regime in which the sovereign government gave over natural resources or infrastructures and limited Persian diplomatic autonomy by forbidding, for example, any European power other than Britain to traverse its territory (1814).

The way China became a part of the international system reveals in yet another way the destructive effects of Western international law and the circumstances that trigger it. We have seen that China's discovery of alterity is very ancient, since it was concomitant with its construction as an empire. The institutionalization and formalization of the effects of this discovery are more recent. They became apparent when it was no longer a question of juxtaposition but of defining one's own space, of specifying the norms that attach one to the center, the significance of borders, and the reciprocal obligations linking self to other. The Manchu period was well aware of this process, since it established China's current boundaries, and since the seventeenth-century conquests put it in direct contact with other actors seeking to take part in the same interactive logic and attempting to define their own territories.

Significantly, China's initial insertion into an international system that was becoming worldwide occurred in a hybrid fashion, only partially corresponding to international law. The peripheral territories had already integrated acquired identities essentially distinct from the logic of the state, and this foreshadowed China's ambiguous insertion into international relations. Manchuria was a territorial possession belonging to the Manchu dynasty in power in Beijing. Mongolia was part of the empire only because of personal allegiances linking tribal chiefs to the Manchu emperor. Tibet was recognized as a religious center under Chinese protection to eliminate the risks of a Mongolian guardianship. The peripheral kingdoms (Nepal, Burma, and what was then Siam) were vassals. Only Sinkiang (etymologically "new territory") had the status of occupied territory with a military administration, clearly taking part in the logic of territorialization in accordance with international law. That is how China became an international actor according to the practices that prolonged an almost 2,000-year-old imperial logic and which, all in all, made few concessions to an international law that it largely ignored. As a result, China first built itself as an autonomous regional system and as a merely potential actor in the international system. Here is a historical turning point that helps explain China's specificity as a hybrid actor in the international scene. With its imperial identity still very real, the complexity of its relations with its neighbors, Vietnam, Burma, and Korea, reveals a very relative conjunction of the Chinese system with international law.[46] Particularly since this conjunction began, as with the Ottoman empire and Persia, on the most contradictory bases of inequality.

China's first encounter with the Western law of treaties occurred in 1689 in Nerchinsk, when Chinese authorities wanted to record the progress of Russian colonization in Siberia and set the boundaries separating the two countries. Significantly, the document was written in several languages, those of the two contracting parties, and in Latin. The discussions included Dutch intermediaries and Jesuits, who formalized the accord. The purpose of China's entry into the international juridical order forged by the Western powers was to define its relations with another empire and to stabilize a process of conquest. Its entry was prolonged by the decrease in diplomatic exchanges in the first half of the seventeenth century. These increased, however, after Nerchinsk, when the Russians relieved the Dutch and Portuguese by assuming more diplomatic activity. But it is the unequal treaties that completed China's membership in the new international order. Thus the Treaty of Nanking in 1842 was a juridical sanction imposed during the first of the opium wars by formalizing the cession of Hong Kong to England, the opening of a certain number of ports for commerce, and, particularly, modifications of China's internal juridical order, such as the suppression of the Cohong monopoly (Association of Cantonese Merchants) and the recognition of the right of extraterritoriality to British citizens within the empire. The Treaty of Tianjin (1858) and the Convention of Beijing (1860) combined certain international institutions of common law, such as, for example, the opening of consulates, and the worsening of certain unegalitarian dispositions that the law approved even though they contradicted certain of its fundamental principles: Chinese customs were placed under the control of a foreigner, new concessions were opened, British textiles were exempt from customs taxes, and foreign fleets could circulate freely on Chinese rivers. In 1904, the Treaty of Shimonoseki confirmed these dispositions and even strengthened them, this time to Japan's benefit.[47]

In sum, the form was largely respected: treaties were in conformity with legal procedure, permanent embassies opened, and an international order of integration replaced the former system of juxtaposition. More important, Western international law had become universalized, accepted, and recognized by non-Western partners as the procedure for regulating international relations. At the same time, however, the logic of universalization entailed a threefold effect. First, the international system was unified around a center that the West intended to occupy, particularly since it had produced the system. Next, it was made uniform according to processes that accelerated the configuration and the practice of the international actors following the model of the state. Finally, it legitimized unequal and dependent relations, thanks to the generalization of the contractual practice of treaties. Thus the conditions of inequality and dependence were softened symbolically by the fact that they appeared to result from the voluntary consent of the contracting parties, hence from their sovereignty.

The Construction of an Interstate System

This universalization of the normative system inevitably affects international relations by promoting expansion of an underlying model of state logic. From this perspective, the Hobbesian paradigm has acquired, internationally, the same relevance it has within each nation: practice and law meet where principles of security and sovereignty converge. The international order that triumphed after the Peace of Westphalia established the transfer of the logic of violence from the individual level to the universal one. No longer can one legitimately use force for religious motives; but that does not exclude a state from recourse to force the moment force becomes legal, or in other words, that recourse to force derives from a state's exercise of its sovereignty. The appropriation of international violence by the state has multiple consequences both internally and externally.[48] For the internal workings of state logic, the appropriation of violence constitutes a precious reservoir of the mobilization of resources and legitimation, while intensifying external insecurity provides a valued means of reactivating allegiances. Furthermore, the state's appropriation of violence has effectively helped to universalize and to consolidate the state and regimes in place within non-Western areas, such as, for example, the military action taken by India against Goa, by Indonesia against East Timor, by Morocco during the Green March, or though less successful, by Argentina against the Falkland Islands. In each of these cases, the process of mobilization valorized and diffused among the local population the primary characteristics of the state–namely, territory and citizenship. In sum, here is an entire grammar whose function was essentially to hasten the integration of the most diverse political orders into the interstate system. Externally, the state's appropriation of violence orients the international system toward the elimination of private wars. Effected with the Hobbesian pact within national spaces, this elimination, which is of primary importance, is confirmed internationally by outlawing and treating as renegade every violent confrontation not pursued at the national level. Piracy, for example, became so intolerable that it was eradicated by a Hague convention in 1907. And precisely because it opposes the state itself, civil war cannot be sanctioned internationally, and interstate diplomacy must disinterestedly ignore its existence as a fact. The territory itself may not take part in international practice: a state attacked or threatened by a terrorist group cannot negotiate with it without risking the negation of the very conventions on which its own legitimacy is founded. Thus the sacrosanct principle of negotiation only from state to state is put forth on all occasions, even as a cautious protection against the slightest clandestine negotiation between a state and a terrorist group.

This reproduction of the nation-state model finds support in two paradoxes that have become the most effective of all dependence practices: the juridical fiction of sovereignty and the game of power. The first derives from one of the best-established principles of contemporary international relations. The international system can be constituted only of sovereign states whose juridical identity reflects that of the Western states, and this is attested by membership in the United Nations. In the effort of universalization, every international normative construction must affirm the sovereignty of each state and the concomitant right and duty to protect itself.

The first element of the paradox comes from the inability of these states, such as they are constituted, to maintain more than a fictional sovereignty. Possessing only the slimmest capacities, they lack the means internally to meet the requirements of the Hobbesian pact. Fragmented social spaces, deprived of a unique and structured civil society, divided by the powerful communal solidarities of which they are composed, issue to the state only the weakest requests for guarantees of security. Because they are weak states up against strong societies, to use Joel Migdal's idea, in reality they represent a largely fictional identity configuration.[49] Diametrically opposite to this logic, the international system invests the most essential of its normative resources and its political practice in maintaining the juridical personality of each state. By challenging all territorial modifications, establishing the principle of noninterference and respect for state sovereignty as the very foundation of diplomacy, and refusing to recognize as an interlocutor and partner in negotiations anyone but the legal governments of states, the international system compensates for internal weaknesses with the maintenance, and even the activation, of external capacities. Whether it concerns Libya, Ethiopia, Chad, or Angola, the lack or absence of legitimacy in the political center, the fictitiousness or precariousness of its authority, the nonexistence of the state's real relations with the governed are at each step compensated for by an influx of international legitimation elicited solely by its identity as a state actor.[50]

Understandably, this contradiction is sustained, particularly by non-Western political systems that find an appreciable guarantee of their hold on power in conformity to the state model. Deriving from a "warrior state," where competition for power involves a Khaldunian-type permanent communal confrontation, Chad saw a substantial mutation in the discourse employed by its political personnel when they acceded to power. The new discourse revealed a fastidious respect for international law, since it provided a distinction from its former guerrilla practice. In the same manner, Iraq's leaders were able to criticize an "imperialist international law" that condemned its invasion of Kuwait while simultaneously expressing a fastidious respect for an international law that allowed it to reestablish its sovereignty during the Kurdish rebellion. Even the Movement of Nonaligned Nations based its own positions on the principle of national sovereignty while simultaneously condemning dependence practices and detaching itself from them.

At the same time, the Northern powers encourage this paradox because they readily benefit from it. Located exclusively in the context of the state as nation, the principle of sovereignty tends to maintain in the non-Western world what Robert Jackson calls "quasi-Nations" or a "negative sovereignty."[51] As a result, it tends to worsen the effects of distance between the center and the periphery within the international system, and it also worsens the conditions that necessitate the exercise of genuine dependence relations. It accelerates the decomposition of the internal functioning of peripheral societies, that is, the retribalization and activation of new modes of communalization from which the religious sects, the social elite, and the independent preachers benefit equally, while it affirms cultural minorities. This composition reduces the sphere of authority of the country's leaders, thereby increasing their propensity to seek the status of client to the states in the center. Perhaps even more serious, the fragmenting of civil society vigorously transforms economic development into a source of confrontation and competition so as to weaken even more the peripheral state and reinforce its dependence. In fact, this contradiction is largely contained in the entirely fictitious idea that the inter*state* system is an inter*national* system, that is, that the divisions among sovereign elements correspond in effect to apportioning off units conscious of their national identity, so that the relation between national sovereignty and state sovereignty occurs in a transitive manner. Conversely, the intransitivity of these categories in the context of non-Western societies leads to a view wherein the universality of the state model is attached solely to the dynamic of international relations.

Moreover, the paradox is exacerbated by the largely fictitious nature of the way the principle of sovereignty itself is transferred into the international sphere. According to this principle, there can be no source of authority outside the state, which is the ultimate holder of all means of constraint. In terms of international relations, only two alternative conditions exist: either states function in a relation of strict equality of power, or they produce normative and institutional conditions that allow the arbitration of their disputes. The second possibility is tantamount to abandoning sovereignty, which is contradictory, aside from the fact that sovereignty was never in effect. The first seems perfectly utopian because, in fact, the states remain unequal to each other, for it creates conditions of international competition that noticeably reinforce the gap between the juridical affirmation of sovereignty and the means by which it can be realized concretely. In this context, the principle of law becomes an ideal that the political elites of developing societies use to criticize the actual political order. Actors in non-Western nationalism use the principle of the universality of sovereign and equal nations in order to denounce inequality. The universalist principle inscribed in the West's history becomes a principle universalized by the actions of anti-establishment strategies.

The paradox of the power game derives from the fact that, in a context of weak institutionalization, the confrontation of powers becomes the sole means of competition conceivable; however, by definition, this means can involve only a small number of states. It falls to the others to define, in practice, an alternative mode of political expression that, by contravening the rules of the game, can be assimilated only through a deviation of some sort and through the exacerbation of insecurity.

From this point of view, the cold war falls perfectly in the norm, for it sanctioned a balance by terror and thus made the mutual neutralization of powers a way to validate the principle of sovereignty. That the East-West conflict became also a conflict of states and ideologies reinforced this verification, since in the final analysis it demonstrated that the confrontation of ideological concepts could only disrupt the reciprocal respect of sovereignty. The discussion made sense then because, in a disciplined competition among states seeking the maximum of unilateral advantages, each side could indicate how far it would go and at what point it considered its vital interests threatened. In short, behind this balance of power lay the implicit affirmation of a principle of equality between states that gave meaning to the hypothesis of sovereignty. Because each party was thus entirely sovereign and took full part in the same state universalism, nothing that was ultimately unacceptable for the other could take place.

The end of the cold war and the East-West conflict strongly shook this model by divesting it of at least its universality. As abstract as it may be, the hypothesis of a North-South conflict presents difficulties: a conflict of power can bring into opposition the countries of the South, as was revealed in the wars between Iran and Iraq, Algeria and Morocco, or India and Pakistan, but in no way can it pit a country of the South against a country of the North. So this second type of conflict can alternatively or jointly take forms that completely violate interstate logic: either by the massive recourse to extrastate modes of action, such as terrorism, the mobilization of transnational groups, the opposition of the state against its citizens; or by recourse to forms of war that, instead of opposing one power against another, tend to reproduce an international confrontation between dominator and dominated, thus making the conflict into a "protest" war.

The process is all the more novel for being explicitly antistate and for jeopardizing international practices: the state's monopoly of the use of violence, the recognized and institutionalized priority of allegiance relations for citizens over the network of transnational solidarity, and the use of force by the state exclusively to protect or define its sovereign boundaries. However, conflicts in the South tend to superimpose the elements of this logic and others that come from its opposite, as revealed by the instability and war that have for decades characterized the Horn of Africa.[52] Before becoming an interstate confrontation, war belonged to a long tradition of structured relations among ethnic groups, tribes, and clans, as indicated by the longevity of conflictual relations between Tigreens and Amhara within Ethiopia, but also among Ethiopians, Somalis, Afari, Issaaqi or Oromos, and equally between Ethiopians and the Muslim nomads of Eritrea. All these conflicts transcend for the most part the structures and allegiances of the state. In the middle of the Ogaden conflict, the Tigreens formed pacts with Italy in the war of conquest between Italy and Ethiopia in order to preserve the right of access to their pastures. Addis Ababa took advantage of the opposition between Muslim nobles and Christian serfs and exploited clan rivalries to contain the Eritrean separatists. At the same time, however, all the conflicts fell into the interstate context. In its conflict with Ethiopia, Somalia's president Siyaad actively sought a Soviet alliance, and confronted with particularly serious internal economic difficulties, Somalia joined the Arab League in 1974 in order to benefit from Saudi Arabia's economic and financial support. Dropped by the USSR, which preferred Ethiopia, Somalia had to solicit the protection of the United States, whereas formerly the emperor had offered the United States the Eritrean base at Gagnnaw with the purpose of obtaining its loyalty, even while he sought rapprochement with the USSR, China, Nasser's Egypt, and Saudi Arabia. Cuba and certain Arab nations even sought mediation according to the rules of international law.

Two superimposed levels come into play, though they do not have the same status: sociologically, all the components of an action that break down the interstate model to substitute other rules for it; institutionally, crisis contexts that reactivate the state interaction mode, both internally, where nations attempt to make use of communal antagonisms, and externally, where Southern nations seek–within the interplay of alliances and protections or insertions into international institutions–the means to compensate for their incapacities and their lack of legitimacy. Here as well is a logic comparable to that by which the political elite seek in state-type alignments a means to correct the weakness of their authority over their governed. In foreign policies the paradox is even more marked, since the excesses in state-like behavior indulged in by the leaders in the Southern societies transcend the tensions and contradictions opposing institutionalized international order to internal social dynamics.

Missing Civil Societies

The extreme diversity of these dynamics contrasts with the most decisive implicit element of the entire machinery that tends to dominate the Western model of political order, that is the postulate of universality that structures the concept of civil society. The historical construction of this concept has often been discussed and is based on at least three distinctive principles: the differentiation of private social spaces from the political space; the individualization of social relations that thus confers precedence on citizenship; and the presence of horizontal relations within society that gives preference to associative logic over communal structures and that, consequently, marginalizes particularist identification in favor of identification with the state.

Each of these principles sustains universality and is easily integrated into a general problematic of development that transcends each group's individual history. This problematic is explicitly associated with a normative and prescriptive approach intended to put the actors of non-Western societies under obligation. The differentiation of the private and public is considered the way to optimally reconcile general interests with private ones, while favoring the realization of a specifically economic space, which is a factor in development. Since the Enlightenment, and even more with nineteenth-century evolutionism, the individualization of social relations has been considered an emancipatory process that enhances rationality. It progressively liberates the individual from communal allegiances, from control by the group he belongs to naturally, and leads to a more free and more critical socialization. Furthermore, it detaches the individual from a natural will of the group in order to substitute a rational will, which opens the door to calculation and evaluation. Horizontal solidarities, for their part, complete the individual's liberation from his particularist identifications to instill in him a sense of his role as a function of a social construct that is not segmentary but rather organic, solidaristic, or functionally competitive. According to this reading, all communitarianism can only be residual, a legacy of tradition and bound to disappear as an entity as the governability of political systems advances. Tribalism doubly negates the principle of universality: first, by hampering the construction of a civil society capable of transcending particularities, and second, by blocking the advent of a universal modern society that would reproduce the same characteristics everywhere and thus conform to a reasoning that could be nothing other than unique.

The universalization of the model of civil society has three mechanisms at its disposal. First, it is implied by the universality given to the state model: it is the duty of the state's founders to reduce the ways by which particularist identities are formed, because these hinder the state's claim of a monopoly over authority and limit extraction and mobilization capacities. Without renouncing the value of his tribal identity, the prince seeks symbolically to substitute for it his identity as father of the nation: without effacing his Sahelian particularity, President Bourguiba promoted his role as "supreme combatant" and incarnator of the Tunisian nation; though he retained his royal title, President Houphouët-Boigny preferred a paternal conception of his relations with the people of Ivory Coast. More practically, the state actively constitutes a civil society by trying to endow itself with voluntary interlocutors that supposedly incarnate different social interests and thus transcend communal particularisms. The neocorporatist effort to construct unions or interest groups closely tied to the state should not be analyzed only as a symptom of authoritarianism, but also as an effort to more or less artificially create social spaces structured as a function of various interests.

The constitution of a civil society also occurs through strategies employed by the intermediate elite: the progressive formation of new professional categories (lawyers or journalists, for example) promotes the rise of associations. Such associations play a considerable role in India, but also in sub-Saharan Africa, particularly Ghana and Nigeria. The alignment of these categories in terms of an associative conception derives from a calculated strategy of universalization: in conformity, certainly, with a model learned in the West, where these categories were developed, but judged equally capable of protecting the specificity of their status and assuring, in the most symbolic and manifest way, their new social position.

Finally and especially, the increase of transnational inflows constitutes a powerful call, coming from the international system as a whole, for the constitution of private associative networks. Professional associations are themselves stimulated by the decrease in international nongovernmental organizations to which, if one is isolated and threatened at home, one adheres all the more willingly. The proliferation of humanitarian and human rights associations amplifies this phenomenon in that, by promoting the constitution of local branches, they accelerate the formation of embryonic civil societies and thus guarantee if not the immunity, at least a not negligible protection for a small local elite that for the most part comes from the first nascent professional associative networks. The jurist Lahidji, who took part in the creation, and then in the 1978 officialization of the Association for Human Rights in Iran, told, for example, how this association was begun by a dozen Iranian jurists and intellectuals in close contact with Amnesty International and with the Association of Democratic Jurists, and was integrated into the International Confederation of Human Rights.[53] Mr. Lahidji also recalled how it was preceded by the constitution of the Association of Lawyers. Another promoter of the same cause, the writer Hajj Seyyed Javadi, noted that it also helped the constitution of the Association of Writers. What is true of this type of association holds equally true for other professional, religious, or ideological associations and extends also to the economic sphere. In short, the international dynamic reinforces pressures–from minority and other individual sources–that support the formation of a unified civil society. It thus encourages a "dual society" composed, on one hand, of all these associative groups and, on the other, of a communitarian order that cannot be considered a mere residual effect, but rather is an integral part of the history of non-Western societies.

Thus the universality of the Western model not only declares its intentions by its discourse, it also manifests an essential practice in the workings of the international system. This system is organized around norms that are unique, but also in place culturally, wherein it obeys models deriving from Western history that weigh on each non-Western political order, as if by doing so it rectifies its own developmental trajectory. The pressure, however, does not stop at the forced universalization of interstate activities. It goes well beyond that to exert pressure notably on economic, cultural, or associative transnational inflows, thereby fostering the paradox of consolidating globally a culture of the state by means that are extrastate in nature.

In a manner perhaps still more determinantal, the tensions that give rise to this universalist logic often profit from the interstate model and even nourish it and support its completion. The mutually affirming incompatibilities between certain cultures and the territorial order help change identificatory claims linked to dominated cultures into territorial ones, thus accelerating their entry into state logic. Such was the case with the Kurdish and Tamil issues. The universalization of international law belonging to Western history leads the non-Western leaders to use its principles in order to claim the rights those principles confer. Interethnic and intertribal conflicts become interstate conflicts precisely because they activate relations among the nations of the region, precipitate or consolidate alliances, and accelerate phenomena of clientelism by the Northern powers. The weakening of internal political abilities proper to the developing political systems pushes the governing leaders to consolidate their status by acquiring a symbolic ability that they derive from their insertion in the international system. Finally, claiming the state principle of sovereignty constitutes the last symbolic advantage the princes can employ to contain the effects of dependence.

All of these dynamics are based on power relations, on a specific mode of resource distribution, and on the use of violence. But they derive as well from an original cultural configuration constituted throughout Western history that reflects a specific articulation of the particular and the universal, and the affirmation of self as a particular identity different from that of another, but all the same universalizable. The principle of the state as nation definitely lies at the center of this duality, since it supports the claims of each cultural identity to accede to sovereignty, but also the universality of a mode of political administration that finds the mark of its virtue in equalizing, normalizing, difference-effacing, and transcending particular interests. Though often incomprehensible in other cultures, the idea of the state nevertheless flatters and attracts because it evokes sovereignty and emancipation. Though subject alternatively to loss of meaning and susceptibility to misinterpretation, the state can nevertheless cultivate ambiguity to its profit.

Yet the logic of exportation finds its limits in the logic of importation at work within the importing societies. Western political models would have only the slightest chances of becoming universalized if they did not find an active reception outside their place of origin, where they were invented. Aside from an infinite number of strategies used by individual actors who benefit from carrying out these practices, the articulation of the processes of importation and exportation emphasizes the diversity of cultural constructs of the universal and, in fact, their irreconcilable nature. Where the Western model is based on a functional and very productive combination of the universal and the particular, other cultures have affirmed different combinations throughout their history, which explains many misunderstandings.

Since Hindu culture already views itself cosmogonically, it cannot be reduced to the same particular-universal distinction. The Hindu world already exists in a universal that contains within itself an infinity of particulars, notably in terms of sects and castes. This construct makes it difficult to assimilate the conception of other and self within Western categories. Hence the great difficulty of defining a Hindu or Indian nation within the international system. Hence, and more generally, the intensity of problems resulting from the need to fit into a different world and through it to accept and integrate its political models.

Islamic culture seems to present another variant. Since it is defined in relation to a universal inscribed in a Revelation, it is accessible to the other's culture, but only in the name of either a proselytism through which it exports more than it imports, or a temporary coexistence with another world that it does not accept as a bearer of universality. Without trying to be exhaustive, one could envision other examples, such as tribal cultures, that of the Nuer studied by Evans-Pritchard or the Kachin observed by Leach, which do not integrate the universal in their political construction and conceive of their moves in this area only as the reproduction of a particularist identity.[54] Tribal culture, which neither proselytizes nor considers itself in terms of a universal, is not easily brought into the dialectic of importation and exportation; this lack of affinity is perhaps one of the foundations of its resistance to incorporation into a statist framework.

These cases of cultural resistance, however, cannot be seen as eternal. They combine with the strategies of actors who find it useful to upset these orientations in order to become importers and thus try to overcome the obstacles that hamper exportation. Hesitation to universalize the Western model is then more or less surmounted politically by a desire for importation.

PART TWO

The Importation of Political Models

Exportation arouses tensions, opens gaps, creates frustrations; but it grows strong and expands. Power and hegemony do not explain everything. Western political models spread and become globalized because–perhaps principally because–they are imported. They are sought after and integrated because they meet the strategic needs of the importing actors, and thus result from individual choices guided by incentives and rewards, hopes and expectations.

For this reason, the importation of Western models concerns both actors and products, the great variety of which explains that this global process is complex, and that it lends itself dangerously well to amalgamation. The designation of sites is just as delicate. Though the opposition between the exporting North and the importing South supplies some answers, as an explanation it lacks rigor. Westernization radiates through the world's societies from a center that includes Western Europe and North America, but the insertion of Latin America becomes uncertain. Claiming its status as Western while aligning more and more with the Indian populations that reject such an insertion, Latin America is both part Western and an importer. This situation clearly differs from what happens in societies that, like Japan, India, or the Arab world, have a different history from that of the West, a different political tradition from what is now being universalized, and an entirely different culture from what makes up Western identity.

With this distinction we can see how importation works. Fundamentally, it designates the transfer into a given society of a model or practice of a political, economic, or social nature, that was invented and developed in a historical context foreign to it and that derives from a fundamentally different social order. The dysfunctions that accompany this process tend naturally to crystallize into acute cultural dissonance; but such acuteness itself is not the founding element. Even if they claim to be Western, Latin American societies live on a daily basis the logic of being borrowers, the tension between their history and that of the exporting societies, just as they undergo the effects of the forced globalization of their development and the methods used by the importing elite who govern them. These essentially compose the dynamic of importation, its constraints and setbacks.

3. Importers and Their Strategies

The principal paradox of importation logic probably comes from the wide variety of those initiating it. Widely criticized as a bearer of dysfunction and failure, the process of westernization is an integral part of the most diverse and unexpected strategies. Though often conceived as a weapon of those in power, the importation of Western models serves the purposes of protest movements as much as it does those of conservative projects. Though the target of most protest movements, it infiltrates their themes and their daily political practices. Though an instrument of action and of government, it is also widely supported by the intellectual elite, regardless of the discipline in which they think and write and regardless of the orientations of their convictions.

The Power Actors

The very workings of power place the actor in the position to borrow his ways of being, thinking, and organizing from an external source. The difficulty, however, comes from the complexity of an approach whose results are not all consciously sought; and when they are sought, they bring a mixture of desired actions and undesired restrictions. In fact, dependence derives from a complex logic that is all the more effective because it places the actor who submits to it in the position of supplicant, wherein he is fully convinced that he receives advantages from his position as dependent. Further, there are two types of dependent positions: either the dependence relative to the foreign country brings the leader new options, or it convinces him that it can in the future help reinforce his own resources of power and thus his chances of emancipation from the constraints of external control.

Importation and Conservation

Conservative modernization represents, at least in the beginning, a reasoned choice: to better preserve his power, the leader tries to adapt it to the new conditions, that is, to an ideal of modernity that he hopes will bring him both additional resources and increased legitimacy. The leader thus tries to present modernity as a neutral and universal category, hence adaptable to any culture. It is thus endowed with a legitimacy superior to what justifies all the particularisms. In this, the leader's actions claim to be superior to those of his opponents, who are consigned to the periphery as representatives of a tradition easily categorized as inferior.

Aside from this option, several strategies are possible. The first was clearly expressed by the Ottoman sultan in the nineteenth century. Focused essentially on external affairs, this strategy was an attempt to shore up crumbling power by selectively borrowing Western recipes for success. The second occurred in the very center of the Meiji revolution and tended to borrow in an effort to satisfy internal needs first. The difference between these two strategies is not clear-cut. It does, however, reveal the shape of different projects whose chances for success are far from equal, as history has already shown.

Variants of the Ottoman strategy appeared in Persia and Egypt, but also later in Morocco, the Arabian Peninsula, and Siam. The Ottoman case is the clearest: moments of heavy importation correspond closely to periods during which military strength weakened relative to the West and sultanic domination within the empire deteriorated. Thus the importation strategy was essentially selective and began in the military. In addition, westernization began under Selim III with the mission of General Sébastiani.*[1] Similarly, it was revived after Mâhmud II's defeat in Syria, with the mission of General von Moltke.† Likewise, Mehemet-Ali began a long process of westernization in Egypt, notably with the cooperation begun by Captain Sève.

---

*Translator's Note: Bastien Sébastiani (1772-1851). Napoleon's ambassador to Constantinople in 1806, a veteran of the Napoleonic Wars, and minister of the navy under Louis XVIII.

†Translator's Note: Helmuth von Moltke (1800-1891). A veteran of the Turkish campaigns (1835-39), a disciple of Clausewitz, and the author of several works on military strategy.

Strictly military in the beginning, the logic of importation extended functionally to the areas of administration and education. Military reforms begun by Selim III condemned first of all the traditional military administration; in particular, in 1807 the janissary corps set in motion a plot that culminated in the assassination of Mustafa IV. These reforms also challenged the local administrative apparatus, which was so decentralized that it hindered both the mobilization of human resources and the fulfilling of governmental functions. The logic of these reforms thus led directly from the borrowing of Western military techniques to a vast administrative reform that practiced the Weberian principle of a state monopoly on power and took over the political functions exercised locally by tribal, familial, and religious structures. During this period, there formed the first coalition of actors uneasy about westernization, in which janissaries found themselves side by side with the local notables and the *ulama*. Significantly, von Moltke's mission relaunched administrative reform by promoting, in the name of Western military rationality, the constitution of a civil service composed of agents receiving fixed salaries. Similarly, the progressive formation of a modern Ottoman army, which in 1742 numbered 400,000 men, resulted in the creation of military academies and the progressive diffusion of knowledge borrowed from positivism and scientism. This phenomenon occurred in Egypt, where modernization of the army accompanied the first administrative reforms and thus promoted the creation of ministries and provincial administrative institutions that initially oversaw conscription and later taxation. Simultaneously, Mehemet-Ali sent the first Egyptian students to Europe for their education. The creation of military schools, such as those of the infantry at Damietta, the artillery at Thourah, or the cavalry at Giza, was echoed by the August 1834 opening of a School of Civil Engineering. The latter supported the diffusion of Saint-Simonianism, where Lambert served as director of the School of Mines inaugurated in 1838; "school commissions" and "councils of public education" spread throughout Egyptian villages, where Saint-Simonians associated with educated Egyptians. In this context the first westernized elite was formed—around Minister Tahtawi, Mazhar Effendi, and the first engineers, such as Reshvan Effendi and Mustafa Effendi—and was influenced by Auguste Comte and John Stuart Mill.

The same phenomenon occurred in the history of Persia, for its defeats in the war against Afghanistan are what triggered the process of modernization and, in fact, of westernization, which first affected the army, following the same logic experienced by its Ottoman neighbors. Yet this development lacked the amplitude of the Ottoman experience because it did not involve directly and quickly enough the Persian bureaucracy, which for a long time remained trapped in neopatrimonial logic. This difference can also be explained by strategic considerations. Though the Persian bureaucracy was smaller and older, it had for a long time focused on individual advancement, so that an individual of a socially modest background had a chance to accede to the highest levels in society. Rather than organize a coherent pressure group that would militate for reforms from which it would benefit collectively, the Persian bureaucracy supported individualized strategies for social advancement or the retention of power, the latter having more to do with maintaining the status quo than promoting westernization. As a result, such efforts undertaken by Amir Kabir and Sepah Salar met with hostility and intrigues from other agents, who dissuaded the monarchs from engaging in policies of change that could be divisive and weaken support already in their favor.[2]

The very cohesive monarchical practice of westernization extended to the military, educational, and administrative sectors; this extension was, however, facilitated by intermediary strategies, some of which were chosen freely and some of which were imposed by force, nineteenth-century Persian monarchs, of course, being little inclined to support a conservative modernization, which they feared would limit the reach of their despotism. Naseredin Shah, for example, inaugurated the first polytechnic school in Teheran, though he was apprehensive about an educated–and thus antiestablishment–elite developing in his midst. Yet the essential aspects of this problem probably existed at another level. Modernization occurred in successive waves: diffusion of the Western model developed here and there, solidly infiltrating the army, administration, and education. But the absence of intermediary support within the administration itself, that is, the lack of expectation of a change from which he could benefit, almost negated the prince's efforts. The most successful aspects of westernization did have this support, as in the Ottoman empire, or as we shall see later, in Meiji Japan. On this point at least, certain developmentalist theses are partially right. The acquisition of a collective rationality and hence an esprit de corps unreservedly promoted the transformation of institutions, even if promoting a Western politico-administrative order did not seem very functional.

This phenomenon has currently acquired an even more marked importance within traditional monarchic regimes. The administrative apparatus and its agents went from merely supporting the processes of westernization to becoming a clear motivating force. Morocco is a case in point. As the perfect site for the promotion of the Western model of the state, the administration became far more than a simple support of the sharifian policy of conservative modernization. Combining their expectations with those of the urban middle classes, the civil servants were doubly motivated by their Western university educations and the reduction in contacts with their European counterparts. They acted cohesively to change the legitimacy the prince possessed from the traditional formula to a "rational-legal" concept in alignment with the Western model of the state. After a point, too strong an administrative support of importation disrupts conservative modernization, since it dangerously compromises traditional legitimacy.[3]

An essential aspect of the conservative modernization process lies precisely in the leader's efforts to simultaneously import Western models and preserve his own hold on traditional authority. The sultan Abdul Hamid II was remarkable in this respect, since he integrated a selective introduction of Western practices and institutions with a reactivation of the caliphate. In this way the sultan supported the return, not of the orthodox Islam he feared would limit his power, but of a mystical Islam that he counted on to help legitimate political and social transformation. The official support brought to the Arab Sufi sects, particularly the Rifai Alep order, is revealing because the dignitaries looked favorably upon Alep, particularly his master Abdul Khoda al-Sayyadi, who specifically wished the reestablishment of the caliphate to take precedence over the establishment of a constitutional order.[4]

Beyond the Islamic world, the nineteenth-century monarchs of Siam brought about the same process of modernization. Rama I, founder of the Chakki dynasty, sought to reintroduce the rites and principles of classical Buddhism into his country and his court; he thus initiated a long process of reform continued by his successors based on a consolidation of traditional royal legitimacy. Siam opened progressively to Western influence, which became more marked as the monarchy transformed and consolidated, and thus retained power in spite of the colonial powers then occupying Asia. The reigns of Mongkut (1851–1868) and Chulalongkorn (1868–1910) resemble what has been observed in the Ottoman empire, since both these monarchs undertook a selective westernization, especially in the military, administrative, and legislative areas, even while they were supported by the restoration of traditional legitimacy. Here, however, the process reinforced monarchical power, whereas the sultan's power in Siam continued to weaken. This weakening allowed the Siamese royalty to impose a gradual westernization on the conservative aristocracy without having to seek the support of other elite groups. At the same time, westernization meant a modulation, even a transformation, of the system of meaning: unlike the monarch of Burma, the Siamese monarch gradually played down the references to various identities supplied by Buddhism, such as Boddhisattva, Chakravartin (world governor), Devaraja (king-god), and Dharmaraja (just king); this led to a progressive secularization of the person of the king that allowed him to fulfill an increasingly active role in political life and social change. This transition to mortal status strengthened the new elite, who both supported the new policies and functioned as importers of Western models.[5]

For their part, the Burmese monarchs chose to concede nothing in the definition of their attributes or the cultural foundations of their power, and to close themselves to Western influence, with the possible exception of King Mindon Min (1853–1878). Thus the principal effect of British conquest was to topple Buddhism's role as cultural referent and standard-bearer in the process of protest mobilization and, also, as the ideology of the governing center. In any case, the difference between Siam and Burma reveals two peripheral political systems that developed in response to the West: a penetration of Western influence undertaken by the leader himself, in the case of Siam; and a closing off to the West, which resulted in a loss of independence and subsequent colonization, in the case of Burma. It is probable that no direct or exclusive relation exists between these strategies and their results, but there can be no doubt that some relation does exist: by aligning with the Western model, Siam reassured the West and at the same time strengthened its resources; by closing itself off, Burma probably hastened both colonial invasion and the dismantling of its political structures by the British administration. The conservative modernization undertaken by Siam corresponded to strategic considerations of adaptation to the international political order and an effort to protect the royal power structure against destabilization.[6]

The Meiji revolution reflects the logic of conservative modernization as well, but it derives from a very different strategy, one that assigned a different meaning to the importation of Western models. The trajectory of Japan's development has always been characterized by a strictly limited and controlled opening to the outside. Penetration by the Jesuits in the sixteenth century resulted in around 500,000 conversions to Catholicism, which precipitated the decision to expel the missionaries; in the eighteenth century the Dutch presence was tolerated only because it spread the ideology of the Reformation and helped balance the importation of Catholic values; it also favored the circulation of scientific and utilitarian ideas. However, the Meiji era cannot be analyzed as the end point of this earlier westernization, which was too weak and too controlled to topple the then-current political order; nor did it depend, as in the Ottoman empire or in Siam, on a tactical adaptation to an international order that had become confining. Westernization did, however, help restore the imperial power to a position central to and above the shogunate and the feudal order. It is significant that the process occurred by the mobilization of Western influence, by solutions very close to state logic, and by the initiative of traditional elite groups–all without provoking the protest and rejection conspicuous in Muslim societies.[7]

Mobilization of Western influence appears clearly in a sociological analysis of the Meiji elite, all of noble families, but marked too by the diversity and density of their knowledge of the West. Three years after the restoration of the imperial order, a large, governmental-level Japanese delegation spent two years in Europe and the United States. The 1889 constitution owes much to the Prussian model, notably in its definition of imperial primacy, and the new government tried to abolish feudal rights.[8]

The solutions adopted closely resemble the construction of the Western state. This was the case with military reform, which immediately built a national army placed directly under imperial authority, toppled the intermediate powers, and established a state monopoly on legal physical violence. This was also the case with the administrative reforms that converted the *daimyo* into provincial governors and the samurai into agents of the imperial bureaucracy. Finally, it was also the case with the tax reforms, which led in 1873 to a new property tax. Constructed thus on the mobilization of military, administrative, and fiscal resources, the new imperial system turned to its own profit the dynamic of centralization that came initially from the Western institution of the state.

This modernization process is all the more conservative because it relies on support from the traditional elite, in contrast, for example, to the Bismarckian revolution, which came about more through political actors than from demands on the part of the elite. Unlike the Japanese aristocracy, the Junkers actively opposed change. The solid conservative base that benefited the Meiji revolution can probably be explained by the absence of a democratic potential in the revolutionary process. Cut off from any popular support and from any reference to democracy, the selective importation of the Western model would be less likely to provoke mistrust on the part of the elite in power. Elsewhere, since the samurai had been dispossessed by the shogunate, they had little reason to invest in a rural and feudal social order; instead, they expected reform to supply them with new social roles in the context of an urbanized society. For this reason, the Meiji revolution could mobilize support from the entire traditional elite, which pressed for conversion to a meritocracy in the domain of employment and that saw a chance for adaptation in the importation of Western models. Here paradoxically, the new imperial order was built on a minimal consensus, as was the case earlier for the construction of the state in postfeudal Europe; on the other hand, selective imitation of the Western model aroused no hostility in the groups that might be victimized by it. Westernization came about more solidly in Japan than in the Muslim world because it was more a function of internal considerations, with no direct or pressing influence from without, in a more controlled manner, and without directly contravening any of the benefits gained.[9]

In fact, in most all of these cases, westernization offered a way to fill "empty spaces" or ambiguous ones. Faced with the decomposition of a feudal order that no longer permitted the shogunate to control certain areas of Japanese territory, particularly in the southwest, the Meiji revolution appealed to the logic of a monopoly on power. The Ottoman sultan tried to enact the same process in order to counter the increasing autonomization of the 'ayan that derailed every real process of mobilization or systematic control of territory. The Persian shah tended to react to the growing power of the governors, who dealt directly, and thus over his head, with foreign powers. In fact, in each of these cases, the principle of territoriality was perceived as the most valuable and essential element among all the borrowings the leaders sought to absorb from the West. Territorial logic fulfilled a double function: it favored insertion into the international order by aligning structures in place with those of the dominant powers; and it replaced a segmented imperial order by a closed, centralized state that may have diminished the prince's symbolic influence, but noticeably reinforced his capacity for decisive action. This action was a calculated risk. It turned out to be effective and lucrative for postmedieval Europe, since it had been effected through the initiative of dynastic centers that were growing in power at the expense of their disintegrating peripheries. For similar reasons, it had a positive effect in Meiji Japan, where the relation between center and periphery benefited the prince even more because the traditional elite had already been deprived of their resources by the shogunate and were pleading for reintegration into the center. On the other hand, the calculated risk was dangerous in certain conservative monarchies of the Muslim world: in the Ottoman empire and in Persia, more than in Egypt or Morocco, peripheral resistance and stirrings on the part of the notables became particularly acute, and thus worked against the construction of a state on the Western model.

The creation of a *new* political system follows a similar logic, for it also requires the formation, even the invention, of a territory, the diminution of peripheral authorities, and especially the creation practically *ex nihilo* of an entire network of institutions. The example of the Middle Eastern monarchies presents a process of conservative action, since a traditional dynastic center was in control. This construction of new states involved the double concern to protect the formula of legitimacy on which the authority of the prince rested and to endow the political scene with the institutions necessary for its functioning as quickly as possible. The need for quick, short-term action became a decisive factor in the more general borrowing from the Western model. In this respect, it is remarkable that the Iraqi monarchy, at its inception, wrote a constitution inspired by the Australian model, whereas the successive constitutions of the Hashemite kingdom of Jordan reflected Western constitutionalism and that the first was of Indian origin.[10] Perhaps even more significant, Kuwait reveals the complexity of a double reference, both traditional and Western. In the 1930s the al-Sabah emirs took up policies that went far beyond the simple tactical will to consolidate their own power. This phenomenon grew stronger with independence, acquired in 1961. Needing to assure its survival as much against Nasser's pan-Arab movement as through its connection to the traditional Wahabite monarchy, the emir Abdallah al-Salem al-Sabah sought a distinct character for his state by acquiring, under British influence, a strongly westernized constitution, dominated by the parliamentary model and by the practice of the welfare state.[11] Paradoxically, the will to distinguish itself initiated the act of importation: needing to act quickly, in the context of a state to construct, but also seeking to protect his own authority from competing models, the prince found in westernization a strategic means to preserve his own power as well as his own specificity in relation to his immediate neighbors. No paradox is lacking in the fact that the protection of identity, or at least of independence relative to an influx of threats, could be achieved by seeking Western influence. This influence has, of course, been limited and, all told, remains precarious, since the parliamentary experience accompanying it has frequently been interrupted.

Importation and Revolutions

The importation of Western models appears also in the modernization processes that invoke revolutionary legitimacy, beginning notably with a more or less selective use of socialist themes. These themes provide the advantage of being able to indict the West and to thereby sustain an anti-imperialist discourse that can explain failures in economic development. However, these socialist and revolutionary references remain essentially Western, as much in the authors who inspire them as in the conceptual system mobilized, and especially in the justification the state derives from it. Even still, one must be prudent here too and know how to tell the difference. Socialism provides both an effective basis on which to organize the state's center and symbolic compensation for the state's ineffectiveness.

The first case corresponds clearly enough to the evolution undergone by the leading elite in India, and more particularly by the Congress Party. As the principal actor in Indian nationalism and the gaining of independence, the party of India's founding fathers had been from its inception profoundly marked by Western influence. Founded in Bombay in 1835 at the instigation of a retired Englishman, Allan Octavian Hume, it initially developed a nationalist, state-centered, and secular ideology, clearly secondary to Indian culture. Its conversion to socialism was actually concomitant with its accession to power. Essentially attributable to Jawaharlal Nehru, this conversion gave the party a way to adapt to the requirements of state construction. The Congress Party was not monolithic. The circumstances in which this direction came to prevail remain very significant, not so much because of the ideological investment in them as because of the deliberate strategies toward a certain number of clearly voiced goals that they evoked.[12]

The first is the creation of a strong state for the precise purpose of overcoming the traditional political order, which was segmented both locally and socially. Providentially, socialism provided the governing elite with a way to counterbalance the centrifugal effects of the traditional conception of politics in India. We know that, contrary to the Chinese model, this conception was basically characterized not only by the breakdown of the caste system but also by a "galactic" conception of politics that traditionally tended to give over a large portion of sovereignty to different territorial units (villages, kingdoms, etc.), which made the Indian world a more or less interconnected assemblage of dispersed entities.[13] For the people attempting to develop a state that reflected the principles of the Congress Party, promoting a unifying and legitimizing conception of a strong and powerful state was an effective way to establish their monopoly on legitimate physical violence, which under cover of socialism, became the central objective of their importation strategies.

Accordingly, the socialist reference promoted egalitarian principles that, in the context of India's construction of a state, became a major asset for the governing political elite. The diminution of inequalities in a society of castes and profound regional disparities had the principal advantage of diminishing the resources of the competing traditional elite and of thus establishing the political arena as the privileged space for the exercise of power.

Finally, socialist ideology offered the new elites of the state, under the cover of a guided and voluntary project of economic development for the society at large, the means to establish influence in society and to increase public property. With precisely this perspective, Nehru set up the Planning Commission in 1950 and launched the first five-year plan the following year. Later, the Industries Act allowed no new industrial enterprise or any significant extension of existing factories to function without state licensing. In 1952 Nehru set up the National Development Council, made up of the principal ministers, which offered supplementary conditions of intervention in economic life. Nor was the agricultural sector forgotten, for it was the primary focus of the first plan, which initiated an important agrarian reform, followed by an attempt to establish cooperatives under direct state control. This important reform, presented at Nagpur in 1959 before the Congress Party, was intended to initiate a genuine socialization of agriculture.[14]

It is significant that the agrarian projects met with a lot more resistance than the industrial ones, which for the most part were successful. In the first case, the peasantry was profoundly marked by traditional culture and refused to accept the socioeconomic order authorities wanted to graft onto it. Nehru's decision to back off in this area was a prudent one. In the second case, socialization of large industry met with active support of a whole new bureaucratic elite, who found in reform a means to guarantee its own position and to reinforce its own power. To these ends, the 1955 Avadi resolution formulated by Nehru was approved. It called for incorporating production into the public sector; and the following year, the operating principle was that fundamental industries had no choice but to belong to the public sector. It is revealing that as Indira Gandhi gained power she progressively allied herself with these same options. In 1966, however, with her appointment as prime minister, she seemed to take the opposite position by seeking a certain liberalization of the economy. Very quickly, she nationalized numerous banks and insurance and mining companies. This socialization developed parallel to a gradual personalization and centralization of power that the daughter of Pandit Nehru sought to develop to her advantage. She kept her own portfolio as minister of the interior, strengthened the police and other security forces, and reinforced the public administration and its direct control. Similarly, though Rajiv Gandhi tried to initiate liberalizing policies, these were offset by the maintenance of an imposing bureaucratic structure and by the progression of his own corrupt activities. The liberal breakthroughs of Narasimha Rao became very fragile by 1991, in part precisely because of resistance by the bureaucratic middle class, which felt threatened and thus resisted them.

A similar logic can be seen in the context of the most radical political systems that have recently achieved independence. Zimbabwe, for example, evidences the unexpected effects of resistance to dependence and the strange combination of importation practices Zimbabweans were subjected to and those they provoked themselves. The Lancaster House accords concluded between Britain and the Zimbabwe African National Union, a Marxist-Leninist inspired resistance movement led by Robert Mugabe, sought to translate into institutional terms the compromise effected between the black nationalists and the white minority, which held economic power. This already precarious balance was conceived uniquely in parliamentary terms, since it allowed a minimal number of parliamentary seats to whites and guaranteed this disposition by defining a complex and restrictive procedure of constitutional revision. More concretely, these accords established a compromise that conceded economic power to whites and accepted for the blacks a political power overseen by the whites.[15]

This curious duality brought the economic sphere into opposition with the political sphere. The first was successful and closely linked to South Africa, across which 70 percent of Zimbabwe's external commerce had to be transported; the second was composed of constitutional institutions taken whole cloth from British models, and was directed by a Marxist elite educated in Christian schools but with no means of imposing its choices. These two spheres contrasted with each other in terms of different capacities. The hegemony exercised by white economic power was evident in its capacity to maintain free enterprise, to engage in close relations with South Africa, to control development in poor rural zones occupied by the black population, and also to diffuse among this population certain models of collective organization. Thus the CACU, which coordinates agricultural service cooperatives that supply black farmers, was modeled on the cooperatives of the white farmers dating from the colonial period. Also, the NFAZ (National Farmer Association of Zimbabwe) brought black farmers together in imitation of the former British master farmers' clubs.

For its part, the political arena failed to attain a position of dominance. Not a single element of ZANU's socioeconomic program was ever really put into practice. The agrarian reform project remained bogged down for a long time; planned nationalizations never occurred, and the effort to transform abandoned "white farms" into state farms resulted in only a small number of conversions. Significantly, attempts on the part of the Zimbabwean "state" to penetrate social spheres controlled by the black population failed completely. The creation of a minister of cooperatives never allowed for leadership in these social spheres, since village social life was structured more around community than around the state representative or the ZANU.

In response to its failings, the central power could manage no more than symbolic gestures. For lack of ability genuinely to affect dependence structures, and in particular the capitalist models and institutions for development, Robert Mugabe opted for a strong ideological investment, for which he turned very broadly to Marxist discourse and symbolism. These were particularly effective among intellectuals and students, for whom socialism provided compensation for the strength of white power in economic life. This inspiration resulted, in December 1957, in the shaky political party that henceforth paradoxically coexisted with a private, ultraliberal economic sector that basically controlled industrial and agricultural production.

Similarly, Mugabe sought to address the genuine problems confronting Zimbabwe (ethnic tensions, social and economic difficulties felt by rural blacks owning small properties, and especially the inability of the central power to penetrate the periphery) by manipulating political structures already in place. Failing to construct a state model possessing political competence and adapted to endogenous cultural givens, the Zimbabwean president tried to control the crisis by enacting constitutional reforms over which he had influence, but which involved the population very little.

Alignment Constraints and Composition Effects

For all its success, westernization has not resulted from free choice exclusively. It has also and especially come about in response–almost forced–to alignment constraints in relation to Western powers. Whether a matter of carrying out the wishes of these Western powers or bending to injunctions expressed in diplomatic and military terms, constraint plays a major role in importation, particularly in financial and politico-juridical areas.

The threat posed by nineteenth-century Russia weighed continually on reform initiatives pursued by the Ottoman sultan. The first constitution of the Ottoman empire, the *Khatt-e-Sharif*, was written in 1839 by Abdel Madjid I and Rashid Pasha in order to obtain an alliance with Western powers. All of its dispositions characteristically reflected moves toward the Western model of the state: the introduction of security provision, of the right to own property (regardless of the subject's religion or nationality), of taxation. This charter also provided for elections and stipulated that the death penalty could be applied only by a tribunal. Similarly, the war with Russia (1853-55) supported approval of a second charter, in February of 1856 (the *Katt-e Homayyun*), which spelled out certain important points: fiscal reform, budget annuities, the rights of Christians. In 1861, the recognition by Abdel Aziz of the empire's debts led him, in order to benefit from support by the great powers, to accept the creation of a stock market and a state bank modeled after those of France. During another disastrous financial crisis, in 1875, Midhat Pasha deposed the sultan and strove to develop a constitutional reform based on the Belgian system, specifically outlining budgetary institutions in order to resemble more the Western model.

The same process occurred in Egypt. The 1876 economic crisis provoked a call for help from the European powers, who required the participation of both English and French ministers in governmental decisions as well as a redefinition of fiscal law, which notably required the prince to submit yearly tax collections set by parliament. Similarly, each military weakening of Persia, vis-à-vis England or Russia, resulted, beyond the acceptance of military missions from Europe, in concessions to Western powers who agreed to forgive debts. Particularly, the protest movements that developed in the beginning of the century led to a progressively more active "mediation" on the part of Britain, who pressed the shah into accepting a constitution very similar to the Belgian one and, in addition, provided for the election of an assembly.

This process was remarkably timely, and it was so for one of two reasons. It could be that the leaders occasionally undertook the same steps in their external policies. For example, Anwar Sadat sought to attract attention in the West by establishing in 1974 a multiparty system that, albeit limited and under surveillance, could at least nourish the fiction of a Western-style parliamentary life. Or perhaps, on the contrary, the Western powers placed explicit conditions on their aid—in particular, they required a process of democratization that they saw purely and simply as the westernization of institutions and constitutional practices. This approach was particularly strong with President Carter and was renewed at the Baule summit at the initiative of François Mitterrand, which led certain African countries to convoke national conferences, to set up multiparty systems, and to hold competitive elections.

The importation of Western political models results not only from choice, forced or not, nor does it always have to do with a more or less forced decision by the actors. It just as often results from a mixture of choice and of social and political processes that no actor controls directly and whose realization is all the more irreversible. Such results have occurred frequently and in other countries as well, particularly in the Middle East and Japan.

Several factors have produced westernization in the Middle East. The primary factor lies in the secularization dominating nineteenth-century Ottoman history, attributable to actions on the part of the sultan, even though he did not always want secularization, which he did not find congruent with his own project of conservative modernization. The sultan wanted his brand of modernization as a means to protect monarchical power and assure his authority. It was based on maintaining a traditional authority that gave the sultan the powers of the caliph, thus sheltering him from internal rivalries, and allowed him to control sociopolitical changes more fully. Nevertheless, the construction of a state logic based on recentralization around a renewed administrative apparatus, and the monopoly of power by the sultanic center against peripheral authorities, put Mahmud II in the position of having to limit the functions of the *sheykh-al-islam*, who in effect, incarnated the presence of a religious personnel at the hub of the empire. The same motives led him to progressively diminish, then, by instituting the *Waqf*, to dismiss the religious commissioners from their positions in the army and to establish tight financial control of possessions held by the *ulama*. Here three essential elements of Western state logic are implicated: the construction of a political center claiming dominance for itself, absolute control of the military and thus of violence by the politico-administrative power, and the public overseeing of all revenue collection from the empire's subjects. The sultans tried to compensate for this loss of authority by a symbolic gesture, which led Abdul Hamid, notably, to claim full restoration of caliphal authority for himself. It was impossible, however, for them to reconcile the logic of monopolizing legitimate violence, within the very heart of the political system, with the maintenance of religious roles based on a centrality built on other principles. Undesired, secularization weakened the prince's symbolic positions, which he had to accept, nevertheless, as the direct effect of a conscious choice for the state option. This choice was dramatic because it provoked a conflict that could set in motion a counterlegitimacy and thus deprive all the conservative monarchies of any other than exogenous formulas. This phenomenon appeared progressively in nineteenth-century Persia during the Qadjar dynasty, and more brutally with the Pahlavi. It also came about in Jordan, Morocco, and the Arab peninsula, and forced the princes to seek protection in institutional immobility.

The effects of national communalization and territorialization are just as formidable. The Ottoman empire's progressive entry into the international system already brought about a territorial logic that was in no way reducible to the plurality of coexisting cultural minorities. The more delicate outcome derives precisely from this uncontrollable transformation of the very idea of minority. Traditionally, it did not amount to a national identity. The valorization of an Arab consanguinity by one Butros al-Bustani implied no demand to leave the Ottoman empire, no more than did the presence of a thousand-year-old tribalism among the Kurds. Minorities found their identity both in the expression of a cultural symbolism and in the claim of autonomy, which is actually one of the principal prerogatives of the imperial order. Yet historians have recently shown that the gradual progression toward a national focus and then a nationalist one owes very little to the direct spread of the Western idea of nation; rather it owes considerably more to a complex mixture of diverse political changes.[16] The well-known channels of entry for a nationalist ideology were in reality very fragile. Christian schools contributed to this in Syria, but they affected just a small fraction of the elite, and even this was undermined by the fact that the Christian minority had strategically chosen Ottoman ambiguity over an Arab nationalism that could potentially entrench them even deeper into the status of minority. There were militant secret societies, influenced by Western ideas, that supported the Arab nation, such as the Society of Young Arabs located in Paris. But they came about late in the game and counted only a few individuals in their ranks. Whatever their importance intellectually, they held little sociopolitical relevance.

Similarly, the classic thesis that sees the middle classes as vectors of national propaganda was gradually questioned. To see a heart and will in a vaguely defined collective subject is an excess that sociologists have often justly rejected. Moreover, historical analysis shows that the principal promoters and pioneers of Arab nationalism were recruited from the ranks of the traditional elite, notably Syrians from the Sunni milieu in Damascus, that is, from the same social context in which the most loyal agents of the Ottoman empire were found. Thus in fact, nationalism initially seemed triggered by competition with the fast-developing political and administrative bureaucracy, whose recruitment possibilities were inevitably limited. Individually, it reflects an exit strategy deployed by an autochthonous elite, disappointed at not benefiting from changes in the imperial order and the effects of a westernizing bureaucracy. Formerly, the struggle for status required one to obtain a religious position or to align with tribal power; but later the construction of "modern" political and administrative institutions became the primary site of competition. Henceforth, the birth of a closed and selective public space took priority over the formation of identifications and left those excluded from that space to define their own identification by claiming another public space possessing a superior legitimacy. As an element in a cultural discourse, the concept "Arab" became the tactical element in political practice and an argument for rejecting the practice of delimiting a sovereign space. Arab nationalism is principally an effect of the importation into the Muslim world of the Western idea of public space. Introducing a new grammatical element paves the way for more new elements to enter the discourse.

This does not mean that Arab nationalism is imputable exclusively to competition among the elite groups, but this process accounts for a significant portion of its genesis and its early evolution. It bears the mark of the ambiguities attending its birth, particularly in that it approaches the masses through the large-scale nationalist ideologies that have punctuated the history of the Arab world over the last four decades. It was supported by the poorly controlled increase in social mobility and especially urbanization, and thus reflects social instability; but that alone does not make it part of a system of significations genuinely integrated by the masses. For example, it rapidly developed into an adherence to a charismatic individual, Nasser being the most famous; it was frequently confused with religious principles; and the mobilizations it provoked were extremely precarious.

Moreover, the rise of a Western-type bureaucracy did not alone engender nationalist behavior. Mobilization by the center also produced similar effects, notably on tribal and community structures. For example, Sultan Abdul Hamid himself enlisted various tribes in an army commanded by the imperial center and thus considerably accelerated the formation of nationalist sentiments in the peripheral areas of his empire. The Hamidiyya was created in 1891, made up essentially of Kurds. By mobilizing tribal groups, by bringing the members closer together, by reducing transfers and placing the men under the command of personnel not of their own extraction, the Hamidiyya transformed Kurdish identity from a feeling of belonging to a community-based and segmentary entity into a sense of belonging to a vast entity with a specific character within the empire. Once again, one element of state logic, this time the mobilization by the center of military resources, led directly to the awakening of a nationalism that played, in turn, an important role in reinforcing a competing Armenian nationalism.[17]

Clearly, colonial practices contributed decisively to expressions of nationalist behavior. There too, however, the construction of a governmental center was much more important than the identity of even its leaders. In Egypt as in Iraq, the British presence was denounced as such by a small nationalist elite, supported in Egypt by rural notables who had formerly supported Urabi Pasha.* For the others, the essentially provincial uprisings in March of 1919 proclaimed the right to maintain traditional autonomy from the powers in Cairo, regardless of the leader in place. Similarly, the October 1920 revolts that shook Iraq were initially tribal, more peripheral than central, and more anti-taxation than directly anti-Western. Since these revolts were traditional in nature, they only gradually became part of nationalist activities, which many saw as due in part to European interests that classified them as nationalist. Though they were initially antipolitical, by virtue of their confrontation with Western-crafted governmental structures, they became the point of departure for the mobilization of the Egyptian or Iraqi people in support of the nation.[18]

Ultimately, the construction of a nationalist logic brought up the problem of territorialization. Now territorialization grew out of a direct constraint imposed from without, notably the Treaty of Sèvres.† But it developed just as much from a conversion of the identification modes found in diverse collectivities into a national sentiment that produced confused territorial claims. British diplomacy tried to turn this conversion to its own profit by promoting the creation of a Kurdish state, which would offer the double advantage of a weakened Ottoman empire and the acquisition of a client state. But this and other operations failed because of the two obstacles that show just how much the territorial principle comes from an unclear exportation: the impossibility of defining a Kurdish geographical space—particularly in the Armenian presence—and the mistrust of tribal chiefs only too aware of what they stood to lose by a strong Kurdish national community. In each of these cases, the elements of a communitarian culture work to relativize and nullify the rise of any national sentiment echoing Western grammar. The superimposition of these two logics is, moreover, easily explained as the competition between Kurdish movements and

---

*Translator's Note: Urabi Pasha, a leader of the Nationalist Movement, who led an insurrection against the British in 1882.

†Translator's Note: Treaty of Sèvres (August 10, 1920). The treaty between the Allies and Turkey that officially dissolved the Ottoman empire.

their leaders, between Sharif Pasha, working alone and residing in Paris, imbued with Western culture, militating for a Kurdish nation-state, and multiple local tribal chiefs working to activate communitarian tribal allegiances. In fact, the case of Kurdistan is not unique. The imbrication of territorial and communitarian logics, the ambiguous combination of nationalist and communitarian behaviors, each of which is sustained by various political practices, are all found in Lebanon, Armenia, and Turkey; in other words, in each case there arises the problem of different minorities in close juxtaposition.

In the westernization of Japan, the same forces were at work. Beginning in the sixteenth century, the shogunate's active political scene required the *daimyo* to reside in Edo (Tokyo) and the samurai to leave their rural residences, in order to limit the autonomy of both groups. This hierarchical restriction of feudal logic had several effects. It limited the political usefulness of land; it soon caused a shift toward the city, pauperized the samurai class, and precipitated their frustration politically and financially, since they lost their employment. It thus placed certain groups in the position of asking to be integrated into the political arena. The participation of samurai and certain *daimyo* in the Meiji revolution can be explained not only by the dissolution of their bonds with the shogunate but also by their efforts to reconstitute their positions of power within a modern state. In addition, the samurai's loss of basic resources led to their involvement in the construction of an industrial economy, which helps explain both the rapid progress of Japanese capitalism, particularly its immediate acceptance by the elite, and the rather massive diffusion of those elements on which Western industrial culture is based. If we compare Prussia's conservative modernization with that of Japan, which have long been considered similar, we can see the specificity of comportment proper to the traditional elite who are both solicited and dispossessed, and thus led to invest themselves in innovation and, in fact, to seize whatever advantages they can find in the recomposition of an imperial state subject to westernization. This only seems paradoxical, for the traditional identity of the elite in Japan supported their active alignment with the Western model.

Two other elements enter the picture. The absence of mass movements, either by peasants or, more significantly, workers, made the importation of Western models all the more selective. Chances to democratize were small, since democracy had no potential importing agent within Meiji society. In addition, Japan's long-standing tradition of isolation, which for centuries had stifled and limited every effort of the West to influence or control the country, allowed for a clear distinction between importation and subjugation; it also reconciled the fostering of fastidious nationalism combined with imitation without risk of institutions imported from Europe. Thus the traditional Japanese elite, whose involvement as innovators and importers was so unexpected and, initially at least, unsought, could gradually and consciously assume this role without fearing opposition.

The Creation of an Importing Class

Lastly, westernization has maintained itself by its own dynamic. In fact, it supports the rise of an entirely new elite whose lasting quality is linked to the safekeeping, indeed the reinforcement, of importation. From the beginning of the nineteenth century, the entourage of the traditional princes was already composed of councillors, ministers, and courtiers who quickly understood that the imitation of European constitutional models and practices could allow them to seize some of the power monopolized by the prince and at the same time to acquire a minimum of autonomy and a mark of their own identity. This was the comportment of the Egyptian Tahtawi, minister of Ismail Khedive, and the Tunisian Khary ed-din, both prudent importers but convinced of the principles of early nineteenth-century European political liberalism. They admired the Orleans charter and successfully used constitutional processes, representative institutions, and political debates to create the conditions necessary to a political life and a public space in which they would be pivotal.[19]

More profoundly, this reformist logic surpassed its creators to form a new generation of westernized elites, who drew their basic resources from their education in Western-influenced schools. Composed of doctors, engineers, officers, and civil servants, these elites were directly absorbed by the state or integrated into civil society, in journalistic, legal, or intellectual sectors. In the first case, they very soon became linked with the state; in the second, much more frequently, particularly in the Ottoman empire, they took positions of control in political and administrative institutions, where they found a legal-rational legitimacy that did not disguise its conformity to the Western model. This strategy, which was particularly that of the Young Turks, led to a rapid increase in the logic of borrowing and channeled political debate in the direction of conflicts among different conceptions of the practical means of westernization.[20]

The prince's vigorous efforts at importation only intensified the debate. Here, as Ira Lapidus notes, the difference is clear between the "Ottoman world" in the larger sense and the other Asian Muslim countries. Colonization is not a decisive variable and plays a much less decisive role than the strategies deployed initially by the center. Under the khedive's initiative, Egypt was able to acquire a positivist-inspired civil elite that, though threatened subsequently by the British protectorate, chose to strengthen itself through its directorship of the Egyptian nationalist movement. Like the Young Turks, adepts of a utilitarian secularism and seduced by Durkheim or Frédéric Le Play,* this national elite thought of itself as Saint-Simonian and excluded the *ulama* from its ranks. In contrast, the importation of models occurred much more evenly in Indonesia or Persia, for example, where the westernized elite was more easily absorbed by the center: relegated to subaltern administrative roles (*priyayi*) where it was considered complicitous with the Dutch colonizers, in the case of Indonesia, or completely co-opted by the neopatrimonial logic of the political system, it left the task of mobilizing the opposition to the traditional religious elite.[21] Thus in Iran the function of opposition crystallized around the *ayatollah*(s), leaving little room for the Mossadeghist movement, whereas in Indonesia it was sparked by a coalition of *ulama*, merchants, and farmers, embodied particularly in Sumatra by the Padri movement, which mobilized coffee growers nervous about commercializing their production.

The unification of the political space around high-level secular personnel does not occur, however, without provoking negative, destabilizing effects. Deliberately excluded from political debate, the religious elite can choose, as in Egypt, to play the card of communitarian investment, which favors the constitution of countersocieties that transform protest into a way out of the political system, as is attested by the reduction in the number of small communities seeking total control of the individual by depriving him of his role as citizen. Similarly, integration of the elite into westernizing forces leads to their separation from the intermediate levels constituted by minor civil servants, teachers, subaltern officers, and students, who are precisely those led to express their bitterness toward a Western model to which they have no real access.[22] Inquiries regarding these groups within the contemporary Egyptian population reveal the ambiguity of their attitude toward the West, that is, their fascination and their fear, both dominated in fact by a presentiment of menace, which is largely the combined ex-

---

*Translator's Note: Frédéric Le Play (1806–82). A French engineer and economist, he was the principal proponent of conservative and traditional social Catholicism. His ideas influenced the late-nineteenth-century movement to restore authority to landowners, bosses, and fathers.

pression of their inability to gain entry into the higher, westernized spheres of the state and civil society. Probably, for these reasons, the menace is perceived essentially in cultural terms: the West is condemned because it saps the values and modes of internal social structures, which progressively divests middle-level individuals of resources that would provide them a basis for their own identity.

This cultural tension reveals the extent of these two groups' differences: those intermediate individuals radicalized by virtue of their increasing identification with traditional values and those leaders whose strength lies in their capacity as professional importers of Western models. A similar process occurs in the "Sanskritization" that M. N. Srinavas had already observed in India in the 1950s. Excluded from a power strongly marked by the predominance of Anglo-Saxon references, the middle classes reacted by investing symbolically in the apprenticeship and mastery of the more traditional cultural domains.[23]

Other elements join with this dynamic to make it a veritable vicious circle. Not only does westernization survive on the elite that it maintains, but it is nourished by its own failures. Confronted with power, the elite measures itself daily by the difficulties and tensions produced by development. The impossibility of finding solutions to demographic, social, and economic problems renders the leaders absolutely powerless, forcing them to direct most of their political efforts in areas that are the least costly, the most spectacular, and most able to sustain the relegitimation of increasingly deficient leaders. This overvaluation of the political arena can appear out of nowhere or in periods of crisis, but it takes the form of massive importations of political practices and symbols from the West.

Zimbabwe, unable to control either agriculture or industry, tried to build a petite bourgeoisie from the black population drawn from an active Africanization of the public sector and the army, and also from an effective economic support brought to the small sector represented by the black agricultural producers who were able to export their goods (covering 4 percent of the land). Whether from the interior or the exterior, this petite bourgeoisie initially merely supported the state; henceforth, however, it was not only bound to the state but also derived its identity from that connection. Since it thus managed to distinguish itself from the large majority of the African population, its method consisted—as it does to this day—in espousing to a maximal degree the Western-style state symbolism that also distances it from other civil social spaces.

The conservative strategy of the black petite bourgeoisie has its counterpart in most non-Western societies. It dips abundantly into the turn-of-the-century state ideologies forged in the West when the underclasses called for an active state intervention to redistribute wealth. Heard by those in power, the eloquent discourse imported by the elite became a new and unexpected form of westernization; it became even less of an appropriation in that it tended to imbue those at the summit of power with the implicit logic of coexistence that belongs to every tribune. A barely softened Marxism in southern Africa, Baathism in the Middle East, Getulism or Peronism in Latin America–these ideologies reassure those in power with a political grammar imported from the West, but which is comprehensible only to a state that retains its power and its exogenous nature.

However, the extension of the economic crisis into developing societies seems to have triggered a substantial change. Politics of "structural adjustment," which the Southern countries have gradually had to undergo, whatever their political orientation, mark a process of disengagement from the state and thus the progressive abandonment of ideologies linked to its interventionist efforts. Algeria presents a remarkable case in point. The FLN ideology, which since independence has been marked profoundly by state socialism, seems to have disappeared in favor of pragmatic concessions to liberalism. Thus the second Algerian plan proclaims the need to spread the costs of development among the state and other economic agents, from the business community to private households. The founding myth of a public sector responsible for development is explicitly surpassed by the announced will to satisfy social needs, to find new sources of financial support, and especially to help relieve the state of pressures from many aid requests. The new Algerian technocratic elite needs, in fact, to differentiate itself from the economic space, even at the cost of assuring the rise of the private sector, in order to avoid the risk of being implicated in a dangerous state bankruptcy. Hence the call for private savings, banking policies, and calls for decentralization of authority over the business sector.[24]

This process of differentiation between the state and the economic sector means first of all a new convergence with the Western model of development. The rejection or the marginalization of these ideologies expresses, in fact, a functional banalization of the state and an alignment in terms of a duality between politics and economics. This process reflects the neoliberalism in effect in the West during the 1980s, which was holding to the idea of a unique and universal way to handle crises. Far from weakening the political elite, neoliberalism guarantees its safety against the aftershocks the state and its personnel would be sure to feel from economic collapse. On the other hand, there are risks: the positions acquired by the state in the economic sector are absolutely necessary in order to contain the emergence of competitive forces. Similarly, the diffusion of socialist and dependentist ideologies allows the state to exculpate itself from economic failures by imputing them to the international capitalist system. By technologizing the economy, the elite risk accelerating and feeling the full brunt of protest activity, as was the case after the liberalization policies mounted by Sadat in Egypt in 1977 (*infitah*),* or after the efforts of structural adjustment undertaken first in the early 1980s in Tunisia and Morocco, then at the end of that same decade in Algeria.

Importing Intellectuals

The intellectual's role in westernization is paradoxical: identified with a culture he holds within himself, he nevertheless imports a system of thought and action from without. However, the intellectual's path in the Muslim world shows that the contradiction is easily explained. As the inventor of his own space, the intellectual quickly finds himself in a double opposition to both the constituted powers and the protests directed at them by traditional sectors of society. As soon as he aspires to equip himself with autonomous sources of power and to occupy a real position in society, he runs up against both princely authoritarianism and the effects of a pure and simple reproduction of religious knowledge that his own efforts cannot contravene. The face-to-face encounter between neopatrimonial power and ancestral tradition presents a fearsome obstacle to the professionalization of the intellectual. For he can escape it only by a more or less massive borrowing from foreign systems of thought, which itself brings other dangers and other failures in its wake.

The itinerary followed by Hajj Seyyed Javadi, nicknamed the "Iranian Sakharov," is revealing. While in exile in Paris, he recalled the important role he played in triggering the 1979 revolution, denouncing the rigorous symmetry between the shah's regime and that of Khomeini; he also recalled that, as an intellectual, he could only be elsewhere: "When the shah was in power, I was not allowed to leave Iran; now during the Islamic Republic, I cannot return."[25] Born in Qazvin in 1925, he completed his secondary and then university studies in Iran, and then went to France for four years for his university education. After the coup d'état that ousted Mossa-

---

*Translator's Note: The *infitah* was Sadat's effort to open Egypt to the West, which exacerbated the economic crisis and triggered the insurrection of 1977.

degh, he worked as a journalist and writer, a time punctuated by arrests, clandestine activity, and censure. Shortly before the revolution, he wrote two "open letters" to the shah, denouncing authoritarianism and corruption, and citing words used by Vaclav Havel to Husak. These letters were enormously successful and spread like wildfire from the university to the bazaars, playing a major role in prerevolutionary mobilization. With Bazargan,* Javadi created the National League for the Defense of Human Rights and fought "for a regime where the king must reign without governing, for free elections, for freedom of expression, the emancipation of women, the separation of powers, the independence of parliament, the forming of a constitutional assembly, and the defense of political prisoners." After proclaiming a state of siege, he wrote an "Open Letter to the Army," for which he was arrested. Once Khomeini attained power, he reacted to one of the Imam's first speeches, in which he called upon women to wear the chador, by denouncing the "noise of fascist boots."

Hajj Seyyed Javadi lived primarily in Iran and was awakened to political consciousness by sentiments of revolt against "the colonial situation in an Iran then pulled between Russia and Great Britain," which made "the fight against imperialism" the major element in his engagement. He had nonetheless, however, developed the basics of his political thought from a Western intellectual production: from his discovery, at age twelve, of Jean Valjean, and his readings in Rousseau and Montesquieu; to his wartime engagement within the communist movement, his participation in the Tudeh Party, his adherence to Marxism, from which he later distanced himself, and his admiration for Pierre Mendès France, whom he considered his model.

Hajj Seyyed Javadi acknowledges that Marxism was nothing other than an imported product, and he remembers having come to it in a context where he had lost all historical memory: "When I was twenty, I had no memory of Iran's past. Dictatorship had suppressed all celebrations of the past, with the exception of the king's and the martyr Hussein's birthdays. The accession of Reza Shah was the only moment in our history that we could celebrate. Marxism was acceptable for a generation that had no memory of the past." This flight toward elsewhere and toward abroad seemed the only coherent way to withdraw from a political system that rejected debate and to construct a place for oneself in a society where tradition blocks any invention of other models: "Persian society was very

---

*Translator's Note: Mehdi Bazargan (1905–95), a reformist Muslim intellectual. He was named the first prime minister of the Islamic Republic by the Ayatollah Khomeini in 1979. He resigned after the taking of the U.S. hostages later that year, fed up with the fundamentalist radicalism of the Iranian revolution.

quickly engulfed by an unrestricted Islam. Moreover, violent contacts with Arabs and Timorese Mongolians prevented any stabilization of Persian thought. From the time of the Safavids, everything was included in religion; all cultural poles were closed by theology, Arabic grammar, the *fikh*."

The way out was henceforth very clear: borrowing Western ideas of modernity, rationality, and sovereignty allowed an escape from the dilemma of a sociopolitical order that offered no role to the intellectual. By opposing Western culture made of rationality to the "Asian culture" of "fatalism, death and the other world," the intellectual designates the place where he can realize his own power. Reason and sovereignty are the two qualities that restore to man the possibility of creating, of inventing outside institutional tutelage; modernity constitutes the legitimization of the work of invention that he sees as his own. Referring to the Aga Khan, Pirnia (Mushired-Dawle), and Mossadegh, whom he considers the first modern Iranian intellectuals, Javadi emphasizes that all three began to rationalize the system by separating power and religion, whereas the establishment of a theory of national sovereignty dominated the 1906 Persian revolution, from which resulted the first constitution.

However, two paradoxes derive from the professionalization of the intellectual. The work of invention that he claims justifies his professionalization quickly evolves into the work of importation. Assigning himself a creative role in the short term, and participating in importation in order to define his functions, reinforces borrowing at the expense of production. For Seyyed Javadi the state is characterized by the separation of powers, the parliamentary system, and regional elections; the republic is definitely modeled after the West, and secularism has to come about "without hurting religion," even if the Arabic and Persian vocabularies have no term to designate what can be called *jodâ'i*, which in Persian means "separation," without mention of its object. In addition, the price to pay is a distance from the people: the Persian intellectual does not have in the 1979 revolution the same status as the intellectual of the French Revolution, for his chances to communicate are of the very weakest. The price of this hopeless rupture is a perpetual exclusion, a permanent exile that the intellectual can stand only with the help of developmentalist arguments, by complaining of the "backwardness" of the people and their lack of culture—a cumbersome proof that draws its actor into a forced westernization.

Significantly, the synthesis between westernization and cultural backwardness is brought about with the idea of nation: the authoritarian regime, like the people nourished by tradition, "causes the failure of the national construction." The regime does it through self-interest, dividing to govern, distancing itself to avoid redistribution, fragmenting to avoid protest. The people do it by an excess of identification with traditional, ethnic, tribal, village, or familial communities. The result is negative in that it incites irresponsibility and dictatorship. On the other hand, the intellectual is the "only one in a position to create the nation," to diffuse national sentiment, to teach its virtues. This function completes his position of power: by supporting the dismantling of traditional sociopolitical structures, diminishing the function of mediation held by the peripheral authorities in the definition of legitimation, and creating conditions of ideological debate and the formation of a public space, this function confers a genuine status on the intellectual, which he could not obtain in any other way. Furthermore, this function makes the intellectual into the importer of Western constructions of nationalism and the idea of nation. Thus to the idea of the national state, Seyyed Javadi gives primacy over all other political action, seeing it as the central element in the conception of the ideal city.

Hajj Seyyed Javadi's adventure is not unique; all non-Western societies are acutely marked by this same tension between an authoritarian regime and a tradition endowed with a strong capacity for social control, as in the Muslim world and as in the worlds of India and Japan. The formation of a class of intellectuals differentiated from society is first of all imputable to the spread of education that dominated the nineteenth century: the establishment of Saint-Simonian schools in Egypt, the rise of a positivist-inspired academic current in Turkey, the increasing success of Christian schools, and also of Masonic lodges in Syria. It relates equally to the new mobility of children of the bourgeoisie and the aristocracy, who continued their studies in the West. Thus, among the new Ottoman intellectuals in the nineteenth century, Ibrahim Sinasi studied public finance in Paris; Ahmed Riza pursued agricultural studies in Grignon; and the Syrian Michel Aflak studied at the Sorbonne from 1928 to 1933.[26]

The strategy of these intellectuals who separated themselves from a strongly integrated sociopolitical order was first of all to acquire a very strong network of associative solidarity that gradually accentuated their identity as importers. The creation of journals played a decisive role inasmuch as the model of the Western press was a privileged source of influence. Thus it was in the Ottoman regimes of Takvimi Veka'i, founded in 1831, of Terjumani Ahval, begun in 1860, and especially of Tasviri Efkyar, who supported by Ibrahim Sinasi, appeared on the scene in 1862 upon his return from France and at a time when he was involved in extensive translations of French literature into Turkish. The rise of literary salons, such as those of Amy Kher or Marie Cavadia, fulfilled the same function of sociability in Egypt between the two world wars, where westernized intellectuals cultivated their distinctness and strengthened the value of their role by addressing each other with honorific titles. There were also libraries, such as Henri Curiel's, in the center of Cairo, and especially the numerous more or less secret "societies" founded by Boutros Al-Bustani at the end of the last century, in part under the influence of American Protestant missions, such as the Association of Turk Derneye founded by the Young Turks in 1908 and the Arab Syrian Congress held for the first time in Paris in 1913.[27]

This associative logic certainly solidified the autonomy of the new intellectuals. The way they extricated themselves from politics also helped. In the beginning, they were all linked with the Western model of the state, in conformity with their vision of the universal and the rational, which corresponded closely with their identity. As children of the upper administrative cadres or themselves in that position, they expressed a close solidarity between their status and the political usage of reason: Abd al-Haqq Hamid was the ambassador to Paris, London, and Brussels; Ibrahim Sinasi interrupted his career as writer and journalist to work in the upper administrative echelons of the Department of Education; the father of the Egyptian Georges Rassim was himself ambassador to Rome, Madrid, and Prague; the Persian Forughi held the highest government positions, just as did the Tunisian Khayred-Din and the Egyptian Tahtawi. When they were not sons of this intellectual caste, politicians marked their attachment to the state by acquiring the attributes of an intellectual: the Persian prime ministers Vosuq Dawle and Qavam Saltaneh pursued parallel careers as translators, and Gamal Abdel Nasser–an assiduous reader of Victor Hugo, Dickens, Napoleon, and Rousseau–wrote an article on Voltaire entitled "Man and Liberty" as well as works on military science and history.[28]

It is evident that, materially, this link can be undone when the intellectual enters into conflict with the state, of which he very quickly became the victim. It is equally clear that the situation became more complex when certain intellectuals thought it a good move to tap into a revivalist construction that would denounce the exogenous nature of the Western state. The depth of their original connections, however, can not be totally denied. The abandonment of all references to state and nation resulted in too great a loss of autonomy and even identity for the intellectual to resolve. The Baathists make this an essential mark of their discourse; as for Islamic intellectuals, they make it the major argument for their separation from the clerical elite: Abol Hassan Banisadr sees in the reference to the nation the source of his fundamental distinction from Khomeini;[29] the Tunisian Ghanushi in no way rejects the concepts of state and nation.

The Indian nationalist movement in general, and the Congress Party in particular, abound with this type of intellectual, who has participated actively in the construction of the Western-configured state that India currently possesses. In the beginning, the Indian Association, founded in 1876 and supported by a series of journals, was effectively constituted by a group of Westernized Indian intellectuals working to create an independent nation-state. Its creator, Surendranath Banerjea, had shown his attachment to Western state structures by successfully passing the entrance exams for the Indian civil service. Having resigned from his position, he traveled to England and returned to India to combine work as an English professor with the promotion of the Indian nationalist movement. His work, *A Nation in the Making*, published the year of his death, speaks in terms of Western nationalism.[30]

In 1925 Sarojini Naidu became the first woman to preside over a session of the Congress Party. A Brahmin and a poet, she also held a doctorate from the University of Edinburgh; she knew Britain, wrote in the English language, and was a militant nationalist. Sarvepalli Radhakrishnan, one of the greatest contemporary philosophers of Hinduism, was able to combine even more significantly Hindu references with a Western education, nationalist militancy, and service to the state. As holder of the Chair of Oriental Religions at Oxford, he militated from within the Congress Party for India's independence; then he began a long political and administrative career that took him to Moscow as ambassador, and then to the presidency of the republic. Written in English, certain of his works have contributed significantly to the work of reconciling East and West, for example, *East and West in Religion* and *Eastern Religion and Western Thought*. Rabindranath Tagore is hardly an exception. As the most eminent representative of modern culture, he most distinctly combines Western borrowings with nationalist expression. After having divided his formative years between Calcutta and Great Britain, he joined the nationalist movement in 1905. He wrote in Bengali as much as in English, being as much a spokesman for Indian patriotism (*Nationalism*, 1917) as for a universalist religious belief (*The Religion of Man*, 1920).[31]

Finally, one can cite numerous cases within the intellectual class, where Western influences are felt as well as an attraction for the state. In London Ramesh Chandra Datta passed the Indian civil service exam and later read

Indian history at the University of London. He subsequently returned to India, where he worked for the state of Baroda and pursued a career as writer, publishing works on Indian history and translating the *Mahabharata* and the *Ramayana* into English. His namesake Michael Madhusudana Datta even converted to Christianity. In his native language, Bengali, he wrote several dramas, one of which was directly inspired by the *Iliad* and another by Shakespeare, as well as numerous poems, some of which were inspired by Ovid and others by the *Fables* of La Fontaine.[32]

The function of the intellectual in the context of the Japanese Meiji is comparable to that observed in the Muslim and Indian worlds, in that it actively participates in the process of westernization. The risk of a break with tradition and thus political marginalization, however, was less because Japanese political culture rests more on the affirmation of the divine rights of imperial dynasties than on a complex religious knowledge claiming to constitute a political doctrine. Thus westernization of thought could occur in a less conflictual manner. Westernization of education was officially begun in 1872, and the interdiction against Christianity was practically eliminated in 1873. Most of the intellectuals who imported Western models came from modest samurai families who had experienced Western languages and sought in such an investment to compensate for the weakening of their status following the crisis in feudal society and their subsequent marginalization. Just as significantly, their insertion into active life came about either by the acquisition of powerful positions in associative networks, or by their integration into the modern state. They spread among the Movement for Liberty and People's Rights (the first political party, created in 1874), and the Society of Year Six, which more extensively represented intellectual elitism. The latter founded the *Review of Year Six*, begun by Mori Arinori, a onetime minister of education, around which clustered Nishi Amane, Tsuda Mamichi, and Kato Hiroyuki (all three senior civil servants), and especially Fukuzawa,* the greatest of the Meiji intellectuals.

Seeking to break with a shogunate that increasingly excluded them, these intellectuals became promoters of a reason more practical than philosophical; they bypassed traditional social structures without overturning the current religious and cultural order, which allowed them to acquire a major role in the definition of a new constitutional order and to legitimize a process of social ascent that they and others like them wanted.

---

*Translator's Note: Yukichi Fukuzawa (1834–1901), author of numerous works that helped to introduce Western civilization into Japan. He fought for the establishment of a constitutional monarchy.

Hence the importance of works that diffused Western law, notably Kato's; hence translations of Hobbes, Montesquieu, de Tocqueville, Bentham, and Rousseau's *Social Contract* by Nakae Chomin, himself named the "Rousseau of the Orient." Hence also the translations of the Christian Nakamura, who provided a Japanese version of John Stuart Mill as early as 1871, at the same time he translated one of the greatest literary successes of the period, *Self Help* by Samuel Smiles, a veritable defense of social ascension and individual success, both of which were conceived as the result of moral experience, work, perseverance, and frugality.[33]

According to Fukuzawa's formulas, the intention was to "leave Asia," to reconstruct a Japanese national character within the West. Because of the vagueness of political models that wavered between German statism, English liberalism, and French democracy, the task consisted in marrying rational individualism with Japanese tradition, of promoting the individual seeking happiness and interest by reason, and condemning outmoded ideas in order to better express the frustration of intellectuals as victims of rigid social structures.[34] This type of borrowing was situated at the exact intersection of collective and individual rationality. The collective rationality was that of the traditional oligarchies dispossessed by the shogunate; "individual rationality" reflected the features needed by the new intellectuals in order to establish themselves as an autonomous category.

The Protesters

The role of protest could seem, a priori, to escape the logic of importation. Is it not an increasingly explicit rejection of or challenge to attacks against independence, against traditional culture and the symbolic structures of the national collectivity? Yet the practice of protest is itself a carrier of westernization, even if the diversity of its origins and orientations makes it a complex and multiform process. The intellectual himself, through his discourse and actions, can be a producer of protest, just like the rest of the liberal political elite, forged, as we have seen, in the very structure of the Western-style state edifice. Both of these actors are, by definition, carriers of values and modes of protest that come from without. But protest can also come from the traditional elite, the very ones who rise up against such actions and feel threatened by them. Far from being marginal, such action by the traditional elite plays a central role because it corresponds with the people, who often seek to understand the transformation or mutilation of their symbolic universe. This protest, essentially a cultural one, can be expressed directly, by mobilizing around its own discourse or, most often, indirectly, by articulating all sorts of protests linked precisely to state construction. In both cases, its insertion into the political scene converts it, either manifestly or latently, into a vector of messages that it had previously opposed or that it continues to simultaneously oppose. More paradoxically perhaps, the context of its action is not the only factor. Protest strategy itself very quickly becomes the carrier of this perverse effect and–in order to conceal its shifts–the producer of an often surprising discourse.

The insertion into the political scene reveals the trap westernization lays for those who rise up against it. Abol Hassan Banisadr tells how the Ayatollah Khomeini's behavior changed along with the growing Islamic revolution, which he hoped to lead. "At Nadjaf, Khomeini did not want to hear anything about the nation because he opposed the idea of national sovereignty, since sovereignty was God's alone, and the nation had been imposed by the West. In Paris, he was made to understand that one could not at one and the same time ask the people to rise up and to refuse it sovereignty. Khomeini accepted this, and then proclaimed that he wanted a national state. He also agreed to speak in terms of independence, democracy, and progress. Once back in Teheran, he again challenged what we others considered as acquired."[35]

This type of shift is very common in the history of Islamic protest. It had already clearly appeared with nineteenth-century revivalism, its first occurrence. The context itself weighed heavily on the situation. Since it challenged sultanic despotism, this current converged with the liberal movements unfolding in Europe; fighting against a tradition that dispossessed it, it willingly affiliated with the themes of progress that sprang from a Europe fully immersed in industrialization; mistrusting certain constrictions of the state, such as the strong tax system, it drew freely from protest modes adapted to the emergence of a strong monopolizing center, such as the first Western social movements constructed; finally, joining a pioneering fight against the first active manifestations of European imperialism, it inevitably acquired a nationalist discourse invented in the West and that it could only with difficulty combine with the tenets of the *Umma*, much less those of Arabism. This adventure, incarnated by men such as Afghani, Abduh, Rashid Rida, or Mawdudi, is not even proper to Islam. It is found in struggles for Indian independence against the secularism of the Congress, in the actions of the Hindu Mahasabha or in that of Dharma Sangh de Svami Karpatri, and, after 1947, with Jana Sangh or the Bharatiya Lok Dal de Charan Singh.[36]

The actors in Iran's Islamic revolution willingly expressed their thematic dependence on values they received from Western revolutionary protest. Thus one mujahideen militant proclaimed himself a "socialist Muslim" who "based his socialism on democracy." He willingly acknowledged that he drew inspiration from other democracies: "[we combine them] with our nationalism, our national culture; it is important for us" and then: "All Iranians who lived in France have been influenced by this democratic culture." Another mujahideen recognizes the combined effect of the influence of two revolutions, Russian and French. From the first, he retains the promotion of "economic equality among individuals"; from the second, he highlights the importation of the concepts of liberty and equality not limited to the economic sphere. He concludes by recognizing that "modernization in Iran occurred with France as intermediary."[37]

In reality, the possibilities of escaping this logic are slim, and experience has shown that to build a strategy on the principle of avoidance leads to perverse results. The example of the *Ulama* Association, created in 1931 in Algeria by Sheikh Abdelhamid Ben Badis, is illustrative. To protect a group that felt threatened and deprived, the Association presented itself as a "religious organization whose goal was to defend Islam through education in the Arabic language and glorification of the past, in order to demonstrate the enduring nature of the Algerian nation."[38] On the basis of this objective, the Association, in contrast to the North African Star and later the Algerian People's Party, made no concession to the Western model of protest strategy and rhetoric. Proclaiming the inseparability of politics and religion, it counted essentially on a cultural effort aiming to save the Muslim community by a return to the Koran, to its lessons and direction. "Resisting the fascination for the West" required the promotion of the genuine spirit of Islam. Hence the Association's first priority was to increase the number of public schools teaching in Arabic.

This imperviousness to Western methods of partisan mobilization came, however, at a price. Unlike the development begun by revivalism, the Association's strategy left no room for any type of political autonomy and thus did not need to make room for any of the themes traditionally associated with it. Political by destination and according to a model perfectly congruent with Islamic culture, the Association's actions had to do only with its religious orientation and its project to reconstruct the Muslim community apart from all borrowings from Western nationalist ideology. The *Ulama* Association went even further: in its eyes, no party could represent the *Umma* or even speak in the name of Islam; no partisan organization could claim legitimacy. The official political scene, that of the *amr*, held only secondary importance, so the Association need have nothing to do with it, which, paradoxically but inevitably, led Ben Badis to pay only slight attention to colonial power, and even, according to some, to accommodate it. Considering that the idea of nationality could refer only to Islam, the *sheykh* in fact distinguished a cultural nationality (*jensiyya qawmiyya*) from a political nationality (*jensiyya siyassiyya*): the first draws cultural resources from language and religion and finds its most natural expression in the *ulama*; the second refers to the articulation of rights and duties of citizenship, but allows for no autonomous political action that would reconstitute partisanship, as Messali Hadj or Ferhat Abbas had tried to do.

Thus the Association limited itself to the conquest of civil society, and eventually dissociated itself from the PPA, which, in order to denounce French colonialism, declared itself a party and espoused methods of political mobilization proper to left-wing French parties, and began to use a nationalist rhetoric forged essentially in the West. The Algerian state derives indirectly from subsequent partisan organizations, notably the NLF; and it draws its westernized state and national identity from this ideological source, which privileges cultural "purity," though it is true that independence and revolution are not concrete objectives within the contemporary interstate community. That the *Ulama* Association and the thought of Ben Badis have deeply influenced contemporary Algerian nationalism, no one has any doubt, as the practice of Arabization reveals. Nevertheless, neither one has been able to extricate itself from the dilemma of cultural autocracy and political ineffectiveness.

This is not an isolated example. Throughout Islam quietist movements have developed a conception of action aligned strictly according to tradition, but that makes no political concessions. The Iranian *akhbaris*, by accepting inspiration from tradition only, acknowledge their own incompetence in political matters.[39] They have followed the example of Ben Badis by playing an important role in socialization, in diffusion of religious values, and repression of deviant sects (notably the Baha'is); they probably contributed significantly to paving the way for the Islamic revolution. Though they rejected all political action and all partisan structuration, they were nevertheless quickly surpassed by the *usuli*, who recognized a political authority in the *marja' taqlid* (*ayatollah*, a model to follow because of his knowledge); and in the prerevolutionary context they were surpassed by the *Sadequiyyeh* branch, who, though a minority group, were determined to acquire all the thematic and organizational instruments of a Western-style partisan action. Here we find the opposition between two *ayatollahs*, Khomeini and Shari'at Madari. The radicalism of the first prevailed over the moderation of the second, just as open political protest proved more effective than the political procrastination of the quietist attitude. The Islamic Brotherhood itself, just like all Islamist movements, was able to act based on a conception of political mobilization inspired more by Leninism than Muslim tradition. Their tribunes, their organization, their method of action, drew more from Chernyshevsky's *What is to be Done* than from the Koran.

In India, the Rashtriya Swayamsewak Association (RSS) found itself confronted with two similar choices. A militant and exclusively Hindu group, the RSS was created in 1925 to fight against the British presence; it was also involved in violence, such as the assassination of Gandhi. Thus it bore no resemblance to the *Ulama* Association.[40] Like that Association, however, it rejected all partisan orientation and professed strictly cultural origins for itself; furthermore, it declared the same rejection of political action, the same active militancy in favor of restoring a sociopolitical order inspired directly by the endogenous culture, and especially the same will to dismantle Western political categories. Thus the RSS vehemently rejected the Western concept of nationalism; it denounced the ideas of borders and territory, and its founder, Hedgewar, considered the valorization of the territorial vision of the nation a "slave mentality" and declared the goal of his organization as the liberation of Hindu society from the degeneration and demoralization the West had inflicted upon it. More precisely still, and closer to the Islamic themes mentioned above, Madhav Sadashiv Golwalkar distinguished between a cultural nationalism and a territorial one, in order to defend the first and reject the second.[41]

Thus the RSS was political only in its goal: essentially cultural, it was first of all Hindu, excluding from its ranks Buddhists and Jains. Its project blended with that of Hinduism. Though it condemned Western-style secularism, the RSS accepted certain of its aspects in order to valorize the plurality of Hindu theologies. Finally, its strategy can be appreciated only in relation to its cultural essence. Just as with many Islamist movements, the RSS distinguished state from society in order to denigrate and marginalize the first. As an expression of the sacred, society can be nothing less than above the state, which is merely a surface addition, imposed from without, an abusive confiscator of sovereignty that loses all meaning in its hands, but to which the RSS, on the other hand, can lay claim due to its nature and divine consecration. Thus all effort was concentrated on organizing the militants, on their education, their apprenticeship in a role destined to cut them off from the state, or in any case, limit their allegiance to it. Regarding the Congress, the RSS chose a strict opposition: not only to construct a nation-state in order to control it, but to eradicate a state and national logic consonant with Western values in order to reconstruct Hindu society elsewhere. Thus Gandhi and his cohorts denounced this movement as "totalitarian" and even "racist," noting Golwalkar's use of the idea of "Hindu race" and the assertion of its superiority. This polemic, which quickly reached the level of murderous violence, clearly indicates the bifurcation between two strategies, that of the Congress, which chose westernization as a vector of the conquest of power, and that of the RSS, which built its identity and mobilization effort around the refusal of any concession from the official political authorities and as a function of a strictly cultural affirmation.[42]

In this context, the strategic evolution of the RSS is as surprising as it is significant. Once independence was attained and the new political scene institutionalized, it slowly evolved to embrace all the various partisan groups. Though it initially functioned only for religious celebrations, such as the crowning of Rama and Shiva, the RSS later acquired, with the Jana Sangh (which became BJP in 1977), a political arm whose structures gradually became electoral circumscriptions, with its members taking roles under diverse headings in Parliament. Particularly, the growing opposition to Indira Gandhi, who as of 1973 tried to outlaw the RSS, brought it to modify its plans significantly. The deliberate will not to lose (by being declared illegal) and to try to win (at a time when the renewal of electoral successes of the Congress Party was becoming problematic) led it to join the electoral coalition, which was victorious in 1977, to transform its platform and abandon in part its religious thematic for talk about prices and corruption, thus presenting an apology for democracy in order to fight against "dictatorship." This turnabout was, of course, due to the simple "attraction to the system" that allowed it, moreover, to be directly associated with power in several states; but even more, it meant the tactical rediscovery of state beyond nation, the need–in order to gain strength–to participate in a struggle for power that quickly veered toward a return to themes more populist than cultural and more statist than democratic.

Such a process in no way entails a loss of cultural references to identity. Neither Islamist movements nor Hinduist organizations renounced–or even wished to renounce–an investment in tradition, that is, the powerful need for meaning that originates precisely in the context of a growing westernization. However, in both these cases, the dilemma of power appears immediately: the discourse of mobilization is effective and credible only if it leads to a discourse of conquest of the decision-making places that require techniques and themes borrowed from the West. One quickly arrives at the syncretic forms that derive from a neopopulism wherein Western references to a sovereign people mix with endogenous cultural reference to a tradition and a system of meaning accessible to the masses.

In Algeria, if one analyzes the words of the Islamist Mahfoud Nahnah used in the rhetoric of the Islamic Salvation Movement to characterize the state, one sees the intensity of this heteroclite formation: legal state, protection of basic human rights, Arabism, nationalism, democracy, brotherhood, solidarity, rejection of alienation, application of the *sharia*. Islam is understood as: "State, faith, law, book, sword, ethnicity, nation, ethics, conduct," whereas "Islamic economic theory" implies the "equitable and just distribution of wealth, encouragement of initiative, establishment of social justice, self-sufficiency . . . , the cultivation of human values previously denied" (by "the Western economic alternative: capitalism or socialism"). This melting pot of themes taken from various Western sources and endogenous references dulls the discourse, blurs it into the most complete imprecision, and in fact stabilizes it into a tribune-based populism.[43]

Western references tend to fulfill a threefold function within protest discourse. First they aim to distinguish a space of thought and of action proper to Western history that is both valorized and presented as universal. Following the example of Afghani or Abduh, modern Islamists willingly take account of what has made the West successful and of what therein can be found in Islam as well. Thus it was with technological progress, but also with the values of democracy and liberty. The Moroccan Islamist Abdessalem Yassin agreed that the values discovered in the west by Abduh– "liberty, property . . . , organization, technology, social peace"–could also be found in Islam;[44] the Tunisian Ghanushi even seems prepared to "redeem" the modern state, as well as the parties and political institutions forged in the West.[45] Thus an entire essential part of Western production is recomposed as culturally neutral, in a way that legitimates its adoption by Islamist movements and facilitates their mobility on the political scene, the definition of their options and their political strategy.

At the same time, Western references legitimate a space of particularity. That the balance sheet of Western history is not entirely negative in no way justifies the "amazement" it inspires in certain elite members of the Muslim world. Even more, since it is culturally materialist, the West cannot fail to "betray" its ideals of brotherhood, liberty, and justice. Islamist movements disappear when a new model of the state needs *inventing*, when a new utopia needs to be shaped; they thus recycle their distinction from the West to both legitimize their reappropriation of history and to assert the superiority of their own political formula over that of their political competitors who neglect or fight against all efforts at the expression of identity.

Finally, according to this logic, reference to the West serves, negatively, to delegitimate the initiatives of the other. This construction appears in striking fashion in the discourse of Abol Hassan Banisadr, who without relying on the most radical Islamist influence, places his political action at the intersection "of the ideals of liberty, modernity, social revolution, and Islam." Thus the Pahlavi regime was denounced as "exteriorized," that is, as an essentially Western production. More strangely, but much more significantly, the *velayat-e-fakih* (government by jurisconsult) established by Khomeini was criticized and refuted as being a "Western idea," "derived from the theory of papal sovereignty" and incompatible with Islam. "Fundamentalism" underwent the same scrutiny, whereas the secularism supported by the former president was presented, in order to better distinguish himself from Khomeini, as "defined in the Koran," as "deriving from Islam and not the New Testament which, in contrast, affirms the total sovereignty of God" where the Koran "places responsibility with man."[46]

4. Imported Products

Dependence does not simply mean imitation. It includes the idea that the imported product is dysfunctional. Developmentalists presume that Western models of government will diffuse without rupture of meaning and without provoking new dysfunctions through cultural dissonance. Challenges to this belief, however, have manifestly reversed the former conclusions of the development theory. Since imported products lose their function, that is, their effectiveness and their power, they take on new meanings that tend to reconstruct the political scene into which they are inserted, with the result that the political scene becomes even more dependent. In addition, this same process applies to both the normative system and the ideological expression and content of political debate.

Imported Politics

In the first place, the example of political parties is particularly striking. As an instrument of participation and political mobilization, partisan organization was constituted in the last century in the West in order to organize a political order that had been shaken by the progressive introduction of universal suffrage. Since it was destined to manage the electoral population, it became, according to the well-known expression of the famous Norwegian political thinker Stein Rokkan, the agent of integration and conflict: integration of a collectivity marked henceforth by political solidarities, linked by a common citizenship and shared beliefs; conflict within the center of a society divided by differences and the free play of competition for power.¹

Behind this double function, which quickly became the natural rhythm of the partisan dynamic, there quickly appeared three non-exportable characteristics proper to the West. First, the liberation of the modes of communalization: with the individualization of social relations and, correlatively, of association, the loss of community solidarity in the nineteenth century initiated, if not a demand, at least a potential for partisan mobilization that brought satisfaction to the individual adherent, which led Weberian sociologists to envisage the party as a "sociation."² Next, electoral mobilization: the West intimately blended party and power by synchronizing the formation of political parties with the extension of the franchise, whereas in colonized countries, parties were constituted essentially in order to claim independence and solidify the more nationalist types of behavior. Instead of competing for power, these parties were created to provide a more united force against the tutelary power. Finally, the invention of partisanship in the West, where it often took several centuries for complex social cleavages to be established, and these nourished both the associative dynamic and the competition for power: strong horizontal solidarities could develop from these long-enduring cleavages, whereas in Africa or Asia long-standing vertical solidarities and various clientelist relations create a more factional political competition that disrupts the principal functions of partisanship. In a political confrontation dominated by this logic, the implementation of development procedures, joint interests, and militant education probably loses any chance of being effective or even of existing at all.

On the other hand, the importation of partisan logic responds to other strategic considerations that carry other functions: to serve as an exit from an outdated political order where dependence and tradition are closely intertwined; to act as a relay for political communication; and to allow for control of a political scene that does not proceed, at least primarily, from the freely competitive exercise of universal suffrage. The logic of *exit* is paradoxically the principal source of the dynamic of imitation. In order to gain independence the elite among the dominated groups freely borrowed organizational structures from colonial powers. The example of francophone Africa is, from this point of view, remarkable, with the creation at the end of World War II of the first large parties in Africa, the *Rassemblement démocratique africain* (RDA) being the first.³ The symbols, structures, programs, and ideologies of these parties were learned and transmitted by the first African deputies at the Palais-Bourbon, such as Félix Houphouët-Boigny, Modibo Keita, or Hubert Maga, and were often presented as modeled on French left-wing parties. The imitation was all the stronger because by it independence could be gained by and for these elites, but only if it was built on a strong political base, that is to say, a base voluntarily ignorant of traditional sociocultural parameters, *and* was resolutely mimetic, that is to say, mimetic in the context of an institutional competence learned by its members that distinguished it from other potential authorities. The rupture thus came about through imitation, a mode that was not unique to this region of the world. This was precisely the course of action chosen by the Congress Party, as well as by the Ba'ath, who very early wore the colors of an Arab nationalism learned in the Christian schools of Lebanon and as a benefit of contacts solidified by its leaders with European socialist parties.

This last example suggests already that even when it makes a brutal and radical break, the nationalist-inspired party does not lack for Western features, though the identity of the sources tends to change.[4] The Syrian National Socialist Party (SNSP, *al Hizb al qawmi al ijtima'i as-suriyye*) was founded in Beirut in November 1932 by Antun Saada, who evoked a language, practice, and symbolism that owed much to visits by its principal leaders to fascist Germany and Italy, and was completed by Saada's own experiences in the Brazilian society of Getul,* where he had been exiled. The thematics of "natural Syria," the promotion of secularism, the separation of church and state, thus structured a discourse brought by a hierarchized, autocratic, and military organization copied rather largely from the Italian Fascist Party and the German NSDAP. The same can be said for the Lebanese Phalanges (*Kataeb*) created by Pierre Gemayel in 1936 and transformed into a political party in 1952, based on the same sources of imitation he absorbed during his visits to the same places. Likewise, the Young Egypt Party, founded in 1933 by Ahmad Hussein and Fathi Radwan, early ancestor of the Workers Party (*Hizb al Amal*), expressed an exacerbated nationalism with themes and methods borrowed from the same repertoire: green-shirted militants swearing oaths of allegiance and the constitution of a discourse on nation that mixed pharaonic and Islamic references with a denunciation of the *Wafd* "plutocracy."

Marxist and socialist-democratic influences are even more numerous. They are evident in the communist parties found throughout the world. They are also seen in the movements that, given the means they had to de-

---

*Translator's Note: The Society of Getul. Named after Getúlio Vargas, who established a populist and nationalist regime in Brazil in 1930.

ploy, aligned more or less with socialist-inspired models. When it was vigorous, the struggle for independence promoted the theme of the "avant-garde" party; for example, it brought the Algerian NLF considerably closer to the Leninist model, particularly in its call for a unanimous national mobilization legitimated very early on its status as the government's sole party. The PAIGC (African Independence Party of Guinea-Bissau) evolved in the same way, as did the MPLA (People's Movement for the Liberation of Angola), the FRELIMO of Mozambique, and the ZANU of Zimbabwe. In all these cases, it was basically the factionalism and rivalry among potential leaders seeking within the repertory of international ideologies a sign that could distinguish them from each other that activated the logic of borrowing and controlled its orientation independently of internal cleavages and social stakes. The process is quite obviously completed with pressure from the international environment that controls alliances and prompts independence movements to find in the left, even the extreme left, concepts on which they can structure their discourse and practice. The search–often forced–for Soviet support was, from this point of view, the deciding factor. It often activated curious overcompensations in the dynamic of borrowing, as in the case of Rhodesia, when Robert Mugabe's ZANU had to use the Chinese model to remain competitive with its rival the ZAPU of Josué Nkomo, who was receiving Russian aid. The essentially ethnic distinction separating the two movements, the first being mainly Shona and the second more rooted in the Ndebele of the south, was thus reconstructed in terms of superimposed antagonisms among persons and factions, as well as borrowed references and disruptive importations.

This same paradox of rupture activating borrowings is also found in the history of the Tunisian independence movement, when Habib Bourguiba reformed the Destour, to give rise to a more exigent and urgently nationalistic Neo-Destour. Moreover, this renewed party mobilized a new elite, distinguished by the Western, secular education of the *Sadiqiyya*, whose graduates constituted an opposition against tradition. Many had completed judicial studies in French universities, where they read Western law and frequented socialist militants and leaders who thus exerted their influence on the new Tunisian party.[5]

A logic that combines rupture of meaning and imitation brings dysfunction in its wake. Once in power, thanks to independence, the parties try to prolong their identity, linked essentially to the struggle against foreign influence, all the while maintaining a discourse and employing practices inspired largely by foreign models. The risks of political alienation and detachment of the victorious party from the population are markedly increased. The ZANU in Zimbabwe provides a significant example: with independence attained, the logic of rupture that sustained it lost all meaning and became a mere instrument of the small elite in power. The efforts to mobilize, following the first legislative campaign in the spring of 1985, led to superficial success. Though official reports put voter participation at 97 percent and records a turnout of 98 percent for Mashonaland–the area populated by the dominant ethnic group–it is known that villagers walked out of electoral meetings and that, as a result, the party's local sections resorted more and more to physical and moral force, with violence not excluded. In short, the first steps toward an electoral process favored the progressive development of a single party system.

In this light, the functional mutation of the Marxist-Leninist-inspired language used by the ZANU merits particular attention. Initially it marked a break with the colonial order, and then progressively evolved into a way to obscure ideologically an economic policy that was, in fact, neoliberal and expressive of the new dependence relations weighing on the former Rhodesia. Faced with a white economic power that had not abdicated, the reproduction of a Marxist-Leninist ideology and a foreign policy favorable to the Eastern Bloc remained the only source of legitimacy for the group in power and the only sign of its political continuity.

The same holds true for most of the parties that built their socialist identity in the struggle for independence. The progressive conversion of this reference into a vague ideological discourse unable to represent the nation deeply separated these parties from the population, thus fueling the formation of fundamentalist and particularlist groups. The success of the Islamic Salvation Movement in Algeria occurred on the remains of the NLF, which could only continue to articulate a socialist ideology unrelated to Algerian culture and belied by increasing privatization and overtures to the IMF. The strong mobilizing capacity of independent sects and churches in sub-Saharan Africa reflects this same logic of particularist attraction in the face of parties using outmoded, ineffective political formulas. This disequilibrium delivered hundreds of thousands of members to Ivory Coast's Harrist church, Zambia's Lumpa church, West Africa's Aladura churches, and also to the Marabout brotherhoods in Senegal and the Maitatsine sect, which in 1984 terrorized the northern Nigerian state of Gongola.[6]

These movements, however, should not be analyzed as organizations of substitution. Refusing to be transformed into political parties, playing instead the card of denunciation and delegitimization of such parties, these movements find their strength in references to authenticity and particularism. In that, they are protesters against the political scene, calling for a way out of the political and entail, in the words of Christian Coulon, a "revenge of African societies," seeking not to take *political* power but rather to give rise to a countersociety. In these conditions a vicious circle quickly appeared. Having lost their mobilizing faculty, political parties did nothing more than support functional rivalries among the elite groups in power; they thus fueled protest–of which they were the victims–by particularist social movements calling for the end of politics and the construction of countersocieties that, in turn, weakened the mobilizing capacities of the traditional parties. As a result, the collapse of partisan resources, which at the dawn of independence were the pride of the new political classes, made these political classes increasingly greater tributaries of foreign support. It is not the least of paradoxes that these parties of rupture became, by their growing inability to renew and adapt, a cause–indirect but particularly strong–of the deepening relations of dependence.

As instruments of rupture, the parties in the developing countries tried nevertheless to fulfill a function of political communication designed to link the governed and governing. This fact, of course, commonly occurs in partisanship within all political systems. It is nevertheless quite a different matter when such communication takes place outside a competitive usage of universal suffrage and in a context where community solidarities and the multiplicity of social networks take over the basic tasks of communication. In such cases, the chances of establishing a common language between the partisan stratum and the public are reduced even further because the usefulness of such communication is infinitely less apparent than it is in a competitive system: for the public, the use of traditional social networks of clientelism and kinship relations is much more effective; for the party, the effort of articulating and transmitting requests is more haphazard because they are not formulated publicly, and the absence of partisan competition makes it useless to take charge of the population's expectations, since no immediate advantage is to be obtained. On the contrary, all developmentalist ideological orientations incite the party to operate in an authoritarian manner and to undertake, from top to bottom, the function of political education that, by definition, refuses to concede anything at the local level. In this scenario, the centralized model borrowed from the West of parties representing large masses tends to become corrupt and radicalized: centralization is only stronger because political education and support for the elite groups in power are activities preferred over electoral mobilization and combined demands.

The parties concerned face a contradiction. The movement toward centralization tends little by little to seriously affect the patronage capacity of partisan organizations closely dependent on autonomy at the local level. This phenomenon has been observed in situations as diverse as in Turkey in the 1970s and in Zambia when, in 1972, the UNIP (United Independence Party) became the only party.[7] Thwarting this tendency thus becomes a major and quite logical concern of the leaders, who nevertheless find it very difficult to effect a real decentralization that risks annoying the intermediate partisan elites and causing them to block innovation. The impossible reforms of which many were victim, among them Nasser's USA, Houphouët-Boigny's PDCI (Democratic Party of the Ivory Coast), and Sekou Touré's PDG (Democratic Party of Guinea) clearly reveal the negative effects of a grafted partisan logic. These three examples show in effect that to reinvigorate local partisan echelons, the party leadership had to either give way to the traditional authorities that escaped their control (as in Egypt or the Ivory Coast), or make themselves into small cells that divested an entire new political class attached to the privileges conferred upon it by the developmentalist logic of partisan and administrative bureaucracies (as occurred in Guinea).

This weak mobilizing capacity had, among other effects, that of turning the political parties in the developing countries a little more toward the exterior and thus the international scene. Their precarious rootedness in the society, and their strong implication in governmental political action, made them often even more sensitive to international stakes: in its capacity as a supporter of demands from the society, the party tends to become an organ of diplomatic and international communication. Thus Nasser's creation of the Arab Socialist Union in 1962 had the principal effect of conveying to other countries the pro-Soviet reorientation of Egyptian diplomacy; the transformation of the Neo-Destour into the Destour Socialist Party allowed Bourguiba to proclaim the radicalization of his socialist options, which themselves marked the end point of Tunisia's break with France and its search for new international patrons.

Thus involved with the international scene and rather largely extroverted, the parties feel the effects of their inability to act within the developing political systems and have a natural inclination to reintegrate, through the international order, into a space more in conformity with their origin. At the same time, this shift makes them at least partial vectors of international ideological and political inflows, and as a result, instruments of dependence.

Because of this very fact, the institutional role of political parties lags considerably behind what it would be in a competitive situation. Political parties in the West were created to organize universal suffrage and were very quickly associated in their history with control by pluralist regimes, to the point even of becoming one with the way a democracy functions. But in a noncompetitive system, they undergo an inversion that can produce quite unexpected results. First, protest has value for the single party whose functions weaken with time, since its specificity with respect to the state fades. Faced with a lessened need for political communication, this type of organization progressively loses everything that signified its originality within political-administrative institutions and finds itself relegated to accessory functions. The evolution of Algeria's NLF is, in this light, notable: as the period of independence receded in time, all the movement retained from its partisan identity was a symbolic and weak hold on the cultural orientation of Algerian society. Because of the party's status as a nonfunctioning unit, the new political elite had good reason to spurn it in favor of pursuing more prestigious and lucrative careers in other state institutions. These other state institutions were powerful, not just in appearance but in fact, which allowed the new generation of young Algerian technocrats to realize their professional abilities and to increase contacts and travels abroad in order to fully benefit from the symbolic recognition that accompanies the exercise of power. Thus the NLF was successively supplanted by the army and then by the new state technocracy, quickly losing the reputation of "partisan monocratism" it had acquired at the end of the war of liberation.[8]

Gradually abandoning its governing function, the single party becomes most often involved in a functional deficit that relegates it to a merely subordinate role, further alienating it politically from society. As an intermediate site beneath state power, it could in the past claim to exercise a patronage function that, as we have seen, tended to progressively disappear, leaving it only a regulatory role in factional disputes. Being geographically diverse and, because of its militancy, retaining a large number of agents, it could also complement the state bureaucracy at various regional and local levels in order to provide services for a small intermediate elite. The 150,000 members of the Syrian Ba'ath party, for example, play a genuine role in local administration; the PRI (Islamic Party of the Republic) effectively managed to coordinate religious leaders and local revolutionary organizations in Iran during the 1980s.⁹ These new functions constitute political inventions, but their performance is precisely contained and limited by the extraneousness of the partisan product: the NLF and Ba'ath are perceived as collective intermediary organizations, just as are the local echelons of single African parties to which the village chiefs are always preferred; as for the Iranian PRI, it was so ineffective that in 1987 Khomeini ordered it to cease activity.

In the context of an open multiparty system, the ability to function leads, in most cases, to inversions no less remarkable; the avowed competition between parties, in fact, reinvigorates traditional forms of authoritarian government. Morocco's monarchy had thus encouraged in 1959 the creation of the Democratic Party of Independence and the reconstitution of the People's Agrarian Movement in order to make all-powerful the Istiqlal Party, which held power in the palace. In Iran of the 1960s, the shah institutionalized the factional struggle by encouraging bipartisan opposition of the Melli Party and the Mardom Party in such a way as to play one against the other and consolidate his own autocracy, just as Sadat was able to bring about a controlled multiparty system sufficiently manifest to legitimate the dominant party and sufficiently restrained not to endanger it. In each of these cases, the importation of the pluralist model generated functional accomplishments that completely contradicted the original characteristics of the imported product, consolidating authoritarianism rather than dismantling it, making the party an instrument, not to spread political power but, on the contrary, to increase its concentration.

Here, probably, lies one of the major causes of the weak performance, even the illusory nature, of most parties in developing countries: their functional decline not only distances the social actors from society and encloses them in an official and artificial political arena but also causes the population to perceive them as extraneous, belonging to a symbolic and human world disconnected from social reality. Of course, the party is not because of that isolated from sociopolitical traditions and can even try to use them to its profit, notably by incorporating the logic of patronage and nepotism: the UNIP in Zambia took over the work of clientelism for farmers asking for credit; within the same party, the Bemba and Ila-Tonga factions used their own distribution networks to provide employment or various types of authorizations. However, the phenomenon began to fade as the UNIP became more of an institution and a single party, partaking of a more state-like and neopatrimonial logic of power.¹⁰ Factionalism and patronage were thus transformed into instruments of a centralizing practice that led the holder of supreme power to place those loyal to him at the head of the party, which happened with President Kaunda and his entourage, graduates of the Sahel in Bourguiba's PSD, the Malinke in Sekou Toure's PDG, the Takriti in Saddam Hussein's Ba'ath, or even Gandhi's family in India's Congress (I) Party.

The partisan dynamic thus combines the effects of a vigorous importation leading to a rapid conversion of its functions with a strong control by executives, which drastically limits its autonomy within the social system. This makeup is increasingly dysfunctional: the control of the parties–most often single parties–by the central power reduces the possibilities society could have to reappropriate the party, thus often accelerating the move away from partisanship and toward associative, religious, or ethnic movements. At the same time, the insertion of parties into the official political system weakens their performance, reduces their autonomy relative to politico-administrative institutions, and reveals the unfavorable nature of importation just as does the disparity between functions fulfilled by Western political parties and the sociopolitical realities of non-Western countries.

Efforts at symbolic correction, the organization of elections offering no real choices, which we know are not merely–or principally–staged, change nothing; that is, they change nothing of the close connection within the very logic of partisanship between importation and loss of political capabilities and, because of this, between importation and dependence. It is remarkable, moreover, that this relation is essentially negative: dependence is created, in this particular case, not so much out of imitation itself as from the destructive consequences that imitation tends to have on the political order of non-Western societies. The "liberal" parties that exist pretty much everywhere outside the West, notably in the conservative regimes of the Muslim world, have not successfully instilled their ideology in the diverse levels of the population, no more than Marxist-inspired parties could in the former South Yemen, Angola, or South Africa. From this point of view, the clear result belongs more to a "de-ideologizing" and thus to a regression of partisan identifications than to a universalization of Western political discourse: the Ba'ath in the Arab world, parties based on African socialism, and the Congress Party produce and express a discourse whose outlines are more and more blurred and less and less in conformity with the ideology of origin learned in Western schools.

In politics the *administration* seems to be another component, also imported, but in a form superior to political parties. The resources of power available to it are incontestably better, for at least two essential reasons: financial support of developing countries comes principally from abroad, aside from choices made by the deliberative powers, which are most often negotiated by the upper bureaucratic echelons; and the advantage available to the bureaucracy leads society to, at least partially and tactically, align with the bureaucracy, thereby initiating a reciprocal adaptation that is probably more effective than what occurs with the parties.

Yet the logic of imitation finds nourishment here. Few concepts have been so extensively identified with the idea of a universal and abstract rationality as that of bureaucracy. To introduce roles deriving from it into a society dominated by development constitutes both a particularly fruitful means of self-legitimation and a consistent way to gain the upper hand relative to traditional authorities. In its Western, Weberian, rational-legal version, bureaucracy offers gratifying and secure positions of employment; it also constitutes a valuable way to conserve power and acquire its advantages. Not surprisingly in these conditions, bureaucracies originating in France were among the first goods imported by the Ottoman sultan at the beginning of the Tanzimat period, and the Saint-Simonian and Comtian ideologies and the very idea of technocracy infiltrated very early not only Turkey but also the Middle East, Egypt, and Persia. At the beginning of the nineteenth century, India began its first recruiting competitions of high functionaries, which later became a model for Britain when it wanted to apply the Northcote-Trevelyan report (1854) and sought to create a structured civil service.[11] It is equally understandable that in the Asia and Africa of today the bureaucracy is perceived by the princes either as a means to link the new, educated generations with their own concept of an imported modernity or as a leading, even obligatory, career for those receiving higher education. This logic led Gambia, for example, to double the number of its civil servants from 1974 to 1984; however, bureaucratic increases and the resulting dysfunctions are increasingly felt pretty much everywhere in the developing world.[12] It was also through bureaucratic development shored up by a strong scientific ideology borrowed from the West that Mustafa Kemal built his own support and acquired a powerful clientele made up of both a state elite and a national bourgeoisie composed of entrepreneurs brought into state capitalism and largely sustained by the public bureaucracy.

It is tempting to formulate the same hypothesis for the African countries that have recently achieved independence and reproduced an administrative model inspired largely by their former colonizers. It is particularly obvious in those former French colonies which, during colonization, became imbued with the former, paradigmatic bureaucratic tradition, which was generously supported by the studies and training the new national elite received in France. Yet several recent studies, notably that of Dominique Darbon, recommend caution: the former colonial administration in no way resembles the Jacobin type of bureaucratic model, since in fact, the new African states inherited an administrative model largely improvised by the colonizers according to the circumstances of conquest, of the management of daily life, and the maintenance of order; moreover, if the structures are imitated, the conceptions and visions cultivated by the agents remain largely differentiated from the Weberian model and, as a result, derive not only from an original bureaucratic culture but also from a particular articulation of the administrative model adapted by the receiving society.[13]

Importation remains decisive, however, at least from two perspectives. Let us look first of all at the structural aspect. Whatever their political or ideological orientation, the African states have taken, principally from France, the naming of ministries, their organization, the delegation of duties, and administrative management. More significantly, the same principle of territorial organization has occurred, even including partitions dating from colonization where only the names of districts or departments have changed: communities themselves as basic units have been ignored, in spite of the decisive importance of their social role, in favor of a territoriality that seems to date from the Napoleonic era. And the height of paradox, the major innovation attempted since independence is a decentralization that differs from the colonial administrative model, that extends well-intentioned political choices (as in Mauritania with the law of July 1986 that initiated local democracy) but which in fact most often adopts modes of decentralization in vogue in the West, such as they are the most actively promulgated by experts in development and by IMF technicians.[14] Community groups are thus immediately assimilated into the local collectivities, losing their own character and being overshadowed by the more visible local echelons associated with preservation of the essential prerogatives held by the center. Just as in the North, the center loses nothing, as can be seen, for example, in the practical results of decentralization policies undertaken in Tanzania.[15]

In addition, the rules of functioning remain the other certain value of importation. African administrative laws are no different from the French model, either conceptually or technically. Public administration remains subordinate to the same rules, just as the population's access to public bureaucracies does. Even if the written law differs in certain stipulations from French law, even if it is not–far from it–the sole normative basis of the administration or those regulated by it, and even if it differs from the "practical law" of Etienne Le Roy,[16] the Romanist syntax dominates, remaining the only legitimate reference for the African states, that is, the only possible way to conceive and organize change. Not surprisingly, in these conditions all administrative reform, even the most vigorous, quickly reconnects with the constitutive elements of the same imported model, thus depriving the state of all possibility genuinely to transform the administrative order, as is suggested, for example, by the well-known fate of the "local revolutionary powers" that Sekou Toure had tried to install in Guinea at the beginning of the 1980s in order to promote participation by the people: inserted in the normative and institutional cadre of a Jacobin-inspired state and administrative model, the initiative was ruined by active resistance on the part of intermediate administrative echelons, who had reproduced a prefectorial type of territorial organization.

In reality, imported administrative institutions present the paradox of combining a powerful conservatism in terms of structure with a need for adaptation to social interaction. The contradiction is, however, only an apparent one: both of these characteristics derive jointly from power resources that benefit the public bureaucracy in societies characterized by the absence of partisan competition, by effective and well-anchored patrimonial practices profiting civil servants, and by the extroversion of political-administrative activities that offer the best perquisites to those in contact with the exterior.[17] This rich endowment benefiting the bureaucracy–which can, moreover, and for the same reasons, be both abundant and parasitical of entire sectors of the society–triggers its efforts to adapt to and insert itself into social life. Yet the limits of social life appear already: the impossible reform from which this type of bureaucracy suffers, the "iron law" that seems to confine it in an imported syntax, enunciating in advance the rules by which its institutional structures are transformed, relegating the dynamics of reappropriation to either the margins of the system or solidly outside its institutional framework, at the risk of engendering a completely dysfunctional dualism.

In fact, the essential element of reciprocal adaptation has to do with the composition of the actors' micro-strategies: while seeking to preserve the rigidity of the imported institutional frame, the bureaucracy needs to penetrate the local society, in order to affect those administered, and detach it from traditional authorities; while valorizing itself by having its own rules shape the rational-legal administration, it needs to safeguard the framework of its own culture and bring that culture within its own sphere; and at the same time, while resisting an institutional model that is profoundly alien to them, the administered individuals need the bureaucracy's services and resources, which are often indispensable.[18]

Numerous means of rapprochement derive from this timely conjunction of shared interests, whose utilitarian nature creates ambiguity throughout a frequently dysfunctional process. The privatization of the administration appears to be the current result of adaptation. A clear means of reconciling the agent's administrative position and his communitarian culture, an easy intermediary to affect a local society foreign to bureaucratic culture, privatization is also activated at the request of the user, who, aware that he requests a rare resource, quickly discovers the advantage of vertical solidarities from which he can obtain maximum benefits personally and for himself alone.[19] However, moralizing about corruption in order to condemn it is, sociologically, just as debatable as discreetly recognizing it in order to establish a "functional dysfunction."[20] In reality, the privatization of the bureaucracy reveals first of all an irresolvable tension between public and private in a sociohistorical and cultural context that impugns it; it reveals the incapacity of both the center and the periphery to communicate, since they can do nothing but contradict each other and reject the constraints of the rules and procedures governing their interactions. In short, the universalist and individualist center must, in order to function, become particularist and communitarian, and thus negate itself and, especially, radicalize all neopatrimonial orientation, which was, as we have seen, one of the surest foundations of dependence. From this double point of view, the corruption in the South differs from that found in the North: though initially an individual practice, it becomes systematic; though initially useful purely internally, it becomes useful to the exterior as well.

Even so, privatization and corruption do not dominate the adaptation process: the convergences between the social dynamics from below and administrative initiatives are numerous, especially when the latter are redistributive and thus reinterpreted as a function of codes proper to the local society. The strong hypothesis developed by Hyden of a "captured" peasantry, torn from its communitarian autonomy by the administration's voluntarist activity, is in part exaggerated, since the Tanzanian peasant finds, as Denis Martin has shown, obvious advantages in the active presence of the state.[21]

However, such logic has its pitfalls: rather than create a durable, institutionalized relation of allegiance among citizens, this exchange of interests supposes an entire group of evasion and avoidance strategies by the administration when the latter's actions meet neither the needs nor expectations of the local communities. After Zimbabwe had won its independence, it found a genuine success in its efforts to build an entire network of agricultural cooperatives from the bottom up. On the other hand, the state's efforts in 1986 to control the cooperatives by creating a Ministry of Cooperatives ended in failure. In fact, the village communities produced their own "clandestine self-administration," to use the apt expression of Ernest Gellner—that, for essential matters, negotiates with the central administration or its representatives for the conditions of its participation in public policies. Whether it concern mutual aid, child protection, health cooperatives, or even credit, the village creates such strong and active participatory structures that the administration has no other choice than to endorse whatever has been decided in the lower ranks.[22] Sub-Saharan Africa is a veritable laboratory where one can observe and analyze this process as well as the resulting frustrations it occasionally provokes in a population poorly adapted to the work of recuperation; yet the phenomenon is found elsewhere, notably in the Arab world, particularly in Egypt.[23]

The articulation is as current as it is perilous: though sometimes profitable in the short term as a useful way to effect certain decisions in the local society, it has the double effect of altering the administrative act and especially of perpetually exposing it to the risk of having no effect when the communities opt for avoidance measures. Henceforth the gap deepens between the theory of a universalist bureaucratic state and the practice of a systematically particularist mediation. In theory, the resulting negative effects could only further relativize the Weberian concept of bureaucracy, further enclosing the imported model of the state within communitarian categories that negate its universalist claim. In practice, however, this setup accelerates the neopatrimonial decline that already appears in the process of privatizing the administration. It drives the bureaucracy even deeper into the conflict between the universal and the particularist,[24] but it especially locks the states involved in this identity into the role of "limping Leviathan," an expression of the growing distance between its voiced claims and its real effectiveness. The ambiguous dialogue between a presumptuous state and a fragmented society, negotiating case by case the conditions of its openness to public action, legitimates the doubling of aid policies, which come, on the one hand, from the Northern states to support public administrations and, on the other, from the ONG to shore up local communities. In reality, the hypothesis of a reappropriation of the imported bureaucracy is limited in two ways: principally in the dangerous blockage preventing central political and administrative structures from changing in order to integrate the particular conditions of articulation into the local society; and also in the resulting obligation for the public actor to play the card of doubling, to accept the diminution of his political abilities, and to thus find himself in a situation that reinforces the conditions of his dependence relative to the exterior.

Imported Law

What is true for politics—partisan or administrative—is even more so in law. Several factors reveal that processes of appropriation and adaptation are at work here more than elsewhere, and to such an extent as to produce more dysfunction. The rule of law belongs first of all to a domain where formalization takes on a very particular operative importance: a written law or procedure reflects not only a system of values but also a more or less performative technical design that derives from a history and a culture. Thus the importation of Western law into the Ottoman empire can be largely explained by formal considerations, in that the jurists of the Sublime Gate found it difficult to be without a codified Muslim common law when faced with special codified laws imposed by international pressure in accordance with commercial or maritime law.[25] This technical imperative gave rise to a debate that led them first to codify traditional law, contained in the sixteen-volume *Medjelle* and published at the urging of Djevdet Pasha between 1870 and 1877. In itself, this production was a typical case of dysfunctional importation: as the first legal code produced by a Muslim state, the *Medjelle* devoted its introduction to a new juridical method, which, in effect, came from the West and enjoyed an aura of modernity in the minds of the elite. At the same time, the project quickly failed, since the *Medjelle* constituted merely a collection of an impressive number of specific solutions, in conformity with the method proper to Muslim law, which is in essence jurisprudential. Since it was neither very adaptable nor useful, the *Medjelle* rapidly sparked intense criticism, which led jurists to abandon it and intensified the arguments of those who favored replacing it entirely with the Napoleonic Civil Code. Here the formal imperative became the basic reason for the passage from one juridical culture to another.

The same steps occurred in the transformations of Indian law. With the Charter Act in 1833, India opened itself to codification, principally at the initiative of Lord Macaulay, an admirer of Bentham and partisan of a juridical method whose practical advantages were obvious: the decree of laws favorable to the unification of a country where the fragmentation of traditional law increased political segmentation. The legislative work begun in 1859 thus led to the elaboration of a code of civil procedure, a penal code, and a code of penal procedure, as well as numerous specialized legislative dispositions. Modern Indian law was henceforth dominated by British juridical culture without being deprived of French Napoleonic influence (even if only in the notion of code) and even some elements of the Louisiana penal code.[26] Independence changed nothing of this borrowing. The newly constituted state, exposed directly to the dangers of centrifugal dynamics, needed urgently to confirm, which it did through Article 372 of its Constitution of 1950, the unifying work of codification, of which it was infinitely more sure than it was of traditional communitarian law. The result, however, was a source of tensions and complexities: from then on official Indian law tended to coexist with more specific laws, Hindu and Muslim, organizing social relations, notably personal ones, at the microcommunitarian level. This breaking up and doubling were matters of even greater concern because they reflected and confirmed the critical distance separating a secular westernized state from a society deeply marked by the communitarian order. This situation has evolved, moreover, toward a more dysfunctional reality: claiming, in accordance with the Western model, to create a unified law and to monopolize political functions, the state has intervened more and more actively in Hindu laws pertaining to the individual. It has in effect taken over that area of law legislatively, has imposed it on the Sikhs, and has subsequently westernized it in order to suppress castes (art. 15 of the Constitution), reform marriage and divorce laws (Hindu Marriage Act, 1955), reform the nature of minority status and that of tutelage (1956), alimony and inheritance (1956), and even land ownership regulations. The process began to affect Muslim law, notably through initiatives undertaken by the tribunals regarding divorce. These practices have fueled community tensions and, in fact, supported the return and maintenance of a purely traditional and social normative system that escapes the center and organizes the reality of social behavior that the state has been asked to recognize. This "law of practice" confirms its significance to the extent that the state tries to unify law: the vicious circle is thus fearsome, for it maintains a logic of dissociation more than innovation.

A somewhat similar experience occurred with common law formalized in French sub-Saharan Africa during the time of colonization: in reality the finished product constitutes a mixture of endogenous customs and a syntax from Roman law; the passage from custom–ancestral norms reproduced by tradition–to common law–codified and written–consecrates an essentially Western formalization and thus tips the balance away from an African normative system toward a foreign law.[27] This observation pertains particularly well in the jurisdictional area, since the enactment of common law has, since colonization, led to the organization of tribunals that, like the Western model, act as guarantors of subjective laws, and are the exact converse of a conception of justice focused exclusively on the reconciliation and regulation of conflicts. The unifying effect of technique and form seems thus to outweigh, at least chronologically, the pressure exerted by rules of Western origin, leaving little place for the mechanisms of reappropriation.

Along with the technical requirement favoring the westernization of law appears a second factor of importation, the vigorous pressure of transnational inflows. The expansion of Western law, even before it reflects political strategies, echoes the need to organize and codify economic exchange relations, both private and public, between non-Western societies and European countries. It is in this perspective that the Ottoman empire accepted Western law by adopting first of all, and very early, the French Code of Commerce (1850), then the Commercial Procedure Code (1860) and Maritime Law (1864), also from France. A comparable process occurred in Persia: in the second half of the nineteenth century demand abroad supported the rise of cotton and silk commerce as well as that of opium, which European societies quickly became interested in. The Greek company Koussi and Theophilatkos, for example, monopolized olive production in Gilan and set up a processing refinery there. Jute and tea production developed the same way, as did tobacco, the monopoly on which fell to a British company. This dynamic rapidly led to the private appropriation of land until then held basically by the shah, who was thereby able to pay his debts. It led directly to the adoption of a law of obligations and a commercial law, both borrowed from France and still in force under the Islamic Republic. By 1880 numerous Iranian commercial and financial concerns had been created, following the Western model, from the Ispahan Opium Company, which grew rich exporting its product to London and Hong Kong, to the Société générale of Iran, which around the turn of the century maintained seventeen exchange bureaus in Teheran. From the beginning of this process, merchants in each city asked for the right to organize themselves into chambers of commerce, meeting with the combined resistance of the shah, the governors, and the clergy. By requiring their release from all these overseers, they hastened the regulating of their profession along the lines of Western economic literature (notably the work of Jean Sismondi,* translated into Persian in 1879) and practices long in use in European cities.²⁸

In China, the 1911 revolution and especially the Nanking regime began the same process that led progressively to the adoption of several codes based on Roman law: the civil and commercial code between 1929 and 1931, the code of civil procedure in 1932, and the property code in 1930, still applied in Taiwan today. There too, the events are not innocent: the Nanking period effectively introduced the Chinese government to the world of business and external economic inflows. Its civil servants were educated abroad, while its primary support, the Shanghai business bourgeoisie, was directly exposed to influences from the large foreign companies there. At the same time, the state profited from financial capitalism at work: giving huge tax exemptions in exchange for political and material support, it compromised itself widely by westernizing its economic and social institutions to such an extent that these institutions become the keystone of a veritable patrimonialization of the society and the political system. Personal bonds grew between state capitalism, such as those uniting Chiang Kai-shek with the Soong bank headed by his own brother-in-law, himself a Harvard graduate. In fact, rarely has the importation of a model of foreign law been such a source of dependence and neopatrimonialization. Nowhere, perhaps, have both of these two logics been so clearly associated in the construction of such a quickly established juridical mimetism. One of the first acts of the People's Republic of China was to abolish the borrowed codes, an act made easier by the fact that the codes they sought to abolish were almost caricatures of their original models, strongly utilitarian and thus very elitist with very little effect on the social fabric. Here, the difference from India is clear: the fact that the Western principle of legality had so bluntly and superficially penetrated India, as well as the subsequent failure of the Soviet model, led the Chinese to abandon a juridical culture favoring the Maoism of the 1960s and its accompanying totalitarian rhetoric. Everything happened as if this failure to import Western law gave free rein to Confucian education and persuasion, which took the place of law and procedure.²⁹

The contrast is just as strong when one compares the experience of China to that of Japan, since the Meiji era began a westernization of law that has proved durable and much more solid. Beginning in 1874, the trans-

---

*Translator's Note: Jean Sismondi (1773–1842), Swiss historian and economist. He rejected the views of Adam Smith and supported state intervention to protect the working class.

lation of French codes supplanted Japanese juridical culture so much that new words were created to assign foreign concepts to categories proper to traditional juridical thought. At the end of the century, the empire was also endowed with a French-inspired penal code (1882), a code of civil procedure influenced by Germany (1890), a code of commerce (1899), and especially a civil code (1898) containing both models. The social use of this law has long remained limited, very weakly adapted, notably in its individualist nature, to the cultural realities of Japanese society. The recourse to tribunals and judicial procedures remains modest, notably in the area of civil responsibility, whereas the poorly valued profession of jurist attracts few individuals. These are so many elements that make a hundred-year-old importation and, it seems, a durable one into a real source of alienation between society and its institutions, though it connects the latter to the international economic community.[30]

This gap promotes dysfunctions that numerous studies of Japan have elucidated. Thus capitalism was established, notably with the help of the westernization of law, without which the categories of juridical individualism do not penetrate into society and provide a counterbalance. Its constructions thus came about along with the maintenance of a "fusional communitarianism" that–the height of paradox–has been adopted by entrepreneurs and politicians alike. The former found a way to limit conflicts in their businesses and progress in a social legislation that could have been in a direct line with the importation of law. The latter refer to it actively in the most diverse ways, fluctuating with varying conditions, but in each case selectively restraining the reach of certain constitutional principles borrowed from Western political systems. It is in the name of "fusional communitarianism" that the traditionalist school of Japanese constitutional law grew, serving as it did in large part as a juridical foundation of authoritarianism at the end of the period between World War I and World War II.[31] Thus the professor of law Uesugi Shinkichi (1878-1929) could bridge the gap between communitarianism and state, which led to an exacerbated ultranationalism that presented humanity as the "desire for order and cooperation" and the state's reason for being as "the unity of natural fact and spiritual operation."[32] The success of ultranationalism was considerably supported by an active combination of a lively traditional Confucianism that an elitist importation could in no way disturb and Western juridical and political categories of thought. The synthesis was as complex as it was clever: Nakono Seigo, founder in 1933 of the Tohokai Party, appeared on the scene at the same time as Hitler and the return to the Japanese community;[33] in 1940 Fujisawa Chikao claimed, for his part, that Hitler had been influenced by Confucianism.[34] Without reaching such an extreme, the ideas of nation and nationalism appeared in Japan as new categories of thought, fruits of this cultural synthesis, as is revealed in the evolution of *kokka*, the contemporary term for the nation.[35] In today's Japan, the process of hybridization sustains the same strategic designs: beyond a nationalism that no longer attains the same heights, the succeeding liberal-democratic governments draw from the same register, making "fusional communitarianism" a counterbalance helpful to the needs of pluralism. Maintaining a consensualist ideology helps depoliticize society, fuels the crisis of party representation and the rise of social movements from outside the system and often just as violent. In the perspective of a politically maintained communitarianism, neighborhood movements (*jumin-undo*) prevail over business unionism, thus revealing the benefits available for the actors from a selective implantation of the principles of juridical individualism. However, aside from the resulting limits in participation, the practice of hybridization helps to no small extent to explain the increase of violence against the state, of which the Sanrizuka movement, created to halt the construction of a new airport in Tokyo, is the best illustration. Remarkably, this movement was organized specifically on a communitarian basis, allying local communities and sects, and protesting as a group against the state's legitimacy and its institutional configuration as well as against the rise of an industrial capitalism that endangered agriculture and, through that, ancestral lands. As David Apter has convincingly shown, the collision between the state and communitarian logic has generated a dangerous dialectic, "violence becoming legitimate and legitimacy violent."[36] As constitutive of dependence, the gap created by the mechanisms of importation between a state having Western law and a society based essentially on its own traditional values also produces tensions and crises all the more fearsome and violent for being part of a system that by definition no longer allows any common ground between state and society. In the name of an endogenous legitimacy, communitarian groups and sects continue the work of imported political institutions.

Technical necessities and pressure from transnational inflows are not the only bases for the importation of Western law. The political needs of the prince and the need for a unified national law in societies dominated by a particularist normative system draw a society to borrow foreign codes endowed with the double legitimacy of modernity and unity. On this basis new African regimes have repudiated the order of custom–whose codification, we have seen, was not often reliable–and have preferred to adopt the law of the former colonizer. Public law has provided good practice: constitutional mimetism contributed to the value of national structures by overvaluing them, and thus it has dismantled a common law that promotes tribal and communitarian structures. The establishment of a unitary and centralized Jacobin* conception of the state helped directly to delegitimize a common normative system that had meaning only in the context of an officially decentralized and pluricommunitarian society. This jacobinization of law brings together, as Etienne Le Roy has shown, mimetism and ineffectiveness in the different areas of administrative, territorial, budgetary, and fiscal reforms, in both judicial organization and laws governing nationality. Similarly, reforms regarding the family and land ownership conform with the French civil code, thereby individualizing social relations and dissociating land from communitarian social structures; they also assure the triumph of the individual as the subject of law, establishing the status of citizenship and thus guaranteeing state domination.[37] At the same time, constitutional law and the administrative law deriving from it are in both word and concept solidly European and specifically French, whereas the experience of Japan shows that the importation of laws relative to work does not necessarily follow.

The hoped-for result, in these conditions, was far from achieved. Being a system of meaning derived from an entirely different culture, law is able to penetrate and function within African societies only weakly. In the quasi-absence of a general social law and a participatory constitutional law, and lacking any ability to incite to action, the integration of law into individual strategies of protection and promotion is all the more difficult. Its principal effect is thus to transform traditional social structures into a site of protest and defense against an institutional assembly perceived as foreign; these structures effect a counterlegitimacy, thereby weakening the state, forcing it to work with them in order to make obedience effective, and this in complete opposition to the desired goal of the importers. The opposition between state and society thus becomes ambiguous, even totally confused, relative to the categories of Western law. In the confrontation of legitimacies it implies, it leads the prince to be more Western than his Western models, which are presented as both modern and democratic, even while he more or less discreetly incorporates the traditional formulas of legitimation. The current growing reference to multiparty systems and

---

*Translator's Note: The Jacobins were a revolutionary club (1789–94), holding their meetings in the former monastery of the Jacobins in Paris. They later became the chief organ of the Montagnards, who advocated a strong centralized regime.

rediscovered political pluralism goes hand in hand with a formal justification of the one-party system practiced in the past. In both cases, there clearly appears the same effort of legitimation by association with, in the past, a Western, socialist, or Marxist institutional practice, and, currently, a neoliberal practice. In reality, this process marks a turning point: it defines solutions destined to consolidate a weakened political order, and at the same time reassure the tutelary Western powers. Its effectiveness remains, however, uncertain, since it attempts to save a political system that falls victim to its own cultural dissonance through principles forged by a legal system from without.

Dependence and importation can also be completely confused, since Western law is imposed purely and simply by tutelary power. The colonizer's role in the diffusion of his own normative system is, as we have seen, considerable, even if it is almost always associated, as in Africa or India, with a formation and a conservation of norms originating in custom: paradoxically, when undertaken by the national elite, as in the Ottoman or the Japanese worlds, importation was more systematic and exclusive. The colonial enterprise is thus perhaps not, for this and several other reasons, the only or even the privileged mode of the more or less forced dissemination of Western forms of domination. The transformations undergone by capitulating practices thus play a decisive role in the transmission of Western law to the states affected. As of 1875, a mixed tribunal system was set up in Egypt: Egyptian magistrates were in the minority there, relative to their European counterparts, who were predominantly French or Italian. Little by little, the regime evolved under pressure from the European powers, who required that judgments rendered conform to Western law. As a result, Egypt acquired new codes that quickly extended to national tribunals. In Lebanon, the French-Lebanese tribunals disappeared only in 1946 and produced a jurisprudence marked heavily by French influence.[38]

The combination of all these importation processes created a chain reaction marked by increasing passivity caused by the very nature of borrowing. Thus, in the name of Arab legislative unity (i.e., a nationalist position), just after its independence Syria adopted a civil code inspired directly and explicitly by the Egyptian code, with the intermediary of French legislation. Iraq's trajectory is more complex, revealing a more sustained eclecticism, exacerbated notably by the juridical influence of its protector, Britain. The Code of Inheritance and Alimony adopted by the Iraqi parliament in 1951 combined rules from Muslim law, the Ottoman *Medjelle*, the Egyptian code, and British common law. Though this mixture is found in the history of Jordanian law, the spread of Egyptian juridical practice has remained dominant in Libya since 1961 and in Kuwait since soon after independence.[39]

Complexity and alienation combine quite specifically to invert the formulas that legitimate law in Western culture. They detach the norm from its natural source as much as from its contractual origin: neither discovered by reason nor produced by a contracting will, the rule of imported law, hybridized and tinkered with, combining at times even rival foreign legal systems, can offer only the political argument of necessity or the more esoteric one of technical superiority to counter the legitimacy of custom or religious law. The task is all the more difficult for the importers of law because where tradition is more vital and more legitimate, political or technical opportunities confront the double obstruction of cultural incomprehension and utilitarian rejection. When Egyptian law stipulates that every marriage must be notarized in order to protect the inheritance and guarantee the payment of alimony in case of divorce, it is immediately perceived as constraining by the social actors, who find refuge in tradition and common-law marriage. It is thus not surprising that modern Egyptian society is increasingly interested in common-law marriage. The same interest has also arisen in sub-Saharan Africa regarding funerals and baptisms of children, where children are given their fathers' names. Even now in Egypt and Japan, plaintiffs avoid juridical proceedings for the purposes of receiving damages, and prefer to settle privately. Thus, in upper Egypt, private vengeance (*tha'r*) has increased significantly and become increasingly practiced in towns, because of rural migration.[40]

This avoidance logic reveals both the individual's strong capacity for resistance and the ambiguity of a normative order that does not realize its objectives, that gives rise to new dysfunctions and brings about the conditions of a renewed independence. The target is almost never attained: appreciated and imported primarily for its universalist virtues, Western law does not create a genuine public space, not in Africa, the Middle East, India, or Japan. Far from unifying behaviors, it fragments them; far from creating the status of citizenship, it promotes the free mobility of individuals among whichever normative spaces most suit their interests. Instead of introducing a state logic into these societies, it in fact imposes an image of civil obedience that contradicts the principles of universalism.

These results are dysfunctional precisely because they try to organize the state against itself. Either, as in Africa or the Middle East, the introduction of a normative system accelerates the state's exit from social spaces, thus diminishing individual allegiances to the center; or as in India, it leads the state to accept the public nature of the plurality of communitarian social spaces, and thus the limits to its own competence and its own universalist identity. Henceforth, the state's survival has to do not only with the accommodation and bending of its own rules, which, in fact, has commonly occurred throughout Western history, but also with a logic of avoidance leading to the reconstruction of a legitimate political and juridical scene elsewhere. The logic of appropriation is thus overtaken by that of doubling. Certainly, the imported laws could, here and there, be adjusted, such as family and land ownership rights in Africa or English law in India, but these adaptations are probably small next to the rigidity of most of the public laws borrowed from the West and the results of the subsequent detachment of the public from the social order. It would be unjust to the receiving societies to say that the construction of a center of authority within them necessarily entails such a loss of capacity that it would ironically be fitting to praise them for their strong appropriation capacities.

This loss is, in fact, twofold. Technically, the effects of avoidance and doubling generate uncertainty and unpredictability, as well as the subsequent weakening of the center. Culturally, it is expressed as an identity crisis that occurs commonly when different, superimposed juridical cultures contribute to the formation of the norm: Jordan and Iraq were, in the space of a half century, exposed to the influence of the Muslim law of the *Medjelle*, of common law, and of French law transmitted through Egyptian law; contemporary Japanese law proclaims its Western-ness and lets its jurists consider themselves translators of a foreign text. This resembles the Roman jurists who at the end of the Middle Ages met the construction of the modern state with a rediscovery of Roman law reviewed and reconceived as a function of the evolution of social thought, the discovery of individualism, and the *aggiornamento* that then affected Christianity. Jurist translator and jurist builder thus stood in opposition in the definition of two different social functions of the producer of law; the function realized by the former inevitably hindered the social creation of the state in order to reinforce its extroversion.

The result is clearly oriented toward dependence. Whether it concerns the education received by the jurists themselves or the education received in the Western universities and hence producing networks of solidarities rooted in the Northern world; whether it concerns the form or the content of a rule of law or the normative mode with which non-Western societies are integrated into international economic circuits: everything concurs in an obvious juridical dependence. Even more profoundly, universal participation in a single legal culture leads governments to meet social crises with solutions based on a constitutional law borrowed from the West, to thereby increase social and cultural discord, to further distance themselves from the people, and to integrate themselves into a juridico-political order in which they are dependent. Such was the case, for example, with the Algerian government when it reacted to the 1988 uprisings by proposing constitutional reforms which they could easily claim did not contribute to inciting a large portion of the population to violence. Such was also the case when President Mobutu tried unsuccessfully in September of 1991 to respond to similarly intense uprisings merely by nominating a new prime minister. This actual dependence linking the governed to a juridical culture, whose extroversion has already been proven, weakens the reactive capacity of political systems, promotes their shift toward authoritarianism, and easily, and most perversely, supports the developmentalist argument that, in a crisis, non-Western societies are unable to respond to requests for reform and cannot meet demands to participate in the political process. The history of the failure to import law is first that of material and technical dependence, and then a cultural one, based, finally, on the insidious, acknowledged inability to use the law to enact reforms.

An Imported Debate

This dependence linking non-Western societies to a self-proclaimed universal juridical culture extends to the entire political and ideological debate. Struggles for independence had placed the idea of the nation at the center of political discourse; in order to be legitimate, this discourse had to actively defend and make known the universal nature of nationalist categories. It was logical that the Ba'ath in the Middle East, the NLF in Algeria, the *Istiqlal* in Morocco, the RDA in Africa, and the Congress Party in India tried to use against the colonizer the hypothesis of a universal right to national sovereignty and thus to inscribe themselves in a political grammar whose usefulness was a direct function of its nature as an imported product. One can blame such actions for the poverty of these movements in the reconstruction politics by an endogenous culture; one can in particular note the rapid decline of their ability to mobilize once they acquire independence. Nationalism is unable to change from being a formula of protest received from the colonizer into a formula of governmental mobilization, as the subsequent experiences of the NLF, the Congress Party, and the Ba'ath attest; recourse to the charismatic formula with Ben Bella or Nehru, or to coercion everywhere else, reveals their inability to mobilize with endogenous cultural symbols, which would have required a complete redefinition of national communalization proper to each of these cultures, a task for which the political personnel had neither the training nor the education.

The failure of Marxism in the Arab countries, then in India, linked notably to the absence of horizontal solidarities and the socialization of individuals in terms of class, reflects the crisis of the discourse of national sovereignty and polarizes the givens of political debate. This debate becomes increasingly simplified, since it opposes a developmentalist discourse, held by the leaders, and a culturalist discourse that emerges from various modes of protest. The developmentalist discourse has a double function: to establish modernity as a primary requirement, justifying the possession by the central executive power of an authority superior to all others, especially any kind of traditional authority; and to defer or arrange the realization of democracy, which can be attained only after a certain level of economic development. The necessarily inflationist use of this argument leads its beneficiaries to insist more and more on the universality and the high value of the imperative to modernize, thus clearing it of the vices characterizing excessive authoritarianism. This orientation is clear in conservative monarchies, formerly in the shah's discourse and now in that of the Moroccan monarchy in its efforts to ally with the urban classes; this orientation also covers the wide variety of revolutionary or reformist regimes: Kemalism, of course, but also Bourguibism, the technocratic and economic planning ideology of India's Congress Party; and also the post-Ben Bellist Algerian regime, for example, in its ambition to rapidly create a heavy industry and with it to set up a national energy system.

The culturalist discourse inevitably works in the same way: aiming its protest precisely at the source of the problem, that is, against a universalist conception of generative modernity as well as symbolic violence and social frustration, the reference to culture as the priority serves as an ideal foundation to every tribunal undertaking. Many different Islamic movements use this same discourse, just as do the Indian RSS and Hindu-inspired partisan groups, the Japanese Komeito, and also the many increasingly successful messianic sects that have become a substitute for fundamentalism, both in Latin America and Africa. This discourse also tends to become more radical: against developmentalist strategies, culturalist protest can easily claim a legitimacy superior to that espoused by the government and make its claim the basis of a political countersociety whose conformity to the law assures its ascendancy over the official political scene. The constitution of such a countersociety is the obvious culmination of the entire strategy of protest: at that point, the taking of real power, such as occurred in Iran, tends to weaken the movement's legitimacy by forcing the movement to make at least a partial compromise with developmentalist practice. The entire culturalist discourse suggests an Islamic (or Hindu) modernity distinct from Western modernity, but without having to enunciate the content. Aside from the fact that this passage to the concrete project implies a partial integration into developmentalist logic, it particularly risks rupturing the unanimity at the basis of a culturalist-type mobilization. In that, the FIS, the RSS, the Komeito, or Kimbanguism support, at worst, a disaggregation or a dulling of the political debate.

On the other hand, the confrontation of these two discourses tends to take place in a democratic context, but in terms very strongly external to the cultural and historical givens of the society in question. For its part, developmentalism serves as the theoretical foundation of a limited pluralism. As a shapeless and eclectic space between totalitarianism and democracy, this strange concept appears as the avatar of developmentalism, describing political systems whose authoritarianism is justified by the need to rapidly construct a modern center and to contain the rapid increase in popular participation resulting from accelerated modernization. As a new and contested power, the modernizing center has to both prove its popular legitimacy and moderate the effects of a political competition presented as a dangerous luxury. Thus democracy is not negated, and even acquires a favorable position in the discourse of legitimation: at the time of its one-party system, Algeria claimed that it was democratic; the consolidation of a single party in Cameroon produced in 1985 the *Rassemblement démocratique du peuple camerounais*; ruled by one of the most authoritarian regimes in Africa, Guinea is controlled solely by the *Parti démocratique de Guinée équatoriale*, Gabon by the *Parti démocratique gabonais*, the Central African Republic by the *Rassemblement démocratique centrafricain*, Ivory Coast by the PDCI, Mali by the *Union démocratique du peuple malien*.

As more and more present, even exclusive in the practice of protest or opposition, culturalism takes over the democratic claim as the coherent end point of its mobilizing capacity. Successor to the RSS, the Jana Sangh entered the electoral fray in 1977 in the name of democracy against the dictatorial tendencies it saw in Indira Gandhi; against Bourguiba, the MTI presented itself as the principal bearer of democracy and clamored to be recognized as a political party; in the 1987 elections, the Egyptian Islamists wanted to appear as the democratic alternative to the controlling party.

Thus the themes of democracy and democratization contain the essential elements of political debate without even being translated into the vernacular languages. Introduced as such, as the grating of two logics opposed by everything else, political debate contains the twofold characteristic of imported word and ambiguous problematic. Paradoxically, developmentalism and culturalism meet to accent the exteriority of the democratic problematic with respect to the history of the societies in question: the first by placing democracy in a more or less distant past, the second by rejecting the definition of its content and keeping only the function of a unanimist and reactive mobilization.

The paradox is burdensome, since it causes actors and observers to think that henceforth the only model for democratization in non-Western societies is the one forged in the West. The democratic order is thus envisioned as a representative democracy with its own institutional methods and its own philosophical underpinnings. In these conditions, the debate over democratization in Africa and Asia quickly becomes sophistic, leading one to evaluate–in the purest developmentalist tradition–the aptitude of the Southern states to adopt, and achieve the same results, the democratic regime as it was invented, over time, by Western history.

At this point, the terms of the debate become very curious. They simultaneously evoke the universality of the democratic model thus defined and its multiple moorings in Western culture. Moorings or at least points of affinity relating democracy and Christianity on at least five distinct levels: all are characterized by a single active and participatory orientation that differs from the contemplative or withdrawn attitudes; the democratic formula of legitimacy draws deeply from the Christian distinction between the temporal and the spiritual; Christianity and democracy share the same construction of individuality, the same conception of delegation and representation, and the same vision of pluralism.[41]

Such an analysis can easily find arguments to support it or, more precisely, bear it out. At its most general, however, it is just as easily refutable. The history of Western Christianity is strewn with experiences that contradict such a hypothesis and that clearly show that the correlation is a weak and by no means necessary one. It at least appears obvious that no single Christian culture exists, for the Roman Catholic, Protestant, and Eastern Orthodox variants are already too profoundly different for one to define, even intellectually, the components and foundations of this affinity. Even within these variants, the social usage made of Christianity can be called democratic at times and authoritarian at others, without either term being dominant: neo-Augustinism, then traditionalism and integrism have served as vectors in the Catholic world for authoritarian and antidemocratic political ideologies, whereas Thomism seems one of the theoretical foundations of the principle of national sovereignty; the Reformation produced as many pretotalitarian experiences, for example in the Republic of Geneva, as democratic inventions, such as that accompanying the Puritan revolution. Similarly, it is less than rigorous to call other cultures antidemocratic hastily, unless one wants to be purely polemical: *Theravada* Buddhism promotes a conception of society founded on both the idea of equality and that of individual responsibility; the great Islamic tradition also inspired a construction of social justice and communitarian egalitarianism that is accepted in the modern Muslim world by all who integrate the idea of democracy into their repertoire of political action.

In reality, behind this too-simple culturalist equation lie concealed two particularly important intermediary considerations. On one hand, democracy came about in the Western world, gradually and at different paces in different areas, as the end point of political strategies of individual and social actors who sought either to demand their political participation or to consolidate their own power by enlarging the participation of others: as a conquest of power in one case, conservation in the other, the practice of democracy consists in constructing formulas of political mobilization by utilizing and enriching the networks of meaning contained in the surrounding culture.[42] On the other hand, and for this reason, the surrounding culture intervenes not to *produce* democracy, but to define its meaning and orientation, to allow the passage from an ideal conception of democracy as an aporia to the reality of a concrete and constructed regime. In other terms, the culture has acted as a factor in Western history to invent not democracy, but *representative government*.

If one transposes this double mediation onto non-Western political scenes, one sees clearly the effects of dependence. First of all, the practice leads to massive borrowing: the existence of democratic regimes already functioning in the West and the socialization of non-Western political actors, which occurred mainly in political organizations or European and North American universities, promote the immediate translation of categories of democratic action into those of a representative democratic order. The first concern of the leaders of Iran's Islamic Republic in its first days of power was to organize a constitutional referendum followed by the election of deputies. In most of the authoritarian regimes in Africa and Asia, parliaments play an important role that is not just symbolic; rather they occupy a central place in decision making and legitimation procedures, no matter how weakly competitive the elections of their deputies may be. The example of Iraq during the Gulf War reveals that, by submitting each important decision to a preliminary vote in parliament, Saddam Hussein took care not only to legitimate his action by a demonstration of consensus, but also to send the Western societies the image of a mobilization supported by the votes of a popular *representation*.

For their part, the strategies deployed by the governing and the governed tend to reinforce the logic of borrowing. Increasingly, the former find in the discourse of democratization the means to obscure the economic and social problems they have no way of solving. The uprisings occurring in Africa, from Cairo to Kinshasa, from Fez to Abidjan, express first of all a profound social frustration on which a symbolic manipulation can have no real effect. Since the governing group meet this pressure by inscribing it in the current constitutional debate, they at least can establish a dialogue between those opposing and those opposed. In this perspective, the least costly solution and the one most practiced by the princes is to reorganize the political class and to assure minimal access by certain elites to centers of power: this is what Sadat did by supporting a multiparty system in Egypt when the new orientations of his diplomacy risked isolating him, or the shah during the winter of 1978-79, when he assigned Shapur Bakhtiar the task of forming a new government, or the president of Benin when in February of 1990 he instituted the practice of national conferences, which was subsequently imitated by the presidents of Congo, Togo, Niger, Zaire, and by the new president of Mali. The conjunction of the effect of demonstration and the need to limit as much as possible the transformation of the political system or the sharing of power leads one to conceive the process of democratization in elitist and representative terms. However, in societies where neither the culture nor social practice valorize the ideas of delegation and representation, such solutions very quickly present the obvious risk of not being received or a fortiori understood by the population and of thus further widening the gap separating political system and society.

Regarding practices of the opposition, the insertion of the theme of representative democracy satisfies several strategic considerations. First of all, it permits a favorable positioning of opposition movements relative to political power. While denouncing the reprehensible imitation of Western institutions, Djamal ed-Din Al-Afghani opposed, in the name of Islamic revivalism, the despotism of the Ottoman sultan and the Persian shah, thereby initiating at the end of the nineteenth century a lasting confusion between the culturalist claim and the call for a democratization of governmental structures. Even if Afghani and the *sheykh* Abduh in Egypt challenged the idea of importing parliamentary and constitutional institutions into the Muslim world, revivalism gained by defining itself as the expression of a popular revolt against the prince and closely associating the defense of reconstructed tradition with the expression of the people's will. Henceforth, the institutional dynamic could very likely complete the process and lead the movements based on opposition practices to claim a place in the political scene and in electoral competition, as soon as the latter began to exist, following the example of what happened after the Persian constitutional revolution at the beginning of the twentieth century.

The culturalist orientation of opposition strategies can, paradoxically, serve this shift and impart an original meaning to the practice of representation. The return to Law assures first of all the promotion of those who know it, established not as representatives, but as intermediaries between the people and a tradition learned and mastered by a very small minority of scientists and scholars. In such a model, the logic of delegation easily comes about, for the twofold reasons of theory and opportunity. The people abandon the political functions to those who know it; the latter can, in turn, advantageously confiscate the theory and practice of representative government simply by modifying the founding formula: elected officials do not represent the sovereign people, but are chosen and delegated on the basis of the competence that distinguishes and authorizes them. Subsequently, the prospect of opportunity lets the revivalist elite be satisfied with imported representative institutions and even draw substantial benefits from them: in the phase of active opposition, they help them fulfill their function as tribunes favorably by penetrating the official political scene, and by controlling municipalities, such as the Algerian FIS, or associative and corporatist networks, such as the Egyptian Muslim Brotherhood; in the process of the conquest of power, they permit them to benefit from the minimum wage laws of oligarchy, to confiscate the advantages of the representative order, and endow it with a formula of legitimation of their own stamp.

Thus did Khomeini move progressively closer to the imported institutions he had earlier violently denounced. Before his arrival in France, the religious leader did not explicitly subscribe either to the idea of a republic or to democracy, though, however, he had for quite some time been castigating the shah's despotism, after the manner of Afghani, and also bringing to light the constitutional violations of which the shah was guilty. The ambiguity was already remarkable, since his oppositional discourse integrated references to constitutional order and reflected calls for democratization. It was, however, on the ideal political order that Khomeini made the fewest concessions: in his theoretical works as in his statements to the press, it was a question only of *dowlat-e islami* (Islamic state) and government by the *fuqaha* (jurisconsults).[43]

It was only on the eve of seizing power that he modified his position: as of November 1, 1978, Khomeini spoke–and for the first time–of an Islamic Republic and democratic government. The expression will be amended, of course, since the idea of democracy underwent severe criticism. The homage, nevertheless, had been rendered and the word figured in Islamist vocabulary at the time of the crucial phase of revolution. In particular, the practice of representative government remained central to the new republic. In a culture that should exclude it, the institutions that inspire it are legion: the supreme Guide is designated by a council of experts itself elected by universal suffrage. At the same time, the president of the republic is also elected by the people and incarnates an executive power balanced by a legislative power held by a National Assembly, also elected by universal suffrage, though its legislative activities are overseen by a council of religious leaders and designated jurists. This produces a hybrid institutional order in which the many elective procedures and instances of delegation fulfill a triple function: to justify internationally the conformity to certain categories that found the "modern" political order; to institutionalize, by the practice of delegation, a new political class that has been effectively composed for the most part of scholars and their allies; and to translate into institutional terms the intermediary identity that theological discourse confers on the religious elite.

Everything happens in reality as if the debate between developmentalists and culturalists opposed first of all two types of mediators whose confrontation reflected political life: conservative or reformist princes, establishing legitimacy on their mediation between a traditional populace and a modernity toward which they intend to lead it; traditional scholars and businessmen, elaborating the formula that bases their authority on the mediation between a desocialized populace and an authenticity that they alone have mastered and toward which they try to lead it; princes encouraging the selective entry of the elite into the center of neopatrimonial power; opposition members claiming a double exclusivity, one based on the esoteric nature of their knowledge and the other on their ability to utilize the electoral practices of representative democracy to obtain mandates and be recognized as a new political class.

This convergence of utilities has evidently limited, even blocked, the capacity for political innovation, since the terms of the ideal state have been quickly transcribed into the terms of the imported institutional universe. As a project of political invention suited to the culture of a specific society, the theme of democracy risks being a subterfuge that, at times, serves the prince as a form of interference or as a mode of adjustment, and at other times, serves the opposition as an instrument of its organization into a political class.

PART THREE

Failed Universalization and Creative Deviation

Since the social sciences have criticized the functionalist, indeed organicist visions that were still in vogue one or two decades ago, it has become rash to think that social systems can a priori and inevitably protect themselves from failure and that they can regenerate after contact with what challenges or threatens their identity. It would be naive to think that dependent states possess the political capacity to emancipate themselves from dominance relations: with rare exceptions, sociological analyses do not venture into this area and do not examine the political production of peripheral societies for the ways it inverts the international system and the power relations that organize it. For the same reasons, it is imprudent to assert that importation practices necessarily lead to a logic of hybridism or that inflows from without tend necessarily to be appropriated by the receiving society, as if a mysterious, invisible hand took possession of goods and symbols conceived and fabricated by other histories and other cultures.

For all that, Jean-François Bayart's hypothesis,[1] in particular, has met with at least four opposing arguments. First, the processes of westernization do not take root only in receiving societies: as inflows, they also belong to the international space that helps make them and organize them, as well as perpetuate them and give them meaning; it is highly probable that the international order constrains and limits the reappropriation initiatives that one or another actor could take. Second, such initiatives cannot be thought of as a priori: their formation presupposes that social actors with sufficient resources find those initiatives valuable; however, we have seen that importation makes sense for those who bring it about, and that there is little evidence that those who benefit from it wish to reverse it. Moreover, the effect of hybridization can be envisioned only as the effect of several actions—strategies, perhaps—about which one can postulate neither homogeneity nor consciousness: if it is clear that certain actors in the receiving societies react to disorders caused by the importation of foreign models, one can, without much risk of error, suppose that their reactions are diverse and contradictory, and that it would be miraculous if they led to a coherent and functional synthesis. Finally, the idea of appropriation finds its basic strength in the postulate of its efficiency: political relations reach optimum effectiveness as soon as they are comprehensible to those whom they affect and would, therefore, suppose a combination of imported data with data derived from tradition. Yet nothing supports a priori the idea that the actors who hold power prefer this formula, whereas formulas of substitution that are valid in the short term do exist: the populist stance, recourse to clientelist relations, and the glorification of particularism often appear as easy diversions from reappropriation.

Nevertheless, the effects of importation remain fixed: importation creates a disorder that, as we have seen, often reinforces relations of dependence; however, this disorder disrupts systems of meaning, processes of identification, modes of collective action, and forms of government: for this reason, it gives rise to new political practices, as well as forms of invention and political innovation. Internationally, disorder is measured in terms of the contradictions deriving from the logic of forced imitation: acute dissensus regarding the legitimacy of law, regulations, and practices; uncertainties around the identity of actors; increasingly clear distinctions between "governing states" and "governed states"; growing dissociation between populations and states; and the spreading of anomie throughout the international scene. Though criticized, nation-state logic doubles as a transnational logic that increasingly interests sociologists and whose effect of recomposition seems as massive as it does complex. Putting into perspective the entirety of these dynamics allows one to locate both the force and the limits of the processes of westernization, to determine what checks and what encourages innovation, to appreciate the reality of possible adaptations, and to evaluate the importance of failed reappropriations.

5. Internal Disorders

The main result of the massive importation of structures of authority is a loss of meaning that strains relations between the government and those governed and even more, the entirety of political relations. Whether or not this loss of meaning is compensated for by a process of doubling or by negotiations between the modern and the traditional, this loss of meaning considerably influences the strategies of both those in positions of authority and those individuals requesting allocations. This is diametrically opposed to Western political history, in that the European state was constructed by dynastic centers possessing a traditional legitimacy, in line with ancient Christian and Roman cultural models and based on differentiated strategies used by social actors seeking their own advantages.

The loss of meaning constitutes an important loss for the official political scene. It discourages the individual in his efforts to adapt to an institutional life that does not concern itself with him. Such efforts thus remain exclusive to the importing political elite, who use exogenous formulas in order to grow stronger and thus stimulate internal competition. Thus it was with the constitutional revisions begun in Algeria following the tragedies in the fall of 1988, twenty years after General de Gaulle used them to calm the crisis of May 1968. The debates of democratization derived from the same logic when the African national conferences attempted to unite the various elements of the elite in order to define the conditions of a multiparty system that could accelerate the formal installation of Western representative government.

Recent research has resolved the paradox of this approach and its lack of effect among those governed. Yves Fauré has shown in regard to the Ivory Coast that competitive or semicompetitive elections were more weakly supported than plebiscites offering a single candidate were.[1] Fauré notes that even for the 1990 legislature, participation varied from 21 percent in districts offering numerous candidates to 99 percent when the PDCI candidate ran unopposed. Clearly, in these conditions plebiscite manipulation does not explain everything. Similarly, the level of political awareness, fetishized by traditional electoral sociology, does not seem to count for much here. The correlation between participation and absence of choice was as clear in the various *communes* composing the urban zone of Abidjan as in the rural districts. Fauré wisely resists the facile culturalist interpretation that emphasizes the African tradition of seniority and consensus. The example of the Ivory Coast–which we saw elsewhere–does not support the commonly held view that a single-party system is the natural or functional formula of government in Africa. The most credible explanation is probably more prosaic: faced with meaningless institutions, the individual recomposes his strategy according to a double–particularist and utilitarian–calculation. Unable to merge into a valorized political community, as is the case with an electoral body carrying national sovereignty, he looks to the electoral process for the formalization of a patron-client relation that offers easy and certain access to the official political scene. In other words, no cultural formula, no symbolic valorization can, as it does in Western democracies, correct or invert the Olsonian cost of electoral participation.

The effect of this loss of meaning is fearsome: it tends to place a burden not just on voting but on any kind of political participation; it locks prospective democratization in a delicate dilemma: either democratization must be completely redefined and thus undergo an "appropriation" occurring in the most fundamental reaches of the society, or it will be revived in an artificial and deceptive manner because the rationale of identity penetrates the electoral scene and assures easy success to confessional or ethnic parties, as in the Muslim world, but also in India, Japan, and even occasionally in sub-Saharan Africa. In the first case, the appropriation is a lengthy process; in the second, it is only the very ambiguous juxtaposition of two mutually exclusive universes of meaning.

As soon as it loses meaning for the social actors, politics undergoes a profound recomposition whose characteristics can be found in the most widely diverse cultures: the institutional vectors themselves produce social movements that tend to construct a competing space of legitimacy outside the official political scene; the political community essentially changes, abandoning its nation-state referent in favor of contradictory dynamics combining particularist affirmation with imperial action; the allegiance of citizenship loses its relevance, which exposes a simultaneous decrease in empty social spaces within which the state can no longer impose its authority; and in order to propagate itself, the leadership must concede more and more to a neopopulism that effectively hamstrings its relations with society. These are such heavy consequences of the importation rationale that, though they can serve the cause of innovation and appropriation, they can do so only in a very selective and very uneven manner.

New Mobilizations

Societies that import Western political models undergo a recurrent crisis of mobilization that evokes new social movements currently at work in certain European countries. The relatively recent crisis of the providence states and the decrease of their ability to react have helped deport a previously integrated and even routine social movement toward a political space beyond the government institutions in place, resulting in less orderly demands and in a mode of action where the symbolic expression and the questioning of values prevail over the strictly utilitarian mobilization identified with traditional union organizations.[2] As a result, identity demands, the denunciation of modernity, the tendency to spontaneity, and organizational flexibility appear as so many major traits. It is not surprising that mobilization took on this type of orientation at a much earlier date in non-Western societies. Little studied by political sociology, it had already espoused most of the traits that the abundant literature devoted to new European social movements is now discovering in our Old Continent. This similarity can be easily explained. Outside the institutional track, mobilization is more successful and legitimate because it substitutes a utilitarian approach with a call for alternative values, notably ones pertaining to identity; weakly integrated in sociopolitical activity that can no longer contain it or neutralize it, mobilization rebels against ritualization, organization, and trivialization.

The parallel probably stops once the convergent effects of extra-institutional contestation become obvious. Such contestation, however, does not have the same meaning when it is, as in Western Europe, caused by a crisis affecting the distributive capacity of the state, and when it derives in other areas from processes of delegitimation and loss of meaning that accompany the massive importation of foreign political models. This importation radicalizes the features of the new social movements: faced with weak institutions that are losing their meaning, contestation claims to produce a direct counterlegitimacy; thus it is even more external to the order in place and emerges as a protest-uprising and as a form of mobilization completely dissociated from expression by the people. For this reason, collective protest, whatever its object, tends to occur in moments of expression of identity, as if all social or economic uneasiness were directly imputed to the work of deculturation by individuals or groups that were its victims.

Many illustrations from various places and times seem to confirm this hypothesis. The Iranian revolution of 1906 was thus partly initiated by a purely categorical economic problem having to do with government regulation of the price of sugar, which had undergone an unprecedented rise caused by the crisis in Russia, Persia's main supplier. Merchants in the bazaar, refusing to lower their prices as mandated by the state, were severely sanctioned. What should have been an uneventful protest action immediately became an expression of identity. Merchants gathered in one of Teheran's main mosques and asked the *ulama* to articulate their requests. To better support these requests, principal ayatollahs decided on a symbolic exile that took them a few kilometers outside the capital to a famous pilgrimage site, where the people came in support. They asked the shah to permit their return and to make certain concessions, including notably the application of the *sharia* in its entirety and the adoption of a constitution. Hesitation on the part of the shah provoked further collective action, leading to an unprecedented action by the shah, in response to which many women demanded that the *ulama*, "which had sanctioned their marriage," be respected.[3]

Such shifts can, of course, be explained by the authoritarian nature of a political system that, outside religious institutions, offers no vectors of protest. They are further clarified by reference to an effective strategy of recuperation on the part of the clergy. This explanation is, however, inadequate: its inscription within a religious context gave protest its mobilizing effectiveness and a legitimacy of substitution that caused the shah to concede and that transformed a categorical claim, that is, the claim of an individual group, into a revolutionary process. This inscription was much more than instrumental, since it gave meaning to mobilization and constituted the very foundation of the denunciation of the political system in place and of its titular head.

This type of articulation was seen again seventy years later in the Islamic revolution. The active protest undertaken by the bazaar merchants against the shah conserved the same crystallization of identity, affirmed all the more because it jointly denounced the government's deflationary policies and the competition imposed by the modern and transnational sectors of the economy. Popularizing the slogan: "Islamic Republic, neither East nor West," the large manifestations of winter 1978–79 explicitly blamed the accumulated frustrations on imitation, making the extolling of Islamic identity not so much a model or a solution, but the very emblem of protest mobilization.

Abdelkadar Zghal interprets the reactivation of tradition in contemporary Tunisia in very much the same way, emphasizing that it derives from several social behaviors, whether they be the reappearance of sorcery and maraboutism in the rural milieu, the reviving of moral proselytism among the local notables, or particularly the return to Islam by the young.[4] This last component produced the MTI, mediated by the religious education circles that proliferated in the 1970s around the mosques in Tunis. These circles attracted a youth population, inserted–but not integrated–into a modern society that offered it no social categories capable of meeting its expectations or articulating its needs in social protest. Under these conditions, the manipulation of Islamic symbols no longer offers a particularly effective context for social protest, but is rather a substitute for it, in that the production of identity takes the place of a failed protest expression.

The mechanism has become common in the Muslim world, where most social movements, springing from the most ordinary disquiet, converge toward the same expression of identity. Hence on February 26, 1986, Egyptian Central Security Force conscripts reacted to the rumor of an extension in their period of service with violence against tourist hotels, night clubs, and cabarets near the Pyramids, completely vandalizing and burning them.[5] In December 1990, the call for a general strike given by the Moroccan unions (CDT and UGTM) was rapidly transformed into an uprising against the city of Fez by the youth and others who felt excluded; this led to the total destruction of the luxury hotel Merinides, frequented by Western tourists, and the appearance of slogans supporting Saddam Hussein. These are two examples among many where social movement evolves into an expression of identity that gives meaning to its mobilization. The difficult conditions of military service, in one case, recriminations linked to the high cost of living, of underemployment, and the restriction of freedom in the other, are as if sublimated into a denunciation of Western luxury assimilated to debauchery and illicit behavior. Protest has no meaning as a demand addressed to the political system; it is legitimate only to the extent that it opposes one identity to another, wherein it expresses the revenge of a culture perceived as dominated against a culture considered dominant. The logic of the rejection and recomposition of identity is violently opposed to the logic of hybridization.

The social movements that have developed in India share in essence these same characteristics. The noticeable increase in mobilizations based on identity and the increasingly important role of religious processions and intercommunity uprisings must be paralleled with the crisis of legitimacy in India that weakened the government's capacity for institutional integration. The model of a secular state dominated by an ideology of importation, articulated by the Congress Party, is increasingly met by a restoration of religious communalism that tends to include and sublimate an entire ensemble of claims and frustrations. One could thus show how the painful economic upheavals that hit Gujarat, and in particular the city of Ahmadabad in the 1960s very quickly transformed into intercommunity tensions. In September of 1969, an anti-Muslim uprising sparked on religious pretexts resulted in more than five hundred dead, according to the official count, whereas on a deeper level, it expressed the exasperation of a small, unemployed Hindu proletariat at the more privileged situation enjoyed by the Muslim community.[6]

From a situation in which socioeconomic frustrations are expressed in terms of identity, we seem to gradually slide toward a new type of mobilization, where the expression of identity alone is sufficient. The increase in community uprisings observed in India in the beginning of the 1980s was fed both by an increased competition between the two communities, as evidenced by what happened in the Ayodhia Temple,* and by continually confirmed fears among the Hindus that pan-Islamic progress would upset the Indian sociopolitical order. The ante is raised here, because the affirmation of identity itself constitutes an intensification of the stakes, confiscating and marginalizing in turn all the other themes of the sociopolitical debate. The "ritual of provocation" that led the Hindu processions carrying vivid images of pigs' heads to pass by the mosques accords with new slogans denouncing "Gulf money" in particular, in order to give the mobilization of identity a central role in political debate. The result is all the more con-

---

*Translator's Note: The Ayodhia Temple is a Hindu temple located in Ayodhia, Uttar Pradesh, the region considered to be the birthplace of Rama. A mosque stood on the site until Hindu fundamentalists destroyed it in 1992. The incident triggered violent confrontations between Muslims and Hindus.

vincing in that the recurrence of communitary uprisings activates modes of allegiance and identification, which is particularly noticeable in a society where hierarchy and divisions into castes and sects tend to atomize the Hindu world into a complex cosmogony that previously limited its ability to organize politically.[7]

Comparable occurrences of this identity-based crystallization of the social movement can be seen in numerous other cases as different as those in Japan and Latin America, which most often benefit religious sects, particularly when they acquire messianic referents. This clever composition allows them to take command of many social demands, as can be seen, for example, in their supervisory function in the protest movements around the construction of the new Tokyo airport, or also in movements developed among the victims of Guatemala's 1976 earthquake. Whether it concern the Chukoku-Ha sect in the first case or the Seventh-Day Adventists in the second, these new entrepreneurs of social movement tend to separate social movements from the state's sphere, to give them their own legitimacy, distinct from their official institutional legitimacy, and to confuse protest with the affirmation of a new identity, one that contradicts the identity on which citizenship is based.

The juxtaposition of these two examples suggests that the identity-based expression of social movements does not necessarily involve direct protest by the national community and the claim for an alternative community. While we have been able to show that the particularly successful sects in Latin America were among the Indian populations who found a sacred ritual practiced in the pre-Hispanic period mirrored in their protest, the sectarian mobilization effected in modern Japanese society in no way aims to dismantle the national community but rather to confirm it. In that respect, articulations of demands and claims by identity movements do not undermine the interaction possible between socioeconomic protest and protest in the national context. It suggests, more convincingly, the defiance of social actors regarding the institutional channels of expression and their surprising availability for making claims that mix the tribunal system with the claim to a substitute legitimacy in order to counter the imported state. Significantly, from this point of view, the resulting type of movement no longer derives from a discourse on the state or addressed to the state, but a discourse on the identity project activating it. The general strike in Fez in December 1990 that disintegrated into a riot denounced first of all the ostentatious luxury and the American action against Saddam Hussein, and thus abandoned the Moroccan interpellation to promote the affirmation of

Islamic identity; the same reaction occurred when those Egyptians who felt threatened regarding the lengthening of their term of military service no longer expressed anything but their desire for a rigorous return to the *sharia*. In the same way, the question of sugar prices reached the maximum of its mobilizing capacity when it led the women, as we have seen during the first Iranian revolution, to defend the *ulama*, which had "sanctioned their marriage." Similarly, the evolution of the practice of riots in India shows that the denunciation of "Gulf money," of the rise of pan-Islamism, or of Muslim claims to the Ayodhia Temple became not only the emblems but the dominant stakes of mobilization, and to such a degree that the state became a passive, powerless and even superfluous actor in the effort of making claims. Paradoxically, this increasing abandoning of the state by a social movement that seems to want specifically to devaluate it promotes a forceful return of international parameters into political debate. The politicization of making claims no longer occurs through an appeal to the state, or even by a frontal attack on the state, but by an identity-based and transnational articulation of those claims.

In these conditions, it is within multinational societies that the correspondence between the making of claims, national identity-based action, and direct protest against the state appears most clearly. The state naturally becomes a victim, since even more than its very nature, its existence as a producer of the political community is attacked. The case of Yugoslavia clearly reveals the same passage from making claims to identity affirmation, accompanied this time by an explicit negation of the state. The active phase of this process began in March 1981 when, to protest unemployment and living conditions, the students of Pristina engaged in collective action that very quickly involved the workers because it immediately took on a nationalist color and evolved into a claim for the recognition of the cultural specificity of the Albanian population in Kosovo. In the entire Yugoslav Federation, 1987 saw 1,623 strikes mobilizing 365,000 strikers; 1988 counted 1,720 involving 400,000. In practically each case, demands for higher wages evolved into denunciations of economic exploitation of one republic by another.[8]

This entire crystallization of identity-based demands is found in a political scene that assures the growing success of the parties evolving there: the Muslim Brotherhood Movement in Egypt and the Sudan, the MTI, later the En-Nadah in Tunisia, the FIS in Algeria, also the RSS, later the Bharatiya Janata Party (BJP), in India, and the Komeito party in Japan are only a few of the most important examples attesting to their geographic and cultural diversity, and thus their presence in areas having nothing in common but the way they treat the consequences of the importation of the Western model of the state.

The irruption of identity parties on the political scene has substantially disrupted the imported rules of the game. The main characteristic of these parties is their promulgation of a type of identification that claims precedence over the allegiance of citizenship and therefore attempts to take its place. Fundamentally, then, the identity party differs from the others: its project is not to compete for political power, but essentially to work for alternative socialization and mobilization and to promote a political identity different from what is officially proclaimed. In this, the identity party has little chance of evolving, as do workers' parties that do not challenge the idea of citizenship, but rather rely on it to legitimate the rights of their members and to call for a transformation of sociopolitical structures. For this reason, the drift of the worker parties toward a tribune function was much more logical, since it wished to lead the working class to full citizenship, and to oppose the idea of a merely formal integration of the workers into society with a genuine integration. By associating itself with exclusionary logic, the identity party seeks to dismantle allegiance to the state in order to develop a more efficient and effective process of reintegration, one that remains if not mythical, at least very strongly and perfectly symbolic. In that, the identity party is essentially the producer of a negative mobilization.

The thematic of these parties is already enlightening. The return to religious law or the strict observance of a sacred ritual applied to civil life, the appeal for the City of God, or at least that of the Prophet, the reference to Hindu divinities or the return to the mystical thought of the Japanese Buddhist reformer Nichiren (1222–82) do not have a programmatic value, but an emblematic one. Similarly, and more concretely, the return to Islamic law has more value as a critique of the imported legal order than as support for a future project. Citing the Islamic renewal in Kenya and Senegal, Christian Coulon notes that the claim for an Islamic law of succession does not correspond to any "quest for a lost paradise" in the countries where this law had no history, but is seen rather "as a critical weapon of existing society" and as "a constructivist vision of another reality." They aim, he writes, "to denounce the misdeeds of western civilization and to imagine another way."[9] It is, in fact, this order of the "imaginary" or of "vision" that strains the programmatic function of identity parties and that, in particular, subjects this function to a preliminary redefinition of the political identity of those to whom it is addressed: it is as a Hindu and not as an Indian, as a Muslim and not as a Senegalese that the individual who answers the call of one or the other of these organizations identifies himself. These organizations are no longer agents of reappropriation of imported political models; rather, they are the very source of the denunciation of a logic of borrowing and its construction as the high stakes of mobilization.

At the same time, this mobilization appears more and more an end in itself. For the RSS, and later the BJP, religious festivals, the crowning of Rama or Shiva, the processions in which it takes the initiative constitute simultaneously a means to reaffirm Hindu identity and to give it a political significance. The phenomenon is even more total in that the participants see an immediate remuneration, since the lower castes and untouchables benefit from an integration into an intercaste movement. This same logic of ritual as a provider of identity is found in the way Islamic parties function through public collective prayers, dress, street processions, demonstrations, and pilgrimages. The services thus exchanged among identity parties and their base, outside of fulfilling traditional political functions, are sufficiently important to discourage their leaders from rectifying their strategy and accepting their integration, and hence their banalization within the current political system.

The Particularist-Empire Dialectic

Yet the awakening of identity concerns is not just an obvious element of political mobilization. Its pertinence extends even to the configuration of an entire political system, principally insofar as it calls into question the realization of that political system as a nation. The latter is openly defied, protested, and destructured as an exogenous political model, according to a process that promotes an alternating drift toward microparticularisms and imperial reconstructions. The instability of the very notion of citizenship and the weakness of its interiorization explain the essential aspect of a process that is, moreover, activated by the failure of integration efforts such as occurred with the governmental crises in Africa and Asia, the arbitrariness of divisions, the regression of political, Marxist, socialist, or nationalist ideologies, and of horizontal solidarities capable of structuring the national political community. This last failure is the construction of a political debate that could validate the state as a category in Africa, the Middle East, or South or East Asia.

Individuals in Africa and Asia respond to the experience of the state, the administration, interest and ideological groups by political action against any form of horizontal integration. In those rare societies where a multiparty system is maintained, the political debate it supposedly supports is increasingly upset by a particularist logic that limits its basic effect. The irruption of identity parties, such as the Komeito in Japan, the RSS and then the BJP in India, or the Islamist parties, intensifies the political debate, which becomes simultaneously a debate *among* citizens and a debate *on* citizenship: instead of activating identification with the state as nation, political competition does it a disservice. Especially since the classical parties are quick to hurt themselves, reinforcing as they do their factional and clientelist structure and replacing their integrating function with the active reproduction of vertical solidarities. The phenomenon is particularly remarkable in the case of Japan, where, behind an apparently successful importation of the Western model of representative democracy, lies hidden the rigorous maintenance of traditional Japanese clan organization. Each deputy is thus endowed with a *jiban*, that is, an electoral clientele personally attached to him, independently of his partisan affiliation and of which he becomes the owner. This client network is itself constituted by a *koenkai*, a support association that prolongs the former limited traditional groups, rural hamlets, or neighborhood blocks, and appears as the true authority of political communalization for the Japanese. As mutual aid associations, sites of sociability, and channels for requests, the *koenkai* mobilize on the community bases they reproduce rather than dissolving them into a national whole: as Jean-Marie Bouissou has noted, they remain the threshold of individual political involvement within a society where partisan militancy attracts very few people.[10] In turn, this clientelist and community structure transforms the parties, notably the Liberal Democratic Party (LDP) in Japan, into a juxtaposition of clienteles and factions, as can be observed in India with the Congress Party, in Turkey with the officially sanctioned principal parties, and even in the single-party systems in Africa or the Middle East.

This failure of national socialization makes, in very diverse ways, the fortune of microcommunitary solidarities: it tends to revive the political importance of the village group, notably in sub-Saharan African societies, and confirm the autonomy of family farms; it also revives "prenational identities,"[11] notably in the tribal states of the Sahel, but also in numerous African countries such as Liberia, Zaire, Rwanda, Burundi, as well as the Horn of Africa, and the entire southern part of Africa. In a different form, the crisis of the nation-state in nearby zones of importation, such as Central and Eastern Europe, activates subnational decomposition into increasingly smaller ethnic groups, all the while valorizing the village group and the peasant microsociety as the privileged site of identification.

The particularist dynamic not only brings about fragmentation but also promotes the constitution of network groups that successfully work against the allegiance of citizenship by transgressing borders. Faced with the state's default of identification, the individual disposes of an infinite number of positions that create many new and active solidarities: insertion into transnational cultural collectivities, churches or sects, allegiance to merchant diasporas, implication in various economic inflows.

The identification of transnational religious collectivities echoes the challenge to the state model pretty much everywhere. The success of the Catholic Church, particularly in Africa, can be correlated with the disaffection felt by the state and the people: the surge of the faithful to Sunday mass in Zimbabwe must be connected to the desertion affecting the official meetings of the ZANU. Moreover, independent churches and sects have more chance to extend their influence in sub-Saharan Africa and Latin America because their messianic message, their stronger adaptability to local particularisms, as well as their greater organizational and dogmatic flexibility, allow them to capture a decisive share of popular allegiance. The election of Jorge Serrano, an adept of an evangelical sect, as Guatemala's president reveals a process that occurs elsewhere: Alberto Fujimori was brought to power in Peru by the Cambio 90 movement, structured and organized by the same allegiance; in his wake, a Baptist preacher was elected vice president, while 20 percent of the deputy and senatorial candidates on this list were Protestants. In Bolivia, home to six hundred non-Catholic churches, President Paz Zamora thought it wise to take part in a day of prayers organized by the Protestants. In South America's Andean countries, the Indian population tends to identify with the new movements that allow them to more effectively express their particularisms: hence the success of pentecostal preachers among Bolivia's Guarani Indians, the strong penetration of Protestant missionaries in the representation structures of Peru's Indian communities, the importance of proselytism in the Quechua language among Ecuador's Chimborazo Indians. Similarly, the Vatican itself counts about 600,000 conversions annually of Brazilian Catholics to Protestantism.[12]

This dynamic is important both quantitatively and qualitatively. It incontestably expresses an identity-based movement, which is all the more vigorous in that it claims, through massive conversions, the way out of an order to which it declares itself exterior. At the same time, the example of sects in Latin America is particularly remarkable, because this explicit manifestation of exit behavior generates in turn a new dilemma of the particular and the universal. Activated by a particularist affirmation, this strategy leads its adherents into an affiliation with numerous networks that, as with the Protestant churches, claim a new kind of universalism. The success of pan-Islamism or pan-Hinduism has the same effect. Through all these cases, we find the same identity-based protest directed against the citizen's relation of allegiance to the state, the same criticism of the universalist illusion, but also the same inclination to reconstruct vast transnational solidarities, sublimating the particularist profession of faith in the adherence to an ensemble that is, in fact, sufficiently vast to contain the microcommunitarian pressure and at least partially reconstruct certain attributes of universality.

The strength of this new associative behavior lies in the constitution of several transnational human networks that increasingly mobilize interactions, as, for example, the astounding vitality of merchant diasporas suggests. The progress of informal economy, particularly in Africa, occurs through cross-border economic flows that disable state control and replace the citizenship relation by other solidarities that currently combine ethnic affiliation and utilitarian objectives such as the smuggling of money, cocoa, or manufactured goods. Certain zones, such as the Nigeria-Togo-Benin group, are so active that the state seems completely outdone by it, sometimes its victim and at others a beneficiary. But the extrapolitical recomposition of social bonds here obeys allegiances that subtly ally the microcommunity with the larger socioeconomic whole, which in any case, no longer has anything of the state about it.[13]

This observation holds for the diaspora of Lebanese merchants in West Africa, as it does for the Swahili along the shores of the Indian Ocean.[14] François Constantin notes the quality and density of the associative movement reuniting members of Muslim communities over and above their citizenship in Kenya, Uganda, Mozambique, Malawi, and Tanzania, where they are particularly in the minority.[15] He also shows how the promptness of the communities to integrate themselves into a transnational network favoring radical Islam has led each of these countries to promote the organization of their Muslim citizens into specific centers and give the local *qadi* considerable juridical power: to better protect itself, the state unravels and relinquishes itself. The equilibrium can appear functional for all parties; nevertheless, it leads to a regression of the citizenship allegiance, to a relative institutionalization of communitarianism, to an officialization of identity-based sentiments, though the logic of transnational identification with the diaspora is not totally broken.

Thus resembling the crisis of the Western model of the state, identity-based expression helps noticeably, but in a very contradictory way, to restructure political space. The disaffection plaguing governments in Africa, Asia, and even in Latin America and Eastern Europe is compensated for by a return to the particularism that reactivates the microcommunitary political order as much as it does transnational groups, whose territory is uncertain and who come into being to the extent that the dominated cultures or those cultures facing annihilation at the hands of the importing state are politically rehabilitated.

These vast ensembles hark back to the traditional imperial order in many respects. They have inherited several of its characteristics: they function like a multinational—or, at least, a non-national—political community; they solidify a valorized cultural identity that they strive more or less to spread; they suppose a weak differentiation between the social and the political, challenging the very existence of a unified and autonomous civil society; their degree of institutionalization is weak, just as is the ability of the central political power to reach each individual subject other than by deploying a military type of overmobilization or very elaborate totalitarian techniques. In these respects, the empire is constituted as a political category on very different bases from those of the state: as a product invented at a certain moment of time, the state was theorized very rapidly, since its history was immediately the object of law; the project undertaken by the founders of the state was sufficiently clear and structured for it to be quickly thought of as a universal, that is, as an entity that could impose itself onto private interests and intermediate groups, but also onto cultural collectivities that produced their own meaning. Public space thus delineated private space, in order not to compromise the state and its citizens with the society of individuals. As for the empire, it was never theorized, or even really thought out: it had no Hegel, no legists, and no law professors. Its identification is uncertain: the comparison of the Chinese, Muslim, and Roman empires reveals that their conceptual ambiguity has to do with the strong tension between the particular and the universal, which, ultimately, explains their success and their fragility. In that they are constituted by reference to a culture that their founders seek to promote above all others, they have a particularist orientation; finalized and legitimated by the explicit postulate that this culture's vocation is to spread, they also have a universalist significance and intent. It is precisely from this tension that they derive their principal characteristics: their militarization, their uncertain territoriality, the ambiguity of their borders, their fervent proselytism, and their weak institutionalization. From this tension comes their incompatibility with the very idea of nation, which is envisioned as a territorializable political community; it is because of this fact also that the empire rests on a more or less assured articulation of microcommunal and macrocultural solidarities.

Thus constructed, the empire appears like a transhistorical and ideal-typical category, one that designates a political dynamic that is more or less in effect everywhere in the world and in the most diverse contexts. History and anthropology can, of course, contrast societies that, like China or the Muslim world, have known a rather strong imperial continuity and, others, like sub-Saharan Africa or the Indian world, which have known only ephemeral empires. The nature of culture and of the social bond have, in turn, been mobilized for explicative ends: here the idea of harmony or of unity, there of a plural cosmogony or a weak disenchantment of the world, rival the idea of community integration, culminating in the production of convincing hypotheses. However, the reflection on the current political order undercuts the debate somewhat. The evolution of communication techniques gives new support to transnational relations and a new future to macrocultural solidarities. Video cassettes and televised images, pilgrimages, attendance by young Muslim Senegalese or Nigerians at the Koranic universities of Al-Ashar or Qom, Filipino students in Teheran universities and their Iranian counterparts on the campuses of Manila—all help activate mobility and bonds within vast cultural spaces,[16] whose simple existence suggests the contours of new imperial spaces indicating new political practices.

These new empires are certainly not new political institutions. Their combination with a state logic that, as we have already shown, conserves important supports, makes their levels of authority even more difficult and fragile, as is revealed, for example, by the vicissitudes and even the failures of the Islamic Conference Organization and a fortiori because it is more demanding, the Arab League.

In reality, the imperial dynamic escapes state control, whereas the interest of the state's leaders is very generally to contain and even to thwart it. Thus this dynamic is composed, either from below, on the initiative of the different "entrepreneurs" of the mobilizing culture, or from above, on that of the prince, who abandons state strategy in order to gain the upper hand by imperial strategy. Imperial order and state order face and oppose each other, worsening as well the conditions of individual political identification. The more or less normal citizens of a state find themselves on many occasions the informal but genuinely mobilized subjects of empires that have no legal existence.

The imperial project immediately evokes the situation in the Muslim world, where the various characteristics enumerated above can be found in conjunction with a continuous tradition dating back almost to the time of the Prophet. The current recourse to imperial strategies is part of the deliberate rejection of the state model and concerns the various types of actors already mentioned: revivalist movements and intellectuals wanted to construct a pan-Islamic space with a real political identity; during the Gulf War Saddam Hussein sought to mobilize the Muslim world against the coalition states, just as did many initiatives of the Ayatollah Khomeini, Muammar Gadhafi and, in his own time, Gamal Abdel Nasser. Article 11 of the constitution of the Islamic Republic of Iran stipulates that "the Iranian government must exercise continuous efforts to realize political, economic, and cultural unity in the Islamic world," whereas article 154 considers it the goal of the Republic to bring "happiness to men of all societies."[17]

The dialectic of the empire and the microcommunitarian is not, however, the prerogative of the Muslim world alone. Hindu revivalist movements militate in the same way for the construction of a unified "society-nation" that transcends the autonomies granted by the confederal system of the Indian Republic, which stretches beyond the current boundaries of the union, even to the whole of the Indian world, all the while finding its equilibrium in the revitalization of the village and the *panchayati-raj*. Other recompositions seem to go in the same direction: the breakup of the socialist states in Central and Eastern Europe appears to give rise to the same dynamic, combining an almost endless slippage of identifications toward small collectivities and a reactivation of affiliations to larger, but less easily territorializable groups. Thus the almost daily discovery of groups claiming sovereignty and inaugurating a real "political microscopy" (North and South Ossetians, Nenetses, Buriates, etc.) is on a par with the rise in pan-Turkism, pan-Slavism, pan-Magyarism, and even pan-Germanism, which finds a political resonance among the Germans of the Volga. The resulting political geometry makes state interaction increasingly uncomfortable, while it encourages leaders to employ imperial strategies for their own benefit, at least when they provide some political or diplomatic advantage.

Japan and China are related to a large extent through this logic of doubling. The first is also characterized by powerful microcommunitarian solidarities left intact by the imported idea of citizenship and by the glorification of transnational Japanese networks that increasingly supply the economic and social life of Northeast and Southeast Asia. As for China, it has long preserved an imperial structure that, in contrast to the others, has conceded nothing in any formal way to the logic of the nation-state. It still prevails because of the ancient political practice of combining the solidarity of familial communities with the force of imperial authority, which has always dominated the nobility. Important recent studies in sinology show the topicality of this data and the pertinence of a neotraditionalist approach that relies on the functionality of these microcommunitarian solidarities, which neither the construction of a modern state nor a heavily mobilizing regime has diminished. It appears, in fact, that during the height of the Maoist period authority was maintained in the factories by strong particularist networks and by the strength of clientelism.[18] At the same time, the Chinese state order was more than ever brought into an imperial dynamic that relativized the meaning of its state borders. First, it comes from a several thousand-year-old history that makes its exterior periphery into the space of "border people," whose sovereignty is uncertain and fragile: Mongols, Turks, Tibetans, Thais, Burmese, and especially Vietnamese have recently known—or still know—this experience. Furthermore, this imperial orientation is strengthened by the diaspora, whose vitality and strong cultural solidarity give the Chinese world a political geometry that significantly overflows its own legal territorial boundaries.[19] Some 30 million Chinese live abroad, notably in Southeast Asia: in Singapore, where they have power, and in Malaysia, where they constitute a strong minority. The Teochew, a particularly active migratory group originally from the northeast portion of Canton province, number 5 million in Thailand, where they control three of the five most important familial economic groups, and one million in Hong Kong, including Li Jiachen, the richest businessman on the island. Juridically, the Chinese state has by turns sought to incorporate them by establishing in 1949 a rigorous interpretation of the *jus sanguinis*, to then reject them during the Cultural Revolution, then to readopt them more recently in order to preserve its relations with neighboring states. This diaspora continues to supply financial and merchant inflows that benefit the Chinese economy (with about one billion dollars in cash per year); it has also created a "sinicized world" that activates its allegiances by an extremely dense associative network that reproduces the principal features of Chinese culture. In sum, these diasporas maintain the networks of integration that for the most part escape the world of states and incite, as in the Muslim and Indian worlds, an imperial dynamic all the more resistant to institutionalization.[20]

Empty Social Spaces

The particular-universal dialectic alone cannot explain the disorder associated with the importation of Western political models. Weakened by the effectiveness of identity mobilizations, the imported state suffers from a serious deficit of citizenship imputable to its precarious legitimacy, its superfluousness, and its political weakness. In the non-Western world, these facts make the "empty social spaces" more important; these are the sectors of society that the official political scene can neither mobilize nor control and within which it deploys forms of substitute authority that garner individual allegiances. The proliferation of these spaces tends also to diminish the internal boundaries of the state, and to decrease and intersect the allegiance networks that integrate individuals.

These empty social spaces cover two principal sites of exclusion common to most non-Western societies: the rural world and the suburban world. The first remains largely exterior to state rationality. When official politics moves into it, it does so basically through clientelist relations, outside all institutional channels. The second is characterized by friction with the state and an order of importation experienced as coercion and provocation. The active and painful frustration of the second corresponds to the passive and indifferent alienation of the first. Thus rural spaces substitute other types of relations, such as communitary personal bonds or bonds based on rank, for institutional political ones. In contrast, suburban spaces privilege active identity-based mobilizations, relying on religious or messianic organizations to attract and manage allegiances, but also on neighborhood associations and parapolitical networks.

The opposition between rural societies and urban ones is sufficiently strong and too unfavorable to the former for there to be anything in imported political modernity that would attract them or give them any reason to align with it. The hypothesis of hybridization stands opposed to the notion of complete alterity, which an entire school of thought formerly called "dual society."[21] But this idea deserves further clarification: while it is difficult to object that African rural spaces possess, as they do in South and East Asia or in the Middle East, enough social resources to make a claim for self-organization, to resist state takeover of its peasantry, and to oppose its own political order to the state, it is also simplistic and deceptive to deny that communication between the two spaces exists. To the state, the rural society adopts an attitude of pragmatic exteriority. Agricultural cooperatives of Zimbabwean companies obstinately refuse to acknowledge the tutelage of the political center, though they do not reject any material or technical help the state provides. Similarly, the Casamance peasant [of southern Senegal] will resist the creation of a local administration, though he does not reject any possible benefits that can be mediated for him by traditional social structures.[22] Even working alone, the individual is not above soliciting clientelist relations in order to reconcile his participation in a local, autonomous microsociety with his desire to obtain unilateral advantage. For its part, the state does not consider itself defeated: aside from the entry offered by patronage, it has been able to find here and there ways to compensate for its weak penetration abilities by trying to restructure the local social order. Its success has been uneven. From the half-failure of the agrarian revolution attempted by Nehru in India to the land collectivization project forged by ZANU during its struggles against Ian Smith, numerous examples illustrate the paralysis of political power against the rural society; agrarian reforms undertaken by conservative princes (such as the shah of Iran in 1962) or progressive ones (such as Nasser's in 1961) have shown even more how perverse the effects of their actions were. Far from giving rise to a new, reliable peasantry that would support the regime, these reforms only brought out the indifference and even the distrust of social actors on whom changes were forced by the political center, according to methods borrowed, in the case of Iran, from Israel and the United States. These reforms are nothing more than political initiatives unable to break through the passivity of rural populations toward the state; they fail to build a synthesis between the imported order and traditional rural society.

Confronted more directly with this importation, the suburban social spaces, on the other hand, exclude themselves from institutional political relations by producing active social movements and by initiating identity-based mobilizations. It is here, in the suburban social spaces, that the revivalist currents find their social base, even if the Turkish legislative election of the fall of 1991 revealed that the Islamist-leaning Rifah party consistently won in the central and eastern rural areas of Anatolia. Essentially, however, the urban concentration of revivalism brings about another dimension of exclusion and another political use of "empty social spaces": to the microcommunitarian withdrawal effected in the rural area is opposed the active and fervent identification with a counterlegitimacy. Beyond its revivalist expression, this counterlegitimacy can assume a messianic and sectarian form, just as it can support the rise of ethnic communities hoping to strengthen themselves by seizing the essential elements of the politicization process. In all these examples, the social spaces in question operate on a formula of legitimacy that, by radically contradicting the imported state order, leads neither to a partial integration nor to a competitive programmatic production, but simply to the affirmation of an identity of substitution. On the level of political communalization, the "empty social spaces" are still not filled. The resulting politicization supports neither the unification of structures of authority nor their hybridization, nor even the construction of a substitute government.

It would, nevertheless, be imprudent to consider this rigid analysis of "empty social spaces" sufficient and to categorize them simply as rural and suburban societies. This would be a return to the developmentalist approach that confuses political alienation with economic backwardness and erroneously opposes a participatory modern sector to a weakly civic traditional one. But the construction of an imported state loosens allegiances even within the new middle classes, whose formation and rise are directly linked to the introduction of modern social roles as well as to the growth of the public sector. Neopatrimonial logic solidly maintains an elite of upper-level civil servants with many material and symbolic privileges, who ask for continual improvement in its standard of living, and an increasingly stronger army of lower-level civil servants, poorly paid and frustrated in their hopes of advancement in the spaces of modernity.[23] The state so privileges the former that they become the active importers of Western politico-administrative models and abandons the latter, who join with unemployed intellectuals and students with uncertain job prospects in radical protest and identity mobilization. One can interpret in this way the interclass nature of revivalist movements, such as the one characterizing the membership of messianic sects or independent churches in Latin America and Africa. The sector of modernity thus contributes to its own undoing, thus leaving room for new empty social spaces.

The Populist Subterfuge

The erosion of support afflicting imported political models does not resemble just any process of political disaffection. Crystallized in terms of identity, this erosion leads to a profound divorce between the governing and the governed; it contests the formula of legitimacy on which the first are based and creates conditions for revivalist conduct by which the second seek, in their own history or in a mythical and messianic representation of their destiny, the sources of a legitimacy of substitution. In this context, the princes possess only limited strategic options: to save their authority by shoring it up with reinforced clientelism, or to manage their own formula of legitimacy by drawing on whatever makes sense to those they govern.

The first approach seems increasingly risky. Urban growth makes the patron-client relation fragile and ineffective, and the dismantling of the upper class substitutes an emotionally based clientelism with one that is considerably more anonymous, cold, and ineffective. The second solution allows few accommodations. The examples of Morocco, Jordan, and Iran show clearly that inserting traditional references into a policy of modernization is not enough to hinder the identity-based reaction provoked by efforts to import Western political models. The Latin American examples indicate as well that the introduction of representative democratic procedures and the advent of political competition are not enough to genuinely involve a politically disoriented middle class and an unorganized working class. Both of these classes experience the same political alienation that separated them from the ruling class, to which they are linked by neither the evocation of former social cleavages, nor the same emblematic vision of democracy, nor the common invention of an endogenous modernity. These impasses were at one time considered transitory and destined to disappear as democracy became institutionalized; they were meant simply to force the Latin American people to opt provisionally for populist strategies that, in time, would be outgrown.

However, these strategies spread instead of disappearing. Latin America confirmed them in essence as the durable way to organize relations between leaders and people, as revealed by the disorderly return of Peronism to Argentina, the election of Alan Garcia and then Alberto Fujimori in Peru, as well as the entrenchment of populism as a way to organize and orchestrate most of the electoral campaigns. Similarly, numerous political systems in Africa and Asia have guaranteed a genuine deepening of populism. Here, cultural alienation is more marked than in Latin America, where the Western referent is only partially perceived as external; the uncertainty burdening the mobilization capacities of dominated or frustrated social categories is reinforced by the essentially identity-based rejection of all models imported from other cultures. Populism thus becomes an almost inevitable technique of government, permitting the prince to reinsert himself into a popular fabric from which his own role as importer of the state had excluded him.

This recourse could already be seen with Nasser and Sankara, with Bhutto and Saddam Hussein; it subsequently grew in Central and Eastern Europe as the Soviet Union declined. Relative to Peronism or Getulism, the practice is managed but not eliminated. Fundamentally, it tries to remain the same by creating a cadre in which the leaders try to govern by "systematically exalting a plebeian reference."[24] Its instrumental function has not really been revised. The valorization of egalitarianism and of the national cadre, the strongly orchestrated resumption of popular themes, the adroit manipulation of traditional cultural attributes, are all meant to bond the masses to the leader, to inscribe the popular sectors within a single political axis that negates the reality of conflicts and counters any identity-based reactive mobilizations as much as possible. In other words, populism is increasingly imposed as a compensatory strategy. Faced with the imported state's lack of popularity and weak legitimacy, populism is meant to endow the prince's discourse and practice with at least some ability to attract and mobilize.

The exacerbation of nationalism, the denunciation of hegemonies and blocks, constituted a founding formula of classic populism. It is in the vigorous condemnation of imperialism that Nasser found the arguments to support his role as tribune; it is in the back-to-back rejections of Russian and American models and in the unified condemnation of their desires that Indira Gandhi drew the most convincing elements of her populist discourse. It is especially by linking exterior hegemony with internal stagnation that this entire orientation made sense and left the first generation of populist leaders with sizable room to maneuver. The large importers of the Western state model could also be the most pitiless critics of Western domination; the convergence of both these roles under the populist banner finally turned out to be functional enough for all concerned.

Since the 1980s, practice has called for a readaptation of the formula. The exercise has become more perilous, even contradictory. Identity-based mobilization has progressed such that it has annexed most of the populist arguments. From modes of government, these arguments have become the credible vectors of revivalist and messianic movements, creating dangerously exaggerated conditions. The rediscovery of identity goes very well with the unearthing of old populist, social, and political traditions, just as it does with literary traditions, notably in Eastern Europe, and religious ones pretty much everywhere. At the same time, the increasing failure of the imported state model makes populism a very delicate strategy for the people: to remain coherent with the requirements of this formula, they must take increasingly greater charge of frustrations engendered by the very functioning of the state; in order to strengthen his legitimacy, the prince must organize the criticisms leveled at his own government apparatus. As a final aggravating circumstance, the exaltation of the nation and the people's rights must henceforth be balanced by respect for the adjustment policies required by the IMF and the World Bank; consumerism and egalitarianism must become compatible with the valorization of budgetary necessities; and the theme of independence must itself be carefully watched so it does not hinder the pragmatic search for foreign aid.

Under these conditions, the populist subterfuge turns out to be unquestionably less effective, and yet more indispensable than ever. The resulting neopopulism seems to play upon its own contradictions to derive its basic benefits. Latin American political life suggests that populism resides essentially in its electoral sites, as if to allow the candidate a credit that he will later have to spend. Argentina's Carlos Menem and Peru's Alberto Fujimori clearly centered their campaign around populist themes, where the defense of the disinherited and references to identity rivaled the celebration of Peronist symbolism, for Menem, and recourse to messianic visions, for Fujimori. Once in power, both invested powerfully in the purest economic liberalism: in March 1991, Domingo Cavallo launched a plan for the "dollarization of Argentinean economy" and organized a vast privatization movement, while on August 8, 1990, the Peruvian president had already administered a "Fuji shock" inspired by the same principles. In both cases, the populist equation was dangerously saved by Fujimori's vociferous denunciation of the corruption of which he accused his predecessor, Alan Garcia, and three thousand of his collaborators, while Carlos Menem decided to declare "war on corruption" when several in his own camp were implicated in corrupt practices. The maneuver became unclear: populist support is there only if the neopatrimonial system is in effect; in other words, the formula is usable only if it denounces certain consequences of the order that it is supposed to legitimize. In the short term, it serves the prince not only at the expense of his entourage but also by undoing a part of the power relations that support him.[25]

Henceforth populism became a blend of equivocation and the last hopes of mobilization. From a simple but coherent discourse, it transformed into a rhetoric oscillating between the banal discourse of ornamentation and a genuine refusal to deal with the situation. More generally, it tried to reconcile unpopular or liberalizing economic measures with the manipulation of unanimist and plebeian symbols having no real effects on the production of public policy: after the political populism of Bourguiba, of Boumédienne, or Chadli during the first years of his presidency, a verbal populism evolved in Tunisia and in Algeria that led to policies of structural adjustment, the privatization of commerce and credit, and increases in the prices of essential goods. Similarly, solidarities formed in the most diverse places, such as formal explanations of economic failures that would directly diminish the state's credibility. Hence in June of 1990, in a very depressed socioeconomic climate, Corazon Aquino launched her own political movement, Kabisig, literally "arms locked together," against protest mobilization by using themes of mutual help among classes.[26] Elsewhere as well, an explicit economic reorientation in Burkina Faso at the end of 1985 moved toward a liberalization of investments and a decline in social welfare: a revolutionary discourse colored by class struggle was followed by a moralizing rhetoric that obscured social oppositions, developing themes redolent of messianism.[27] This ornamental populism is not negligible, however: it constitutes the last chance of legitimacy for governments that cannot count on a communality of meanings able to bind the populace to them, nor on the performance of a state with continually diminishing functional capacities, nor on the mobilizing effects of programs shackled by the rigors of dependence as well as by the decline of the great Western-imported ideologies. The glorification of the Arab, Indian, or African peoples remains, in effect, the ultimate vector of mobilization when the "third-world" variations of socialism or nationalism lose their attraction and when the only viable debate taking shape on the rubble opposes identity-based renewal to an imported ideology of modernity. The populist ornament becomes simultaneously a screen to mask this delegitimizing rupture and an exclusive source of symbolic production organizing the word and image of the leader, his paternalism, his national authenticity, and his status as tribune of the underprivileged. Thus, in January 1984, Habib Bourguiba heard and understood the food riots that drowned out the voice of Prime Minister Mzali.

Wherever it exists, this ornamental populism remains contained, because it can affect neither the rigor of public policies nor the orientation of foreign policies: as Guy Hermet notes, this new realism makes even the populist leader into an "illusion breaker."[28] This function is formidable, since it brutally deprives the political practice it inspires of the basic benefits it formerly enjoyed. The transgressor blinds the prince to the facts: by freeing his tribunate from all constraints, the prince abandons the project of reconciling it with austerity policies. Reference to the people and the underprivileged, the glorification of national values, and the call for equality integrate his basic populist practices into an international system. The leader hinges his mobilizing strategy on a militant denunciation of a worldwide hegemony that makes him an exile among nations, as happened with Gadhafi and Saddam Hussein. The rise of extremism is all the more intense because this pure and difficult populist recomposition is no longer, as it was during the time of [the] Bandung [conference] and nonalignment, part of a bipolar and competitive international order where diplomatic populism was both a legitimate refusal to choose and an associative strategy that considered itself the bearer of counterpropositions.

Invention's Share

Identity mobilization, particularist drift, deficits in citizenship, proliferation of empty social spaces, just like the populist response, do not produce disorder only. They illustrate how importing practices "corrupt" the logics they increasingly contradict. Where the imported product declares itself universal, it increases particularism; where it claims to build a monopolistic political order, it provokes the dispersion of social spaces; where it wants to be rational-legal, it encourages a neopatrimonial management of the state. Disorder makes sense only in relation to the target model and desired syntheses. But does it allow the growth of innovative sites, of places where the state's failure is sufficiently patent to provoke the birth or the rebirth of a new political order that would launch another adventure? Two of these sites can be retained as possibilities, precisely in the interstices of a failing state: local society and extrapolitical social networks.

Local society has always been favored by revivalists. For Hinduist movements, decentralization and a return to the village unit are key elements in their proposals. The justification for the *panchayati-raj*, a system of government that assigns leadership of the village to a council of five elders, links the RSS program to an old tradition already followed by Mahatma Gandhi as a counterbalance to the westernization of the Indian political order. This valorization is found everywhere that the Western state model is denounced.[29] Significantly, in the nineteenth century, populist thought constituted a central argument for protest against the new Balkan states created after the breakup of the Ottoman empire: the Greek Ion Dragoumis criticized the new bureaucratic state, calling for a political-administrative system founded on the local community; Serbian Slavophiles opposed the "natural" Slavic institutions to Western influences;

Bulgarian populist writers stigmatized bureaucratic corruption, imputing to it the decline of village life; the Rumanian poet Mikhail Eminescu saw the true nation in peasant society, while his compatriot Constantin Stere distinguished Western industrial society from Romania, which, he thought, should keep a purely agrarian and decentralized basis in order to protect its own personality.[30]

This type of localism, which is both protest oriented and romantic, is expressed in Gadhafi's criticism of urban society and his call for Bedouin communitarianism as much as it is in the movements that, in Latin America, mobilize against the state in the name of messianism or revolution. Behind the diversity of these occurrences, the defense of local society barely conceals its program's lack of focus. First of all, its visionary quality clearly prevails over its capacities for invention, particularly in that its protests within the urban fabric noticeably weaken the reference to village society, preferring instead a communitarian return to local life. Through their mobilization efforts and their daily activities, Hinduist and Islamist movements, as well as messianic sects, celebrate microcommunitarian solidarity and mutual help among neighborhoods as much as the benefits of autonomy.

As events unfold, then, a localism praising a return to the land shifts toward a much more political expression valorizing the principle of local autonomy for the social actors. Those who protest against the imported state are less and less apt to risk attacking industrial society or even modernity itself. Rather, what comes under fire are the state's claims to centrality and the monopoly on legitimate physical violence. The argument is strategically very coherent, based as it is on a triple challenge: contrary to the Western state, the imported state is essentially constructed from the top, outside of any dealings with the periphery; its failure is largely due to the difficulty of penetrating local society and surmounting the communitarian resistance with which it reacts; and protest mobilization is all the more effective when it meets individuals' expectations for microcommunitarian integration. These elements make the localist reference the foundation of an especially effective political strategy.

The value of this reference is, however, not exclusively instrumental, for it can bring about innovation. The imported state has conquered the peripheral spaces in form only. The colonial administration itself not only had to respect these autonomies but knew most of the time how to build on them or, at least, to work with them. Premodern political systems had in no way eliminated them, as the Western state has done vigorously since the Renaissance. The Ottoman empire recognized for the *ayan* and even its own governors an autonomy that European bailiffs, seneschals, and stewards had never enjoyed. The same freedom can be found in the Persian empire, both under the Safavids (1502-1736) and the Qadjars (1794-1803), in *raj* India, and even in imperial China, where mandarins and nobles shared the daily management of local society. In the Arab world, traditional political systems were constructed on a complex combination of a more or less institutionalized central power and a collection of autonomies recognized in tribes and brotherhoods.[31] The coexistence of a segmentary tribal order and the sultanate was not rare, as the Kurds had until the end of the nineteenth century in their harmonious combination of scrupulous respect for segmented autonomies and the unchallenged legitimacy of royal power.

None of these various potentialities were ever truly eliminated. When the Ottoman empire abolished the power of the Kurdish emirs in order to complete its conversion into a modern state, the *sheykhs* who were leaders of the religious brotherhoods easily found their place and thus assured the continued existence of the structures of local autonomy beyond their institutional dismantling.[32] Similarly, the failure of statist integration in sub-Saharan Africa resulted in an ongoing reevaluation of the role of village notables in order to make them indispensable agents for public policies and even titularies of a true autonomous political power. Also, the very many political conflicts, whether internal or external, some of which have been extremely violent, reveal the disastrous effects of political projects that build themselves on the negation of local autonomies. This is what has occurred for most of the civil wars in Africa. Behind the one that is destroying Somalia can be seen the irreducible personality of the northern and southern clans, each one incarnated in a different political party and playing its own programmatic card in order to better preserve its own autonomy. Thus the Hawiye, who constitute the base of the CSU, established themselves after the overturning of Siad Barre (himself a Merehan) by publicly and officially defending the idea of a national conference, in spite of opposition by the Majertein and the Ogodenis, grouped respectively in the FOSS and the MPS.[33]

These examples reveal evidence of a bifurcation between the European state and the imported state: the first is made up of weakening resources in the local society, whereas the second finds its real substance *outside* the local society. Western society has clearly distinguished between countries like England, where the local society was only very little undone and the state remained weak, from those where the crisis of seignorial peripheral power was sufficiently active to allow a real redeployment of the political order. In the latter case, the state was continually strengthened by peripheral resistance, which it met in an unequal combat with the production of new institutions that enriched it and created in the local society attitudes of dependence and the demand for tutelage.

This stratagem is not exportable because the equality of powers is not at all the same. Subsequently, pressures from the periphery produce a profound redistribution of skills and possibilities for innovation. The difficulty is twofold. As integrated parts of the protest process, pressures from the periphery lend themselves all too well to the tribunal processes that distance them from the logic of innovation. Used by brotherhoods in Turkey and Senegal, by messianic movements in the Andes, and the notables in sub-Saharan Africa, these pressures are invariably cast as negative. Though occasionally cast as an apology for the golden age, indeed the myth of the Good Samaritan, localist visions still draw much too deeply on tradition to be spontaneous bearers of innovation. Yet local society basically everywhere capitalizes on two important resources. The failure of the state and development policies from above leaves it to local social groups to deal with numerous initiatives, such as the reactivation of agrarian or health policies, and the definition of relations with the NGO, or the setting up of cooperatives or savings networks. Moreover, faced with the imported state's institutional rigidity, local society profits from its own suppleness in order to define new modes of individual political participation. The fervent search for a democracy that would be local first and national second, that would be based on a real allegiance of the people rather than a forced or artificial identity of citizenship, is a theme embraced by intellectuals in Africa, the Middle East, and Latin America. Similarly, the solution to identity-based tensions that most often find no territorial expression seems deeply confused with the reordering of local autonomies. This, in any case, is the proposition most often advanced by Kurdish intellectuals and leaders who hope to reconcile the need for identity affirmation and the difficulties presented by the construction of an independent and sovereign Kurdish state.

The rise of associative networks can also be considered a vector of innovation.[34] The imported state's weakness leads inevitably to the composition or activation of social solidarities that escape political tutelage. The phenomenon comes about first in the very interstices of the state, in places it can neither reach nor fully control: mosque networks in Iran, the *ulema* in Indonesia, brotherhoods in Morocco, Senegal, the Sudan, and Turkey; churches and Christian movements in Kenya, Burundi, and the Philippines; monasteries and Buddhist associative networks in Burma and Vietnam. Nor do religious entities monopolize this interstitial capital: the autonomy enjoyed by the rural sector in numerous developing societies confers on farming associations a strong ability to organize social interactions in the agrarian milieu. Such is the case, for example, in Kenya and even more so in Zimbabwe, where such associations have successfully defied agrarian policies defined by the state and have established their own, autonomous bases for a direct cooperation between blacks and whites.

At this level, the very logic of authoritarianism and neopatrimonialism tends to reverse itself. The social actors are effectively confronted with a choice that can not only break the vicious circle but seems eminently able to destabilize the reigning state. In such a logic, the acquisition of power and goods involves a strategy of collaboration with the political-administrative order: to distinguish oneself from the state and create a civil society constitutes a costly yet ineffective objective, since the state controls the principal access to wealth. In this perspective, the chances for an economically autonomous bourgeoisie to develop are slim, but the reproduction of a state bourgeoisie seems to correspond to the rationally thought-out interests of each individual that composes it. However, such a calculation is not universal and seems increasingly doubtful. First, as we have seen, it has never included the "interstitial actors," whose interest lies, like that of religious or rural organizations, in applying a strategy of differentiation that will allow them to subsequently capitalize on growing benefits. Furthermore, this strategy will grow less and less interesting to the social actors who can construct their own autonomy from the accumulation of resources they derive from their functions as tribunes, their affiliation with transnational networks, or, most often, both of these. Thus it is, for example, with journalist and jurist associations in several English-speaking countries in sub-Saharan Africa, including the efforts in Nigeria of the Lawyers Association to oppose the trying of cases involving political corruption before military courts.[35] Thus it is also with the role played by the Writers Association in the fight against the shah's regime in the years preceding the Islamic revolution, and also with student associations in Egypt and Morocco, but also with unions as, for example, that of the miners in Zambia. Finally, the poor results experienced by the imported state led it to increasingly disengage itself from the public sector and to fragment, thus freeing up more new zones of sociability. Beyond economic effects, the process has sociopolitical consequences in places as different as the Maghreb and the Indian subcontinent, where it led to a veritable dismantling of the bureaucracy. Such consequences have made it useless to go through a state phase and to obtain the complicity of its agents: the neopatrimonial strategy that fuses social actors with the political space is challenged to such an extent that it avoids behavior that could lead to the constitution of civil societies. Privatization, private enterprise, the establishment of stock markets, as in Casablanca, and the proliferation of savings banks move clearly in this direction.

Yet the convergence of all these facts does not lead clearly to the constitution of a civil society. Horizontal networks of solidarity remain selective in terms of the limited number of social actors, whereas others benefit from the continuation of microcommunitary solidarities. Moreover, the rise of an identity-based mobilization, which, as we have seen, increases alienation from the imported state, constitutes an obvious and probably lasting hindrance to the establishment of a structured civil society. The success of the associative peasant movement in Zimbabwe is doubly limited by constituting itself essentially in the privileged framework of the village, where it combines with microcommunitary solidarities, and by remaining obedient on the national level to influence from the ethnic cleavage between the Shona and the Ndebele. Similarly, the associative network linking certain liberal professions in Nigeria enters into play with ethnic solidarity and religious identity movements that can lead, as with the Maitatsine movement, to messianic type mobilizations. In addition, this combination does not lead to the disappearance of empty social spaces, but to their fulfillment by movements that only secondarily aspire to integrate into a civil society in which they would be only one entity among others. Neither revivalist religious organizations, nor messianic sects, nor identity movements are disposed to a banalization that would mean the loss of their own specificity. Here we see the cultural alienation that is the primary hindrance to the constitution of a civil society, making improbable the construction of a market economy on the remains of the neopatrimonial order. This economic upset could have opened another path leading to a structured and differentiated civil society: the incessant progress of the informal economy in Africa, Asia, and Latin America; rural enclaves; and the repeated failure to individualize social relations—all reveal the improbability of reproducing and universalizing a differentiation similar to that which grounded the Western model of the market economy.

If innovation does not pass through a stage of autonomous civil society, it can come about through a combination of the different mobilizing actions enumerated above. The local site and the associative site can also be vehicles of invention in that they constitute two places where the individual experiences both a minimal political control and a maximal constraint on innovation: villages and networks are, in effect, of very little concern to the state, but they must act urgently to meet daily needs. In this sense, the distance and the inability of the political center are functional in that they hasten the move toward autonomy. At worst, the simple fact of enduring is already an invention, since it presupposes a very complex adaptation and especially a calculated transgression of the universalist rules produced by a center that cannot be totally ignored.

The difficulty lies, in fact, in the effort to confederate all these microinventions into a coherent model of political invention, to pass from daily innovation to the production of a mobilizing utopia at the level of the entire society. The process is even more complex in that the progress of localism tends to "ghettoize" innovations. The social actors who realize these innovations on a daily level have no strategic interest in generalizing them. The production of a utopia is thus abandoned to organizations that make the denunciation of alienation the principal mark of their political action. The utopia is thus moved toward a place—national or transnational—that lends itself even less to invention. It is, moreover, taken over by a collective actor whose strategic imperatives distance him triply from the work of sociopolitical innovation. Since he mobilizes through reference to identity, he constructs his discourse on praise of a tradition that defies history and social change. Since he is interclassist and unanimist, he needs first not to be countered by a too precise and too engaging programmatic production. Since he denounces the noxious effects of an imported Western order, he seeks to optimize his gains by mixing a normative and mobilizing discourse with the language of the tribune. As Abdelkader Zghal correctly stated about Tunisia, the success of Islam among the young depends on its ability to address the problem of social injustices as well as that of cultural identity.[36] Such an effort can be found in all identity movements, and separates them from conventional partisan logic such as it appears in the most current typologies in political science.

The resulting discourse is all the more difficult to attach to a problematic of innovation because it federates by a moralizing rhetoric that reflects all the virtues it seeks: it is normative, it denounces and denigrates the imported order, it valorizes identity, it is unanimist and sufficiently imprecise regarding concrete matters to be acceptable to all. In fact, it allows the unification of all social demands addressed to a suspect state that will be rejected regardless of its answers. Society is rethought through the minimally compromising filter of a rigorous moral code abandoned by its corrupted actors. But we learn nothing of what the state should be.

In fact, one can postulate that the question of modernity shares these organizations rather than reuniting them. Though Islamism wants to be more revivalist than fundamentalist, and hypothesizes a modernity that could reconcile with revelation and tradition, the debate over what meaning should be given to this reconciliation remains. Whereas in the last century the controversy over the created or uncreated nature of the Koran opposed those who believed in the adaptability of God's word to history to those who refused to even consider that possibility, the contemporary period divides Islamists according to how they view the idea of a modern society and the projects that accompany it. Thus Algeria's FIS integrates, around Benahdj, the salafists* who prioritize tradition and the Djeza'ara school of thought that, centered around the petrochemical engineer Hachani, militates for a genuine Algerian revolution that would bring about another modern, national, and more just social order. The same opposition in Iran distinguishes Khomeini from Taleqani, as if all identity-based protest, far from bringing an ideal model of the state, would erect the state into an unresolvable debate.

Internal political interactions blur rather than promote the logics of innovation. The increasing power given to international considerations and their growing interest by the social actors can henceforth be understood as a search, at times conscious, at times unconscious, of ways to unblock the system.

---

*Translator's Note: The salafists were adherents of the salafiya, an Arab-Muslim reformist movement that, at the end of the nineteenth century, advocated a return to the original doctrine and the reconciliation of science and faith. This movement is associated with a cultural renaissance in the Arab World.

6. International Disorders

Social actors invest increasingly more in the international order because of several factors: globalization of the economy, advances in long-distance communication techniques, increased mobility of individuals, and the crises of the nation-state. In response to numerous pressures from importation's negative effects, the actors in non-Western societies deploy their own strategy on the international scene, as if impossible internal innovation activated a compensatory external movement. This is to say that the results of such choices are potentially more symbolic than real: the resulting multiple factors have just as many remarkable destructuring effects as those occurring internally; it is not unthinkable, however, that axes of innovation can derive from them.

The International Order's Loss of Meaning

In this perspective, international disorder is twofold: in the beginning, it relates to the destabilizing effects of importation logic; then later, it is aggravated by the consequences of internal protest on the international scene. The first of these phenomena is particularly extensive: the protesting actor irrupts onto a scene that is already affected by a loss of meaning, that is destabilized and challenged by the crisis affecting the universality of political models. By reinforcing relations of uncertainty, this destabilization increases the effectiveness of all protest practice: it helps us understand the passage from the internal to the external and the crystallization within international relations of sociopolitical tensions deriving from dependence and from the diffusion of the Western model of government.

By leading to the crisis of citizenship allegiance, the failure of the imported state supports the rise of more or less formal transnational inflows that bypass state institutions and deliberately ignore their claim to monopolize diplomatic and military functions. Identity mobilization lies in the center of this process: uncertain in their allegiance to a state to which they feel foreign, individuals invest in networks of transnational solidarity, where Algerian citizenship competes with membership in the Islamic world, where Liberian citizenship rivals identification with the Mandingo people, where Ecuadorian citizenship is defied by an increasingly active insertion into networks of messianic sects. The usual exposure to inflows in transnational communication, radio and especially television, to economic inflows governing production and consumption, and to eventual demographic inflows tends to confuse the uniformity and exclusivity of the citizenship allegiance.

In this context, identities are increasingly supple and mobile. While microcommunitarian identifications are reactivated, the individual finds himself simultaneously part of an often clashing plurality of spaces that relativize the gap between national and international. At the same time the logic of multiple affiliations weakens citizenship affiliation and, in particular, lets the individual decide which affiliation to privilege and thus the identity he will value in any given time or situation. In the context of the Gulf War, the unemployed inhabitant of Cairo or the student in Casablanca could, in fact, chose to define himself as a citizen of his own nation-state or as a member of the Muslim community, whose solidarity Saddam Hussein invoked. The reality of this choice is all the more vivid and dramatic in that the individual participates directly in the construction of international relations and that these relations are increasingly dependent on the makeup of an extremely large number of microdecisions. As a result, the relations of uncertainty increase drastically, and the states' diplomatic decisions are all the more risky because, in contrast to what is theoretically presupposed, many partners are involved in the decisions. Unable to anticipate what all the individual microdecisions will be, the states have no choice but to ignore them or to underestimate their eventual effects. This, among other events, explains the constant determination of the Western powers to control the various conflicts that fragment the Muslim world politically and diplomatically and to discount all the forms of mobilization and transferals of allegiances these conflicts produce among the people.

As James Rosenau has stated,[1] this fluidity of allegiances counters the diplomatic weapon with the increasingly strong resource the individual derives from his quasi-sovereign decision to cooperate or not. Here we are very far from the paradigms on which the classic theory of international relations is based. Clearly, this renewal does not come solely from the indirect effects of dependence and the forced universalization of the Western model; it is particularly strongly stimulated by the increase in transnational inflows that reveal other logics, such as the choices made by economic actors who, in deciding whether or not to cooperate in effecting an embargo, support or reject a diplomatic decision taken by the so-called sovereign states. The same process and the same effects have occurred in numerous other transnational relations that carefully circumvent states and at the same time attack their sovereignty: the drain or transfer of capital, variation in manpower, the brain drain, informal economic progress, and the diffusion of images and sounds, of cultural and artistic media. In each of these cases, the strategy decided upon by the private actors is crucial, for they leave the state little influence while conferring upon the individual the role of international actor.

Yet between this upset and the forced universalization of the Western model, deep bonds exist that, from several points of view, unify them. The processes of westernization hasten this change because they weaken the abilities of the peripheral states, because they accelerate, as we have seen, the relativization of citizenship allegiances, and also because they have the unusual effect of reactivating transnational cultural actors. The political visibility of Islam, of Hinduism, of the Catholic Church in Africa, of the Orthodox Church in Eastern Europe and the Lutheran Church in Central Europe, and their actualization as transnational forces have much to do with the call of empty social spaces linked to the bankruptcy of imported states. More deeply, the decrease in importation strategies and their apparent profitability in the search for power and material advantages encourage the elite in non-Western societies to intensify transnational inflows, to integrate into these inflows, or even to provoke new ones. The Meiji period in Japan, the rise of nationalism in India's Congress, the first reform movements that affected the Ottoman empire, Egypt, and Persia, instigated the first transnational inflows toward these regions and inaugurated numerous individual strategies to diversify them: official missions and especially private travel; study abroad; membership in clubs or transnational vocational groups, whether the Freemasons or the old Oxford networks; conversion to Western religions, as in Africa, or though more limited, the Christian missionary groups in China, Persia, and India; the creation of colleges modeled on those in Europe; the opening of hospitals or various technical centers modeled after Western cooperatives; and the establishment of branches and representatives of foreign businesses controlling a considerable portion of the interior market. Finally, to the extent that these practices hamper internal innovations, they have helped considerably to amplify and generalize the logic of inflows: initially sector-based, these practices increasingly encompass the whole of sociopolitical activity, with the importers supporting ideological and institutional models and thus stimulating the inflow of ideas and thought, but also of norms and juridical techniques.[2]

Since it is present in the early stages of transnational flows, the universalization of the political model is also stimulated by strengthening communication media. The ability to receive television programs from France 2 in Tunis, to be exposed to Radio Free Europe broadcasts from the popular democracies during the cold war, the ease with which video cassettes circulate, cheaply and ubiquitously, constitute some of the many other examples of effective vectors for massive diffusion of cultural models. The rupture is even striking in a more recent time, when importation affected only a small elite who made it the mark of their distinction and who cultivated, relative to the masses, the exclusivity of its contact with the West: even in the 1930s this role could be played by few travelers, polyglots, and those who frequented the Curiel bookstore or a small number of salons in Cairo, the French Club in Teheran, or the learned societies in India.

This change in scale quite obviously amplified the importation of Western models by giving them access to the masses and by no longer orienting them exclusively toward the reform of institutions and places of power, but more and more toward the transformation of individual behavior. Yet such ruptures gave rise to new disorder and extra tension more than they genuinely harmonized social relations within the importing country. Two contradictions appear, in fact, in the wake of this fully expanding international communication: the clear weakening of the non-Western states' mastery over changes in the media, and the formation of a potential international public prey to anomie and thus to unpredictable behavior.

The principle of state sovereignty already appeared too fragile when imported political theories applied it to peripheral political systems whose cultures did not always conform to intellectual constructions of Western constitutional law and whose real functioning, in particular, revealed the marks of dependence and clientelism. The same principle collapses completely when we establish that the capacity of media production in non-Western countries can no longer rival, on their own territory, those arriving from abroad.³ Three press agencies–AFP, Reuters, and AP–have a quasi-monopoly on the circulation of information; the United States alone controls most of the distribution of cassettes and films; cable and satellite usage promotes the almost infinite extension of media diffusion. Remarkably, it is by recourse to a strict usage of the constitutional principle of sovereignty and a rigorous reading of international public law formulated by Western jurists and practitioners that African and Asian states have protested these practices, thereby revealing the contradiction. As of September 1973, the Conference of Non-Aligned States held in Algiers demanded the collective appropriation of communication satellites and, three years later in Delhi, called for the creation of a pool of press agencies able to balance the flow of information put forth by the Western agencies; in October 1976, at the request of UNESCO and under pressure from African and Asian countries, Sean MacBride wrote a report in which he recommended the formulation of national communication policies in each of the developing countries, the respect for cultural identity, and a wide diffusion of scientific and technical information, notably toward the least advantaged sectors of the population. The following year in Nairobi, a vigorous debate in the context of UNESCO saw the United States pitted against those who, following the Tunisian Masmudi, claimed a new era in information: the argument of freedom advanced by the former was echoed by that of sovereignty in the very definition of what a people can know . . . and not know.⁴ The evolution is, in fact, significant: it shows just how extensively the governing elite in an importing state can reconcile its client status with its function as leaders. As it happens, the communication debate also reveals a contradiction and an impotency: the contradiction in a logic of state clientelism that cannot go so far that it compromises the government's chance for minimal control of socialization–and thus political education–of the people; the impotency of peripheral states that cannot abolish the inflow of tutelary communication, widely concerning, moreover, rather far-flung private actors, who in any case lack both the attributes of international partnership and any reason to subject themselves to the discipline of the desired new order.

The international public constituted in such a manner is far from reflecting media diffusion. The effectiveness of the Western cultural model at influencing the masses without rival and abolishing national borders or cultural boundaries is far from being an undisputed fact. The related hypothesis of a unified international public opinion regarding the large common categories is equally unfounded. The functionalist hope has been disappointed: There is no unified cultural code corresponding to a global international system; quite the contrary, for the complex experience of transnational inflows of communication confirms that the importation of Western political models has more to do with a conscious strategy of actors and that it in no way corresponds to the image of a growing wave that would submerge the entire world equally.

Studies on Iran have shown that receptivity to media messages was essentially selective, that they penetrated to the interior of the society rather than unified the society under the banner of a communication mass structured in the West. The sensitivity to musical programs from Los Angeles or London essentially affected the elite who had already become, socially and professionally, importers of Western models of modernity. Even more, in Iran as in Nigeria, the penetration of external inflows reactivated primarily the traditional channels of communication used by other social categories. In the case of Iran, the process was very beneficial to the mosques, to the *hayat* who gathered a small number of faithful in private places, especially during Ramadan or Muharram (the monthlong celebration of the martyr Hussein), but also the bazaar and its mazes: so many places where information and the cultural message were all the more legitimate precisely because they opposed those media made suspect by their cultural inaccessibility. In the case of Nigeria, the establishment after 1960 of radio and television based on the BBC, managed and developed by BBC-educated nationals, resulted in a failure intensified by the coexistence of 178 languages in the national territory. Henceforth, it reached only a small westernized elite, who as a result, were even further cut off from a populace that had no other choice than to confirm its communitarian growth and to sustain its traditional channels of communication by returning the role of *gongman* to a new generation of youth.[5]

The media imperialism thesis is too simple and thus inadmissible, as is that of the "universal village" postulated by the constitution of a world culture. Rather than the formerly accepted image of an object such as a ball launched in one direction, the more convincing and currently accepted image of the boomerang describes the failure of a media inflow that turns against those who transmit it and that encounters the obstacle of identity and the will of the receiver.[6] The resulting recomposition is as familiar as it is deceptive: it mixes, as occurs in the daily life of African or Asian towns, the debris of exogenous cultural flow–jeans or Coca-Cola–with a system of meaning that continues to provision itself from without; it distinguishes socially and culturally two worlds within each of the non-Western societies, two positionings defined precisely by reference to the usage of these inflows. This opposition, often too fragmented to be politically sustainable, clearly gives rise to populist strategies of reappropriation: in India as in Latin America, traditional culture is associated with the media and encouraged politically in such a way as to inflame the allegiance of the receiving public and to prevent the traditional culture from serving the ends of protest activity. Thus cultural neonationalism is henceforth more political than social and, in turn, distinguishes between the political elite and the socioeconomic elite who see no advantage for themselves in it.[7]

All this reveals that the resulting international construction is particularly complex and unpredictable. The actors move into the international scene, where obstacles abound and cultural inequalities create the conditions for a growing disorder. On one hand, the inflow of information remains produced, organized, controlled, and diffused essentially from the Western world, unilaterally, placing the non-Western actors in a situation of dependence, rupture, and, even worse, weak communication with their own citizens. On the other hand, cultural inflow, failing to constitute an international public, paradoxically fuels the reconstruction of particularisms and feeds identity movements. More seriously, instead of a unified or at least a homogeneous public, different publics nourished on particularism are formed that everything conspires to bring onto the international scene: the growing visibility of international factors responsible for their frustrations; alignments more or less marked and more or less accepted by their own governments along the lines of Western-fabricated institutional and normative models; and the increasingly obvious and established impossibility of initiating solutions and responses to social, economic, and political stakes that emerge on the interior political scene. Moreover, this international mobilization is all the more aleatory because it is not governed–nor is it governable–by any institutional authority; further, it gives rise to uncertain cultural schemas, formed of references to identity and of various elements taken from the repertoire of Western modernity. In that, it simultaneously limits the sovereignty of states that have less and less hold over the international conduct of their populations and represents a new factor of uncertainty for the international order.

This logic of disorder is all the more fearsome because it deprives the state of everything that could validate it as a reliable international actor and a fortiori everything that would make it an international actor hierarchically superior to all other actors. Three foundations of the state's diplomatic action are thus imperiled: its claim to sovereignty, its function as guarantor of security, and its demand for the exclusivity of international partnership.

State sovereignty is breached at several levels: clientelism, economic dependence, cultural dependence, and the deficiency of citizenship already seriously affect the non-Western states; the rise of transnational currents hamstrings all states indiscriminately, keeping them from any chance of power. More seriously, by provoking a clear divorce between state and society, the processes of forced westernization free up internationally social spaces, identity groups, and collective actors and populations on which no political sovereignty can be truly exercised. The observation concerns, though unclearly, the acquisition of an international personality by all the elements that detach themselves from a state order suffering directly from this divorce: Lebanese clans; tribes in Yemen, Somalia, Ethiopia, and Liberia; Muslim religious minorities; Sikhs in India; Berber linguistic minorities in the Maghreb; Kurds in the Middle East; the overlapping of peoples in Eastern Europe, but also the Islamist community in Egypt and Algeria, brotherhoods in Turkey, the diaspora of the Chinese in Southeast Asia or the Lebanese in Africa, informal economic networks of merchant elites, social movements of the unemployed, youth or rural migrants in Arabic population centers, and so on. All these reflect social processes that are neither intrinsically modern nor essentially traditional, and which are to be distinguished from phenomena of transnationalization linked to the increasing intensity of global exchanges: in reality, they are born by the very failure of their integration into the heart of a state-controlled institutionalized order. The international scene is thus dotted with spaces of power that sometimes overlap on the same territory, sometimes extend beyond that territory. In its bankruptcy and failures, the diffusion of the model of the state frees up a great many scraps of sovereignty that escape the state, weaken its capacity, and decrease the effectiveness of its attempts to respond diplomatically. Similarly, the increasing shrinkage of state sovereignty reduces the area reachable by the policies of cooperation the patron-state attempts. Intergovernmental clientelism thus loses a good part of its efficacy and especially of its effect on the societies concerned, to remain only an instrument that reproduces links between the governors of the North and the governed of the South.

Similarly, this logic of disorder separates the state even more from its security function. This function played an active role in state order, since it also legitimized its existence and organized its action both internally and internationally, and very effectively, since no institution rivaled it in this function. The secondary effects of forced universalization on the Western model do not alone explain the threats to this logic; they do, however, play a significant role, as do all the other processes that contribute to the dismantling of the state. On one hand, the reactivation of microcommunitarian solidarities leads individuals to seek within their community the security that they should have sought from the state. On the other hand, and particularly so, spaces of sovereignty that the state can no longer claim for itself seek more vigorously to control autonomously their own violence. The takeover by revivalist movements of Hindu or pan-Islamic communitarianism amounts to a transferal of the instruments of legitimate violence: processions by the BJP in the streets of Baghalpur and Hyderabad publicize their claim to protect the Hindu community from the intentions ascribed to the Indian Muslim community as much as to the Muslim world in its entirety; as vectors of a dissemination of violence, they promote community integration, but they also discourage the rival community and persuade it to abandon the positions it occupies. It is significant that Hyderabad community uprisings cause Muslims to flee; their properties are then bought cheaply by the promoters of the Hindu community; it is also revealing that, in this type of mobilization in India, Africa, and the Muslim world, but also in the community uprisings in large Western cities, militants and sympathizers find themselves involved with an underworld for whom violent collective action is a way to express its marginality and its role as social deviant.[8]

What is true internally is doubly so internationally. First, communitarian violence grows in intensity as it crystallizes around international objectives, whether it concerns the denunciation of pan-Islamism in India, or the "privilege" accorded to Western targets in the uprisings afflicting African, Maghrebian, or Middle Eastern cities. In particular, the inability of many groups to realize their ends in conformity with the model of the nation-state tends to transfer their action onto the international scene and to thus further disseminate violence. The inability to deal with Kurdish, Armenian, Palestinian, or Lebanese issues through solutions offered by the state structure has hastened the conversion of organizations that attempt to deal with them into international actors opting deliberately for a strategy that seeks its effectiveness in an increase of violence within the world community. Hence solidarity grows between the denunciation of a Turkish, Iraqi, Israeli, or Christian Lebanese order and an international system presented as collectively responsible. In a more prudent and less radical manner, the increasingly numerous liberation movements seek acceptance of their own use of violence through international recognition. Henceforth, a decisive part of international interactions consists of changing intergovernmental relations into relations among actors who possess a violence sufficiently credible to achieve legitimacy: Max Weber's thought regarding the state is here inverted and, with it, the entire conception of security that founded the diplomatic-strategic international order.

Last, this entire process cannot fail to rebound onto the Western state itself. Can this process work indefinitely if the international order evolves to modify its diplomatic actions so much as to make its interlocutors into actors unaffiliated with the state? The state order postulates universality and monopoly: the system created by the Peace of Westphalia inaugurated an order in which the states were stronger and more institutionalized to the degree that they dealt only with other states: this reciprocity is not respected when a Western state must negotiate with nonstate organizations for the release of hostages, for the non-use of terrorism, or respect for its territory, all of which occur frequently in negotiations that imply an infringement upon the actions proper to the legal state. More generally, in churches and other religious organizations, in cultural actors, and all identity-based countermobilization movements, state diplomacy encounters so many partners that it could dominate only at the risk of losing its own legitimacy.

This disorder is finally completed by the breakdown of the international discourse from non-Western societies, within which several different logics conflict in a more or less organized manner. The discourse of the institutional elite, in principle the only one able to result in diplomatic action, meets competition from the many actors who control the extreme diversity of mobilizations and expressions of identity: religious, ethnic, economic, and demographic networks possess a foreign policy and an active presence on the international scene that does not necessarily acquiesce to the state. As for the state, from it derives a diplomatic voice that speaks on at least three, often contradictory, registers whose coexistence eliminates a good part of its meaning and its normative coherence. First, the non-Western state can, through its diplomacy, haughtily espouse the practices and norms of international relations as they were fashioned by the European system. The states of the Muslim world have given many proofs of their realist conception of international relations, frequently invoking the jurisprudence of international law more quickly than the Islamic counterpart; some of them have refused to sign the Geneva convention on the law of the high seas, basing their position not only on the argument of cultural uniqueness, but on that of state sovereignty, which is not respected sufficiently in the final document.[9] Similarly, African states frequently call upon the principle of state succession to zealously defend the inviolability of their borders, as much from external claims–as with Chad in its relations with Libya, Somalia with Kenya or Ethiopia–as from secession movements, such as Nigeria and the Biafra issue or the former Belgian Congo with the former Katanga. There is a remarkable flood of solicitations with international institutions by African and Asian governments, as occurred with the Saharan question, or that of Kashmir, or the Iran-Iraq conflict over the Chatt-al-Arab. The Islamic Republic knew how to utilize its most astute experts in international law to actively negotiate a settlement in its dispute with the French government, relying when necessary on numerous precedents clearly drawn from a Western-wrought juridical repertoire.

At the same time, however, these very states wisely build a diplomatic discourse and practice that nourish their own particularism, fabricated for the occasion into a legitimate source of law. It is precisely the illegitimacy of a border drawn by Western colonization that authorizes the Iraqi state to challenge the existence of Kuwait; it is the same arbitrariness denounced by the Moroccan state to emphasize the artificiality of Western Sahara, as it was formerly to reject the existence of Mauritania in the name of the traditional institution of the sultanate and thus a fundamentally nonstatist political order. It is also a two-thousand-year-old tradition that creates uncertainty around the border between China and Vietnam, for China traditionally declared its neighbors to the south as border peoples and refused to recognize the dividing line as a "border between two equal states." Constructed and institutionalized by France, this border thus became an essentially colonial production, a Western formalization of an old institution that was much more complex, allowing ambiguities and fragilities to exist, thereby maintaining a duality of discourse where juridical formalism and particularist cultural references alternated with each other in order to justify diplomatic and military challenges. The same happened with relations between Vietnam and Cambodia, where a similar formalization produced comparable effects: the extraordinarily complex relations between the Khmer and Champa kingdoms reflected an impossible cartography and a conception of alterity difficult to grasp in an interstate culture; the administrative boundary markings required by the colonialist power ignored the extreme subtlety of the notion of limits, thus encouraging, particularly in Vietnam, a double practice that drew from both the repertoire of the succession of states and that of protest in the name of historically ambiguous borders.[10]

Finally, the critique of the international order incites the states who engage in it to draw from a third normative repertoire, that of the world of the excluded and disinherited. The discourse of exclusion replaces that of particularism without, however, becoming confused with it: the international order is not rejected because it falsely claims universality, nor because it destroys histories not inscribed in the Western trajectory; rather, it is denounced as the producer of domination and thus exclusion. The word of the state victimized by this discourse is, for this reason, necessarily derogatory with respect to the norm: to international order is opposed justice; to formal equality between states is opposed the inequality between the haves and the have-nots. In a critical conception of justice similar to that elaborated by John Rawls, the state tends to valorize a particular law destined to balance its lateness, and that, as such, negates the classic enunciation of an international order presupposing strict equality among sovereign states.[11]

The state of exclusion is itself complex and multifaceted. It is based on a superposition between nonmembership in the Western order and the exclusion from international resources of power, whether that power has to do with economic, social, or political resources. Inequality can be evaluated in terms of debt, the GNP, poverty statistics, the development of sanitary or educational infrastructures, and the capacity to control and influence innovation. In this respect exclusion relates not only or even necessarily to poverty but also to the transfer of technology, the eventual inability to fully and autonomously use products of modernization, and to organize the passage from previous conditions to the conditions of modernity: the example of the Gulf states reveals a situation of exclusion made from the forced importation of engineers and technicians, from dependence on others for food-stuffs, banking activities, and weapons. The control of innovation also concerns the capacity to control the production of institutions and ideologies: dominating technological innovation, often more successfully than others, Japan only partially controls the mechanisms to construct its own political modernity. Finally, the phenomenon designates the capacity to dominate international political choices, and to influence the evolution of stakes and conflicts that implicate each of the states: the exclusion from international decision making affects unequally an entire hierarchy of states whose role goes from that of almost total effacement before an international interaction that completely transcends them to an alignment of diplomatic positions that quite obviously are imposed on them, such as what Europe and Japan experienced during the Gulf War.

On this account, very few states totally escape exclusion. The *discourse* it inspires has, however, a considerably more restrained influence and affects only those states for whom exclusion creates not only a real and conscious frustration but also leads to such deprivations that they find themselves very obviously relegated to the periphery of the international system, stuck in a dominated position.

The same situation prevails both internationally and internally: the actors denounce a situation only when they accumulate the negative effects with no hope of even minimal benefits. Thus partial exclusion–from which, however, a state like Japan suffers greatly–does not produce a discourse that deviates from the international norm: at most, one observes the attractive effect of this type of discourse in certain categories that remain in the minority and that enrich Komeito. At the same time, when this exclusion becomes systematic, when it sensitizes large sectors of the population, but also a large portion of the frustrated elite, and combines with an atmosphere of cultural alienation, it frequently inspires a discourse of global protest against the international order and will potentially find multiple echoes and active support within society. Reconstructing the stakes of internal politics in terms of international politics and conceiving internal failures in terms of external responsibilities become attractive for certain political organizers. At this level, the forced westernization of the international order favors powerfully the credibility of the discourse of denunciation and hastens the emplacement of a new diplomatic enunciation, which becomes that of the disinherited.

In such a context, uncertainty is twofold. On one hand, the international actors must wait to see the evolution of their non-Western partners among three, often contradictory roles that they choose according to these conjunctions: the alignment in terms of the classic interstate structure, the militant reference to their own system of meaning and their own history, and the demand for rights linked to their role of disinherited. On the other hand, the non-Western actors must continuously seek to reconcile each of these formulas and to withstand competition from those who, in their own country, militate for a more tribunal international strategy. In this increasingly anarchic distribution of roles among actors, the international order loses a good part of its meaning, whereas its efforts to achieve uniformity aimed at the opposite goal.

Strategies of Disorder

One can, henceforth, postulate that certain actors try to take advantage of this disorder to realize benefits that the interstate structure cannot offer them. Non-Western diplomacy has for a long time oscillated between the strategy of clientelism and that of nonalignment, which were both functional for the international system: the first reinforced a relation of state to state by reconciling it with relations of domination; the second furthered the political and diplomatic action among the Southern states according to practices that drew liberally from the repertoire of public international law and that were largely inspired by a vision of the state, politics, the national, and nationalism clearly borrowed from the West. In addition, this third order—or this "third world"—fit almost perfectly in the system of peaceful coexistence, knowing how to play more or less adroitly off the rivalries between superpowers for their own advantage. Until recently, the code of international relations thus remained unified.

Currently, international disorder incites certain actors to step out of this codification. The coincidence between cultural alienation and exclusion makes it very rational to use the emblem of a "dominated culture" as a weapon against the "dominant states." In the clientelist relation, as in the workings of nonalignment, references to non-Western cultures stayed discreet; often even logic led one to censor them in order to privilege a secular construction of politics. In a context where disorder leads to a mobilizing reactivation of cultural emblems, confrontation can take an entirely different configuration. The Gulf War shows how, at any moment, a populist leader can risk defying the world of states, its laws, codes, values, and actors by inscribing his diplomatic action in another register, one entirely exterior to the classic relations among states. Saddam Hussein believed he could win by opposing a protest-based international order to the official international order, resources linked to cultural solidarities to the mobilization of state-based resources, and the order of the disinherited to the order of domination.

Such a diplomacy is certainly not totally new: decolonization and nonalignment, and certain more recent conflicts such as Vietnam, had already begun a functional and mobilizing usage of imperialism and its denunciation. Yet this prelude had not truly shaken the old order: the Suez or Vietnam crises followed the explicit and implicit rules of peaceful coexistence. The subsequent rupture revealed several new elements: the word and action of the dominated were henceforth inscribed in their own repertoire and not that of the international community; they aimed at confederating the disinherited rather than building a new order; in particular, the gain sought could no longer be measured in terms of power or the accumulation of state resources, but in the capacity to mobilize and destabilize. In other words, we see spreading in the international space what could already be detected within non-Western societies: rather than seek power directly, countermobilization movements sought first to establish a protest-based political order that they could prove was more legitimate than the official political order.

The transposition worked out with this strategic schema can seem remunerative for any prince confronted by a series of failures that become well known: the inability to mobilize the governed around a culturally exogenous state; the difficulty of circumventing the revivalist countermobilizations that went into action within the society; the impossibility of defying the international powers on their own territories; and the precariousness of the advantages received from interstate clientelism or from the practice of nonalignment. All these blockages, both internal and external, led those involved to compensate for growing political incapacity by vociferous protest on the international scene: the dominated actor substitutes a tribune strategy for a power strategy, thereby seeking an entirely different usage of conflict. He who goes this route no longer tries, as the classical theory of international relations would predict, to increase his own power or to reduce that of another, but to obtain dividends from his role as tribune. The conflict is no longer a dead end, because his losses on the interstate scene can theoretically be compensated for by advantages acquired by the mobilizing capacity of the people.[12]

Of course, the precedent set by the Gulf War casts doubt on the whole idea: Iraq's war costs clearly outweigh the gain made in mobilization of the people, which were less strong than Iraq's president had hoped, but still much more significant than Western diplomats admitted. Nevertheless, this conflict reflected a big step, since, for the first time, the protest war occurred in its entirety: an actor took the risk of engaging in a conflict where military and diplomatic defeat were certain, with a goal, not to win, but to effect a protest. This objective was largely met, since the promotion of Iraq's cause rallied all the protest movements in the region: diverse Palestinian organizations, Maghrebian social movements, Pakistanis or Bangladeshis, and especially Algerian, Tunisian, Jordanian, and Sudanese Islamist movements all chose alignment with Baghdad over Saudi aid. Similarly, the sensational conversion of the Iraqi Ba'ath to a militant Islamic identity shows the rapidity with which cultural alienation can supply identity-based emblems to protest wars; it also reveals the extreme mobility of calls for international engagement and the facility with which the solicitation of the citizen's engagement can be replaced by other engagements that clearly diverge from the state.[13]

From this perspective, the break is profound: from an international order constructed on the mode of universality, we slide clearly toward an exploded order that mixes different and contradictory repertoires. In addition, the actors play on this plurality to acquire new advantages, whereas earlier the Asian and African states acceded to international relations only by means of the Western repertoire of diplomatic action, by conforming to ideological models found there as well and, in order to be heard, by exaggerating their claims to a stronger state and a greater sovereignty. This cultural explosion of the international system increased in turn the external function of all mobilizations that, within each society, made reference to an identity discourse. The communitarian uprisings in India, proselytism by Protestant groups in South America, the progress of African Muslim brotherhoods, just as the Islamist mobilizations in Maghreb, in Machrek, or on the Indian subcontinent increasingly integrate an international enunciation of their action and thus a management of their international relations. Continuity and rupture appear here quite clearly: religious and sectarian mobilization develop in Latin America wherever guerrillas loyal to Castro are no longer successful; the transnational relevance of Islamist movements and engagements from which they benefit now occupy the place left empty by Nasserian nationalist diplomacy; and the active production of a militant vision of the foreigner–Muslim or Western–is substituted–in India–for the mobilizing effects of Congress's "third-world" diplomacy. All these new elements, taking over in their own fashion the old frustrations or exclusions, can do nothing more than, in time, consecrate a new international life: either because these new mobilizations have already, as we have seen, a direct international effect, or because they constrain the heads of state, and thus limit and shape their own diplomacy, or finally, because they cause some of them to change modes and divest themselves of their diplomatic instruments in exchange for resources linked to this new type of action.

The constraint of diplomacy appeared clearly during the Gulf War, in Pakistan, Morocco, and Tunisia. The first two had sent a contingent to the anti-Iraq coalition, while subsequent popular opinion favored the opposite position, which caused Pakistan to be more discreet in its war efforts and the Moroccan government to support the January 1992 demonstrators. As for Tunisia, pressure from Islamist movements caused it to refrain from taking a position or even attending the Arab League meeting that was to issue a condemnation of Iraq. The substitution effect allows us to interpret a large portion of Iraqi diplomacy, but it already clearly appeared in Iran's confrontation with the United States in the first years of the Islamic Republic. The complexity of Iranian diplomacy has to do with the fact that Iran knew, much more than Libya, how to combine the tribune function with a realistic approach to state action; it also knew how to federate the disinherited by playing off rivalries between the USSR and the United States, and by profiting as well from the possibilities offered by state-to-state bilateral cooperation. The reconstitution of Iran as both a regional power and a transnational force of protest fits right into the two present dimensions of the international order, and in a way that it hopes will maximize its own gains.

By this very action, the function of a tribune for the "disinherited"–to use a term originally from the Koran–projects within the international scene the elements of its own characteristic rationalism, and thus becomes an essential component of international interaction. Basing itself on protest and not power, on horizontal solidarities and not national interest, this function comes as much from the instruments as from the ends of classical international action. For this reason, it aims neither at negotiation as an intermediate objective, nor at international integration as a final objective. Negotiating is only one mode of expression, only one way to give voice to the causes one shepherds. To link Kuwait's liberation with that of Palestine is not the same as negotiation, but simply a mode of international communication that becomes, in turn, the only final objective sought realistically: the tribune function that unfolds on the international scene does not entail an order of substitution any more than the tribune function within a society entails a political program or even a real intention to accede to power. The accompanying rhetoric finds here its principal limit: drawing its force from the exemption to define the contours of a new order, it must be satisfied with the at least partial reproduction of the interstate order it fights. As with all tribunes, the international tribune maximizes its gains when it retains its protest role.

The rationality founding classical international interaction tends to explode: the cost-gain relation no longer means the same thing to the actors; certain very costly action becomes foolish in the context of international relations but appears coherent and rational in the tribune context. In this situation, the partner's behavior is less predictable, and the very principle of dissuasion can get confused. Incomprehension between Western diplomacies and certain diplomacies of the Muslim world depend not only on the ambiguity of cultural mediations but also on the extreme difficulty of reconciling the two, which, by definition, are irreconcilable.

Clearly, protest strategy is unequally distributed throughout the non-Western world. The fact that it exists principally in the Muslim world confirms that it reflects first and foremost the exclusion and denunciation of the failed universalization of international relations. From this point of view, Islam's ability to organize in force transnationally and to criticize the Western model's claim to universality must be seen as a serious explanatory variable.[14] But it would be culturally naive to make it a primary variable and especially to distinguish a priori between cultures that entail tribunal undertakings and those that do not or cannot. The diffusion of tribune strategies can certainly occur outside Islam, can occupy other cultural spaces, and, especially, structure other types of conflict. Thus in this context particularly, what tends to be used is a populist diplomacy, where international engagement in the tribune mode extends very obviously the orientation of internal policies followed by the prince, which occurred, for example, with General Noriega in Panama: here the construction of an actively anti-American foreign policy corresponded neither to an ideological alignment, nor to the search for new patronage, nor even to a renewed conception of neutrality, but rather to international protest devoid of any representation of what the "new world order" should be. It is precisely for this reason that such a strategy has little chance of producing change, but it does stand to gain from prolonging the current international disorder.

The Process of International Innovation

In this context, the possibilities of invention can appear reduced: the interest in change appears as slight as the latitude left to the actors to transform the rules of international interaction. Just as in the internal order, deviation also has creative virtues. Though the reactivation of dominated cultures has little in common with other resources, it can upset the state model and promote a new process of world regionalization; it can also, in the long term, bring about new modes of articulation between internal order and external order. The two hypotheses can be verified empirically to demonstrate that this change is not merely theoretical, but has in fact begun.

The Regionalization of the World

The regionalization of the world comes from the diverse realizations that, combined, transcend the political map of states and accept another division of the international order, one that takes into account to a certain extent the givens of cultural particularism. Four formulas emerge here: the formation of vast cultural groupings that crystallize around transnational cultural inflows, that contest, and even combat states; the elaboration of unions of states according to procedures aiming at the integration and then the transcendence of state logic; the constitution of regional poles around powerful states, combining in an ambiguous manner their identities as states and the will to dissolve those identities into vaster entities; and efforts to resolve the problems linked to infra-state particularisms by constructing regions distinct from states and claiming autonomy.

There are several contradictory ways to carry out the first of these formulas. The reactivation of cultural inflows within the periphery of the international system creates "imperial spaces" corresponding largely to protest ends; the reconstitution of a Muslim or a Hindu world appears initially as a way to enunciate a critical discourse: protest against domination by the Western model; protest against the national unit as an integrated space uniting different cultural or ethnic communities; protest against the state as a way to organize political society and even as a source of secularization; and finally protest against the governors in place, their authoritarian practices and their sociopolitical failures. Both these worlds, and potentially others (for example, that of Indian-ness in Latin America, of African-ness on the dark continent, or of pan-Turkism in Asia or Europe), create sustained interaction between the protest practices unable to merge with the workings of the state and imperial cultural appeals presented as possible substitutes for defiance. Revivalist and neotraditional intellectual movements alike emerge as vectors of this new production of a space that consecrates a large part of its discourse to distinguishing itself from the Western-style state: the *dar al-islam* is that of the believers; the Hindu world of the BJP is not that of the Indian nation-state, but refers to a mythical space that excludes other communities, but which does include the Himalayan states and Sri Lanka. This cultural regionalization constructed "from the bottom up" produces timid echoes in institutional initiatives, which give it a positive orientation even though, there too, their beginning can be seen as a protest response to a challenge: the Islamic Conference was organized in 1969 to protest the burning of Jerusalem's El-Aqsa mosque.

This type of institution unites states jealous of their prerogatives and has no mission to institute a new mode of regionalization, or even to structure a space that grassroots protest initiatives have helped significantly to design. The Conference's charter stipulates the "respect for the sovereignty, independence, and territorial integrity of each member state."[15] On the other hand, medium-range institutional initiatives can have a much more significant structuring effect, as suggested by the rise of the IGO and especially the NGO uniting Muslim intellectuals, academics, technicians, and merchants, and thus constituting the beginning of regional communalization. "Community of pain" and "community of usefulness" produce the first connections of cultural groups and guarantee their international existence: the recent success of the Turkish community party in Bulgaria, the anti-Turk repression in Greece, the organization of the Muslim community in Bosnia, the development of relations between Turkey and post-Stalinist Albania, and the exit of Turkish-speaking peoples from the defunct Soviet Union are numerous events that escape state diplomacy and that create, de facto, an internationally relevant regional space before even the Turkish state can take a clear position on the question.

The *union of states* can appear as another variable in the process of regionalization and supplanting of the state model. Contrary to the cultural whole, the union of states is first of all the product of a diplomatic rationality and a choice from above; it is, however, marked by two novel characteristics that it shares with the preceding model: the hypothesis that this union can give rise to a new mode of political communalization; and the conviction that it will lead to a challenge of the state context and the rules of the game comprising it. In the very center of the Western world, the European construct has already begun to shake statist-national structures by replacing citizen allegiances with the interactions of multiple allegiances that, paradoxically, revitalize particularisms: the reduction of trans-state pan-European networks promotes, in fact, a resurgence of identification both European and subregional. Lyons, Milan, Frankfurt, or Barcelona–all wish to redefine themselves as European metropolises, while the development of regional leagues in Italy, the revitalization of regions in France, and the *Länder* in Germany crystallize new particularisms. Initiatives and the move to federate on the part of the states menace their own survival, and at the same time become a source of innovation for the international order.

The phenomenon stands out much more starkly, and thus with greater uncertainty, in the South. There the union of states validates a regional group whose cultural identity is more confirmed, whereas at the same time the leaders are more prudent, more jealous of their sovereign prerogatives, and much more intent on preserving the attributes of statehood, of which they have made themselves the importers and that guarantee their own survival. The progressive and sensitive construction of the Union of Arabic Maghreb (UAM) clearly reveals this tension. Established in February 1989 by the Treaty of Marrakech, this new authority first marked the end of an era of conflict among its five member states: Algeria, Libya, Morocco, Mauritania, and Tunisia. Fundamentally, it is a coalition in strict obedience to state rationalities and possesses all the means to protect itself against any attempt from the statist-national level to dismantle it. The end of the 1980s saw the advent of a situation in which several common requirements led each of the states to opt for coalition: the convergence of crises and constraints linked to debt, economic difficulties, and the negative effects of a similar type of social mobilization; the recourse to the same "improvement" revenues, at the time when Algeria turned toward the IMF and the World Bank, and when it accepted privatization and proceeded to denationalize; the appearance of common stakes whose processing implied a policy of cooperation, particularly regarding the development of territory, irrigation, and food distribution. Moreover, these crises were apparent enough and presented sufficiently threatening political implications to convince each of the leaders of the need to help one another, including with internal repression, and to not risk, through rivalry, creating places of refuge in the neighboring states for its own opponents. In short, the union of states made sense as a way to stifle the constitution of a Maghrebian community of pain and protest. Finally, to this was added the need to counter the constitution in the North of a European Community: the importation of the state model was followed precisely by that of the confederal model.

The result of these choices is, however, ambiguous. Institutionally, the projects that risked damaging state sovereignty were rejected; thus Libya's project of total fusion failed, as well as Tunisia's model, which militated for a structure resembling the institutions of the European community. Nor did fiscal harmony, monetary union, or a customs union figure among the selected objectives. The only ones put in place were bilateral and multilateral accords, which were quite numerous and always timely, concerning education, commercial exchanges, and cooperation for energy and mines, such as, for example, the gas pipeline linking the Algerian oasis Essafsaf to the Libyan city of Zwara, and passing by Gafsa and Zarzis, or the one linking Hassi r'mel to Tangiers. Yet the basic idea is not there: the very project of a UAM, following three decades of testy nationalism and, especially, in the almost complete absence of cooperation, helps reorient individual behavior in a profound way, particularly that of the leaders. The free circulation in the Maghreb zone of technicians, intellectuals, and civil servants of the five states concerned significantly renews the very conditions of their socialization and, in the long run, the nature of their interests. In any case, such circulation noticeably strains their bond with the state model and helps them think of their identity and their project in a regional context, where history, culture, and the community of needs faced with other regional groups can provoke other interests and conceptions of political action. In short, the very hypothesis of a state bourgeoisie defined as the surest vector of importation of the Western state model tends to grow weak and thus open the way to greater possibilities for innovation.[16]

It appears clear that beyond Europe and the Maghreb, this type of regionalization tends to spread and to find an additional boost, notably since the crumbling of the iron curtain and the attenuation of the ideological division in the world: examples of this include the reactivation of ASEAN in Southeast Asia; the strengthening of regional accords in Latin America, particularly the reactivation of the Andean Pact and the creation of Mercosur uniting the Southern countries; the decrease in the number of inter-African cooperative entities; and proliferation of links between the Chinese coast and its immediate neighbors through special economic zones (SEZ), which the People's Republic had to allow. In each of these cases, one can see the beginning of the same movement toward recomposition of political geography, the same relaxing of state uniformity, the same search for a new conception of international relations in which the rise of a still very relative multipolarity connects with the affirmation of cultural spaces relating to a particular history.

New regional poles can thus form around power states with more or less confirmed hegemonic tendencies and create other types of innovation, but also other types of paradoxes. The current Japanese practice of *kokusaika*, that is, of internationalization, contributes to a Japanese sphere of influence that spreads well beyond its own political borders and that combines elements of state rationality and a cluster of extrapolitical inflows in a rather complex manner, borrowing significantly from codes that govern classical international order. There is a strong tension between the prudence of the Japanese state, which has long ceased trying to acquire international diplomatic clout, and the wide variety of practices from civil society that produce a regional space dominated by Japanese economy and culture. Officially, the Japanese state still follows the doctrine of *Datsua Nyuo* (i.e., let's leave Asia, and turn to Europe), developed during the Meiji period; strategically, the Japanese state remains profoundly marked by the cost of the imperialist adventure that preceded and accompanied World War II. As a response to such institutional diplomacy, the inverse doctrine of "return to Asia" brought considerable progress, heightened by Japan's crisis in cultural identity and also supported by appeals from peripheral states. The rigor of the state cadre is thus softened by the dynamism of Japanese universities, which recruit 70 percent of their scholarship students from the best students in Southeast Asia, and educate the executives of subsidiaries and branches of Japanese firms in Indonesia, Malaysia, and Thailand. The same occurred after the Meiji period, when Chinese, Korean, and Malaysian students attended Japanese universities in order to enter the elite in their home countries. A "cultural sphere of ideograms" formed, and Japanese financing brought new strengths to this regional solidarity: at the end of the 1960s Japan placed 27 percent of its investments worldwide in Southeast Asia, that is, almost 10 billion dollars.[17] Japan was the largest foreign investor in Indonesia, Thailand (where it controls 55 percent of the investments as opposed to 7 percent by the United States), Malaysia, Singapore, and the Philippines. The role of the large Japanese companies is determinantal, though it does not imply a real transfer of technology: resulting financial inflows lead to a de facto control of Southeast Asian economies, without risk of the latter endangering the regional hegemony of the Japanese investors. Divisions appear here that quite clearly refine and design this new space: electronics in Malaysia, agribusiness in Thailand, heavy industry in Indonesia, and services in Singapore.

This type of evolution entails many contradictions. First, it clearly opposes two political geometries: that of a Japanese nation-state rigorously based on universal rules and interactions, scrupulously assuming its role of imitator and political client of the United States; and that of a somewhat imprecise sphere of Japanese influence, indeed, hegemony, with an uncertain and altered institutionalization constituted of resources taken from civil society and crystallizing into an economic and cultural order. In the long run, this first tension nourished claims for political emancipation from Japan and thus for an end to dependence, as is already suggested by the debates surrounding the third renewal of the Japan-American treaty in June 1990. Significantly, this review–which also implied a review of the constitution and thus of the internal political order—aroused great interest among the young generations within the economic ministry.[18]

At the same time, however, this new cultural space is not formed from a rupture with the Western model. Though Japan exercises increasing control over the education of Southeast Asian elites, Japanese elites continue to study at American universities; though the dynamic in civil society disrupts clientelist bonds with the United States and further shakes a political system quite obviously in a state of crisis and only weakly legitimated internally, protest movements offer no other model to replace the current political order. Henceforth, the possibilities for innovation are more connected to the evolution of the external dynamic than the internal one and are more a function of regionalization than a real capacity to detach from Western tutelage. In other words, the change is regulated, not by the crisis of the international system occurring within its own center, but by the effects of innovation that the regional orders create at the periphery of the international system. Similarly, the accumulation of material resources does not seem to be, either today or yesterday, the motor driving these transformations, in contrast to the developmentalist view: Japanese economic power has not in itself created antidotes to westernization and political dependence but has actually amplified these trends. Rupture seems to come from the construction of spaces damaging to the international order, specifically in the chain of consequences of a regionalization that reactivates cultural logics and solidarities totally autonomous from the codes organizing the international order. The disappearance of the Soviet reference, which formerly gave meaning to regional regroupings that was directly compatible with the dominant model of international relations, merely reinforces such a process.

Corresponding to a union of states or a hegemony of one state, the proliferation of regional poles tends to have a restructuring effect, though tempered and limited by mediation from the state entity. Everything seems to indicate that the capacity for control exercised by this entity constitutes the key aspect of innovation processes: European integration, the UAM, the new Far Eastern space, and even the "Muslim world" are bearers of invention in their ability to effect networks of transnational solidarities, of new identification modes, and especially of new forms of insertion into the international system that escape traditional diplomatic logic.

Regionalization of the world also refers to the formation of sub-state or trans-state groups destined to resolve problems linked to the existence of national minorities and the difficulties of their coexistence with the principles of the state model. The founding distinction between public space and private space and the postulate that the individual is first and foremost a citizen supposes that the state knows only the individual divested of any intermediary identity. For this reason, national minorities have always been dispossessed of an international personality and no one has ever recognized their right to accede to the international order or the institutions that structure it.

However, interstate interactions very quickly brought perverse effects. Minorities have quite often become de facto international actors, notably because they were used by states as instruments of rivalry. The evolution of the Kurdish question is particularly significant. As a particularism coming to consciousness of itself, it crashed headlong into state logic: it can realize itself only by upsetting and challenging the state model in its region. Its formation and especially its growth are to a great degree the result of political and diplomatic maneuvers initiated by the states in the region. Thus Soviet diplomacy upheld the formation of a Kurdish identity and encouraged the 1946 proclamation of the Kurdish Republic of Mahabad, principally with the view to weaken the region's states and establish its own sphere of influence. In the same way, but later, the Iranian state materially supported the Iraqi Kurdish movement of Mustafa Al-Barzani in order to get the upper hand in its strictly interstate border dispute with Iraq during the Shatt-al-Arab affair. At the same time, the shah decided to abandon his policy of Kurdish support, which had suddenly become cumbersome, for the reconciliation of the two partners in Algiers in 1975. In turn, the Syrian state, though menaced by the reawakened Kurdish movement, helped the Turkish Kurds several times in order to pressure Ankara; it also helped the Iraqi Kurds in order to settle its dispute with the Ba'ath power in Baghdad. In turn, the Iraqi state supported the Iranian Kurds in their rebellion against the Islamic Republic, while the Turkish state, in conflicts with its own minority, discreetly opened in 1978 its border to the Kurdish *peshmergas*, even while it developed the means for military intervention and "police operations"[19] in Iraqi Kurdistan.

The Kurdish example merits particular attention because it so clearly reveals the contradiction: threatened in their very identity, the states involved are led by their own logic to actively participate in a mobilization that leads to their negation. Though more attenuated, the same phenomenon accompanies the development of most of the identity movements concerning several states: Tamils in India and Sri Lanka, Druzes in Syria and

Lebanon, Azeris in Iran and the former Soviet Union, Baluchis in Pakistan and Iran, and even the Basques in France and Spain. With each of these groups, an identity-based regional space emerges, beyond that of the state, in which all are energized by their own interactions.

National minorities isolated within a state do not give rise to the same contradictions, and no longer, by definition, provoke this strange suicide of the states in question. Nevertheless, these minorities do tend to insert themselves into diplomatic activities and to transform international interaction into a production of identity legitimation: Muslim minorities in the Philippines, India, the former Soviet Union, and Ethiopia supported by diplomacy and even military aid from the Muslim states needing to reactivate their religious legitimacy; Turkish minorities in Cyprus and East Europe who become stakes in the political debate in Ankara and thus sources of intensification; Tibetans supported by India as a diplomatic counterbalance to China; Lebanese Christians encouraged by Baghdad during the Taef accords in order to weaken the Syrian Ba'ath position. Thus states do not function like a closed club protecting its precious monopoly that, theoretically, should allow them alone to control the international scene. Their action at this level leads them irresistibly to participate in the construction of regional cultural spaces that, over time, tend to negate them.

This dynamic reflects not only political-diplomatic interactions but also works within states as an extension of the internal functions of political systems, and notably of rivalries that intensify during the quest for power. The Kurdish example is, again, significant in the evolution of the Turkish state: more westernized than its neighbors, and thus more intransigent in its Jacobin and integrationist visions, Kemalist Turkey has had to slowly evolve toward de facto recognition of a Kurdish personality: the Kurdish language is accepted as an aspect of a subnational culture; at the same time, contacts in the highest level of the state with Kurdish leaders are no longer secret; the massive acceptance of Kurdish refugees following the Gulf War and the role officially conceded to the United Nations at this time signaled the beginning of a recognized internationalization of the Kurdistan question. Significantly, a large part of the initiative was assumed by the Social Democratic Populist Party, which is, from the partisan point of view, the direct descendant of Kemalist orthodoxy: from its ranks come the eight Kurdish deputies who participated in the 1989 conference in Paris on the Kurdish question, which, of course, later on caused their expulsion from their party; but it was also with the goal of recapturing votes that the Kemalist party decided officially to open its ranks to Kurdish candidates for the October 1991 legislative elections, and thus to receive almost all seats for southeast Anatolia, but also to prefigure a Kurdish representation in the parliament in Ankara. At the same time, in Iraq an active repression alternates with quasi-official negotiations between the state and Kurdish representatives. These dealings clearly respond to political moves on the part of the prince with a view to maximizing his chances of remaining in power: that is to say that internal politics, in all its forms, leads, at least in certain conjunctures, to manifestations of recognition of minorities, perhaps precarious recognition, but sufficient to shape a space that can no longer be effaced.[20]

The state, in both its internal and external functions, contributes to the emergence of regional cultural spaces instead of containing them and discouraging their formation. Whatever the rigor of the Jacobin model explicitly present in every imported model of the state, particularisms are in the end confirmed by the interactive processes that are both inherent to state logic and a source of its extinction. Moreover, the crisis of citizenship allegiance and the subsequent reinforcement of communitarian identifications support from below a dynamic that, surprisingly, is also activated from the top. Though particularist slippages are initiated by the states only in certain national or international conjunctures, but subject to reversals and even repression at other moments, everything concurs to render the effects of these explosive processes indelible and irreversible. Everything happens as if the state order instigated an entropic logic that could be considered a bearer of innovation: the resulting regional cultural spaces are not only a pure negation of the idea of the state; but as they form, they too tend to define themselves positively in relation to existing political spaces, to the international scene, and to other cultural spaces. Their difficult territorialization thus leads to another forced innovation: taking away the state's monopoly of international action and decentralizing this action toward the individual and the group, these new regional spaces reconstruct internal and external modes of articulation.

Internal and External: End of a Segregation

The most significant innovation, which in the long run promises the happiest result, probably has to do with the reconciliation of the internal and the external. In classical theory, with traditional diplomacy and the declared designation of roles, internal order was that of individuals, citizens, and subjects, while external order was the province of the states alone. The international scene was an exclusive club from which the individual was excluded. In this sense, decolonization marked a rupture of sovereignty, but proclaimed a continuity in both theory and practice: the principle of state succession was firmly retained by the new princes, which shows just how effective the distinction was.

Rupture here comes from the chain of effects resulting from international disorder: the proliferation of allegiances, the activation of transnational solidarities, and deterritorialization place the individual increasingly in the position of arbiter for the multiple identifications and mobilizations soliciting his help. The international scene is henceforth only the guarded space of collective actors, and even less that of states alone: the international scene is peopled with an infinity of individual actors and is sustained by a composite of an almost unlimited number of microdecisions. Of course, states do not abdicate; of course, individuals are "recommunalized" into numerous aggregates that produce a new socialization and new solidarities. But still, when the individual accedes to international responsibility, he profoundly shakes the order of what was until then presented as "foreign." Theoretically, the consequences are already enormous: losing its role of obligatory intermediary between internal and external, the state abandons a large part of its legitimacy and its functions; the very hypothesis of a public space cannot fail to suffer from this transformation, which the international extension of private social spaces relativizes from without, the idea of national interest supported, nevertheless, by the classical theory of international relations.

At the same time, this individualization is associated with a recomposition and a reactivation of cultural spaces that the state frowns upon. The public sphere is this time damaged by the rise of particularisms and by the substitution of cultural identification with the universalist orientation of citizenship. Individual logic and cultural logic can, however, be balanced harmoniously, with the first softening the effects of the second by offering it a minimal mobility. Individuals are not imprisoned by permanent identities, which sociological critique shows do not exist, aside from the slightest of ideological constructions suggested by these identities. For this reason, the "primordialist" vision of cultures and nations affirms a hastily constructed and poorly understood doctrine regarding the awakening of religious revivalism. One must admit, however, that such an induction is incorrect and that it obscures the conjuncture of the logic of cultural alienation and the process of reactive mobilization supporting such movements. If one effaced these last parameters, the cultural referents would certainly not disappear: integrated at last as organizing principles of non-

Western states, they would inevitably be combined with individualist logic and the decrease in solicitations from the growing diversity of transnational inflows.

Numerous studies have, in fact, shown that the individual is not incompatible with any culture:[21] the acceptable and fruitful hypothesis of a "communitarian culture" does not exclude that of an active and cunning individual; it merely distinguishes a way to organize social relations, which is a way for the individual to give meaning to his insertion in urban society, to conceive and practice his sociability, to construct his relation to the group, and to define himself within whatever exchange relations are in effect. One can thus distinguish the main axes of a communitarian culture in which political space relates to the group more than to a fixed governmental center, in which power relates more to a conception of authority included in the workings of the community rather than to an abstract system of delegations, in which economics relates more to a group of practices "recessed" into the social structure than to an individual positioning in the marketplace. All these elements qualify what can–or could–be a communitarian mode of social innovation in the definition of civil obedience, institutions, the normative system, or economic transformations. Though they construct the individual's role differently, they nevertheless do not efface it. Though they tend to negate individualism, they in no way reject the relevance of individual action.

Henceforth, the simultaneity of the individual's ascension on the international scene and the profusion of particularisms entails no major contradiction. On the contrary, it can bring about innovation, as long as the affirmation of cultural identities ceases to have first and foremost a tribune orientation. As long as it is limited to mobilizing against a hegemony that crystallizes all the frustrations, the militant cultural identification has no chance of producing new utopias and being a factor in change, as is suggested by the great poverty of national and international programs undertaken by revivalist movements, no matter where they develop. Though it also becomes the foundation of a rearrangement of political spaces, the reconstruction of identities can profit from the activation of the individual's international responsibility. Faced with the growing fragility of territorial categories, the uncertainties that weaken the imported state, the challenge to the very principle of nationality misinterpreted as universal, the autonomy conceded to the individual offers him the means to construct his own identity, to distinguish between the various references he confronts, and to divide his action among the various allegiances that appeal to him.

This arbitrage perspective concerns not only an uncertain future: it is already at work in more than one region of the world where the accumulation of different levels of allegiance cannot fail to lead the individual to choose, even if this choice is still restrained by the entirety of constraints linked to dependence relations. The formation of new republics in central Asia has happened in the context of crisscrossed pressures that appeal to the individual through the renewal of the state framework whose artifice has discreetly improved after fifty years of common history, the pan-Islamist mobilization, the Persian reference, and the call for pan-Turkism: political history, religion, and languages rival each other for loyalties where, in the end, only individual choice makes any difference.[22] What can be said about the Horn of Africa, between the Arab world and the African world, the Muslim world, and the Christian world? Of Sahelian Africa between identification through the *dar al islam* and identification through a culture and networks that find their roots or ramifications as far away as the shores of the Gulf of Guinea? Of the Hausa, between the bonds of brotherhood, ancient allegiances to the sultanate, and the paths toward the Niger delta? For maps of cultures are never rigid and identities are not innate: because potential identifications are fortunately always multiple, the individual finds, in the end, the means to choose and have an effect in his growing transnationality.[23]

He also acquires a greater possibility of integrating so-called "foreign" events into his political choices and his networks of identification. The Gulf War was an unexpected factor in the rapprochement of the Hindu and Muslim communities in India in their shared hostility to U.S. intervention. The exacerbation of the Azeri and Armenian conflict, particularly apropos of Nagorno-Karabakh and its visibility in the media, recently helped change the conditions of political mobilization in Turkey, to support pan-Turkish and anti-West appeals, and to fuel debates within the political class, thereby upsetting the diplomatic strategies elaborated at the European Community summit. The revision of alliances in the Indian subcontinent was interpreted as obviously socially motivated, once the loosening of bonds between Pakistan and the United States and the rapprochement between the United States and the Indian Union were accepted as a dangerous simplification of the Kashmir conflict, which thus became the exclusive expression of a confrontation between the Islamic world and its adversaries.

These internal and external events share the common characteristic of coming about due to mediation by the social actors. Such processes help structure the political actions of individuals, to complete their socialization, and to orient their identifications. At the same time, they limit or hinder the state's omnipotence in the elaboration of foreign policies and increasingly substitute the acuity of transnational alignments for the socializing role of the state and the discourse on national interest. Henceforth, the growing confusion of the internal and the external clearly weakens the state's logic, freeing many new sources of change.

International disorder is thus creative and not limited to entropic effects only. Even so, it is not only and not necessarily a factor in innovation, which occurs only if four conditions are met: the factors of resistance do not prevail, the elements of change are not principally manipulated for protest ends, the sources of incoherence do not win out, and especially, the logic of dependence does not neutralize the process of transformation.

Certainly, the elites of the state do not lack the means to resist. They possess instruments of force and find resources to confront upheavals in their role as importer; they acquire from their client position assurances of the international community's protection in critical moments. Even in open conflict with the West, Saddam Hussein received serious offers from the West to preserve the status quo from the threats to international order posed by the Kurdish movement. This slant is doubly intensified, by appeals to the exterior and authoritarian practices, and risks further discrediting the imported state.

Protest logic is itself a source of blockage. The vast tribunal recuperation of all contemporary modes of thwarting the state invariably contributes to blocking innovation. First because those who undertake it settle into it and derive their effectiveness from the vagueness of their program. Then, because no mobilization would have the same unanimist virtue or the same intensity if the promotion of cultural identities did not go hand in hand with a timid particularism and a tendency to exclusivity, which paralyze their innovative effects.

The risks of entropy are no less negligible. Before being innovative, disorder creates a situation of anomie that all sociologists agree is a factor in conflict. The crisis of universality has up to the present brought more tension and violence than the invention of new models. This state is even more prominent because anomie causes individuals more often than not to construct their identification negatively, in response to mobilization processes that oppose them to other collectivities: Hindu processions *against* Muslim processions, Islamist demonstrations *against* the United States or the West, Gagauz movements *against* the Moldavians, Armenians *against* Turks and Azeris, etc. In addition, one of the major stakes that challenge the state model has to do precisely with the state's monopoly on the use of legitimate violence: the most immediate effect of international disorder is a very strong spread of this type of violence, of which terrorist movements are the most obvious illustration.

All these changes can be understood in a context of power that cannot be abolished by decree, not even under pressure from individuals or collectivities. Because dependence does not derive from a plot or conspiracy, but from a characteristic of the international system and the way resources are distributed, it would be naive to think that protest against this order could lead invariably to a transcending of it. In reality, the most constraining element of dependence logic is that it is the principal source of the international order and that it thus helps expel into the sphere of protest everything that could threaten that dependence. To rigidify resistance in protest actions is probably the most reliable guarantee of the durability of the international order.

Conclusion

Dependence takes form in culture, in imitation, and in the image. Its startling symbolic ability prevails over the effect of infrastructures, diplomatic burdens, and even military constraints. Both internationally and in microsocieties, the weight of conformity, the pressure of social control, and the supremacy of the dominant model have been able to look effective and durable. Though it did not put an end to coercion, cultural dependence became the most promising principle of world unification: it is without a doubt the clearest foundation of what is called the "international order."

On the other hand, the awakening of peripheral cultures quickly became an instrument to denounce hegemonies, the "weapon of the poor," indeed, the ultimate resource of collectivities relegated to the margins of the international system. As emblems of resistance, factors of mobilization, and means to reconquer identity and sovereignty, cultural revivalisms have accomplished on the international scene the double function of reintegrating individuals in the often very vast transnational whole and of reconstituting particularisms that seem to proliferate infinitely. Princes and protest leaders have quickly understood–in Africa, Asia, and even Eastern Europe–the course of action they should take, but also the threats and uncertainties that could result. Political in their ability and goals, cultures have also become political in the rhythm of their awakening and their confrontations, political in their very essence.

Thus today, dependence and its protest refer to a curious opposition of strategies: to diffuse one's own culture to better dominate the others, and thus make one's particularism into the universal; to import the elements of the dominant culture to give one the means to more surely govern collectivities that are foreign to it; and to make the quest for identity and its hazards the basic element of a protest strategy that is both national and international. This means that by dint of being solicited, indeed manipulated for political ends, to govern or to oppose, identities have paradoxically increasingly become the *instruments* of political action. Thus, far from being outdated or rigid, these identities are in essence mobile and multiple; they evolve and transform according to need and situation, but also as a function of initiatives taken by the political actors who make them a decisive element in their strategy and their rivalry.

Under these conditions, cultural dependence cannot be a simple–or simplistic–vision of an opposition between dominators and dominated. It has first of all to do with the composition of very complex actions that lead numerous individuals and groups to find in the importation of Western models multiple advantages that cannot be reduced to a simple cynical calculation. The process is even more significant and probably more lasting, since many of these actors, in the very repetition of such practices, count on it as their best chance of survival and often see in it their only hope of political effectiveness.

Moreover, while one can locate the dominant culture in the universalist enunciation that the Western model of the state makes of itself, it is obviously invalid to tally up the dominated cultures. Created in a space of political confrontation, mobile and diverse, these cultures reflect in their instability the inanity of essentialist theses so often put forward in history books. It seems particularly clear that behind the facile formula of "dominated cultures" lie first of all the perpetually reconstructed systems of meaning that form at the confluence of expectations supported by alienated and frustrated social actors and efforts undertaken by professionals of protest who hope to find some profit.

Here we find the very heart of two major contradictions. Forced westernization generates both order and entropy: it imposes universal rules without being able to make them work; it enunciates a unification of worlds without unifying meaning. It is, however, dangerous to confuse this entropy with the organized affirmation of countermodels: this shaky order mobilizes cultural references against itself that serve as emblems rather than substitutes. The chances for innovation are thus limited in this curious opposition between a "culture of government" and identity-based mobilizations that exhaust their resources in reactive strategies.

For example, it would be false to state that the opposition between Western culture and Islamic culture conditions the insertion of the Muslim world into the international order. This idea can, of course, refer to failures of meaning affecting Western political models when they are forcefully transposed into this region of the world. But on the other hand, the idea of opposition is illusory: instead of a site of confrontation between two cultures, multiple political enterprises proliferate to mobilize cultural symbols taken from Islam in order to rally discontent under the banner of rejection of the Western model. Entropy offers chances for protest; but it clears only the smallest of paths to innovation.

In these conditions, culturalism can bring the best and the worst, in both theory and practice. By showing the diversity of systems of meaning, by criticizing universalist postulates, and by evaluating the effects of the diffusion of models, culturalism accomplishes great progress for knowledge, particularly on the international scene. By reifying and rigidifying cultures, by forcing their characteristics so much as to back them into ghettos, and by pushing relativism to the absurd, culturalism has replaced its naive universalism with the vision of an international order that is by definition impossible, condemning everyone to chose between domination and disorder, between the uniformity of the Western model and the infinite shattering of cultures.

A cultural analysis "revisited" and emancipated from such simplifications can help us think of intercultural relations in other terms. These can, in effect, have an entirely different meaning when they are no longer dominated by the dialectic of importation and resistance, of negation of difference and exclusion. The international scene as the entirety of the societies that compose it is de facto multicultural, just as the theories of social communication had already intuited in the past. This multiculturality has not abolished cultures: on the contrary, it seeks to downplay difference. The stakes that emerge from this observation have to do with the institutionalization of plurality in terms of global relations and national relations. Such stakes presuppose the reconstruction of many categories familiar to us, and engage a debate on the transformation that history imposes on the concepts of the state, nation, and territory; this is the debate that discusses the future of failed universalization and in which lies all hope of future innovations.

Reference Matter

Notes

Chapter 1

1. Among an abundance of sources, these are notable: Amin, *Impérialisme*; Cardoso and Faletto, *Dependency and Development*; Kay, *Dependent Development*; and Prebisch, *Economic Development of Latin America*.
2. Lenin, *Imperialism*.
3. Luxemburg, *Accumulation of Capital*.
4. Cardoso, *Politique et développement*.
5. Morgenthau, *Politics Among Nations*; Aron, *Paix et guerre*; cf. W. Smith, *European Imperialism*, pp. 78ff.; Wesseling, *Expansion and Reaction*.
6. Tilly, "War-making and State-Making"; Rasler and Thompson, *War and State-making*.
7. Schumpeter, *Impérialisme et classes sociales*.
8. Galtung, "Structural Theory of Imperialism."
9. Callaghy, "State as Lame Leviathan."
10. These recent publications may be consulted: Sandbrook, *Politics*, and Médard, "L'État néo-patrimonial."
11. This is revealed by the surge of literature on ethnicity, particularism, and segmentedness: see, for example, Horowitz, *Ethnic Groups in Conflict*; Vail, *Creation of Tribalism*; Amselle and Mbokolo, *Au coeur de l'ethnie*; and Chrétien and Prunier, *Les ethnies ont une histoire*.
12. See Théobald, *Corruption, Development and Underdevelopment*.
13. Moore, "Clientelist Ideology and Political Change," pp. 271ff.; Miller, "The Dowreh and Iranian Politics."

14. Field, *The Merchants*.
15. Banfield, *Moral Basis*.
16. See in particular Chazan, "Patterns," and Lemarchand, "The State."
17. On-site inquiry, August–September, 1987, *Quarterly Digest*.
18. See, in particular, Lubeck, *African Bourgeoisie*.
19. Frank, *Le développement du sous-développement*.
20. Cardoso, "Associated Dependent Development."
21. Gilpin, *War and Change*.
22. O'Donnell, *Modernization and Bureaucratic Authoritarianism*.
23. Hobsbawm, *Les Primitifs de la révolte*.
24. See, particularly, Wade, *Governing the Market Economy*.
25. Adda and Smouts, *La France face au Sud*.
26. For the classic definition, see Médard, "Le rapport de clientèle," p. 103.
27. On this subject, see S. Smith, "L'Afrique poubelle," p. 117.
28. On the effects of a change in patronage, in the case of Somalia, see Compagnon, "Somalie," and Laitin and Samatar, *Somalia*.
29. Pahlavi, *Réponse à l'Histoire*, pp. 242-47.
30. Beblawi and Luciani, *Rentier State*, p. 11.
31. Najmabadi, "Depolitization of a Rentier State," pp. 213ff.
32. Ibid., pp. 216-18; Mahdavy, "Patterns and Problems"; Al-Kuwairi, *Oil Revenues*.
33. These figures come from the *Rapport Mondial*, pp. 138ff.
34. Beauge and Roussillon, *Le Migrant et son double*.
35. Leveau, "État, société et rente pétrolière," p. 670.
36. Flory et al., *Les Régimes politiques arabes*, p. 497.
37. Good, "Congo Crisis," p. 49.
38. Strange, *States and Markets*.
39. Rosenau, *Turbulence in World Politics*.
40. Bull, *Anarchical Society*.
41. See Katz and Wedell, *Broadcasting in the Third World*.
42. *Le Monde*, April 10, 1991.
43. Piscatori, *Islam in a World of Nation-States*, p. 55.
44. Ibid., p. 50.
45. *Herald Tribune*, December 3, 1990.
46. Constantin, "Les relations internationales," pp. 237ff.
47. *Défis au Sud*, p. 73.
48. Adda and Smouts, *La France face au Sud*, p. 275.
49. Ibid., pp. 275-76.
50. According to the sources cited, ibid., p. 277.

51. *Le Monde*, December 5 and 7, 1990.
52. Camau, *La Tunisie*, p. 85.
53. Ibid., p. 78.
54. Baduel, *Maghreb*, p. 13.

Chapter 2

1. Ehrenberg, *L'État grec*, pp. 42 and 131.
2. Bell, *End of Ideology*; Fukuyama, *La Fin de l'histoire*.
3. Durkheim, *Les Formes élémentaires*, p. 599.
4. Durkheim, *De la division du travail*, p. 274.
5. As Parsons suggests, in *Société*, p. 148.
6. Weber, *The Protestant Ethic and the Spirit of Capitalism*, p. 23.
7. Durkheim, *Les Formes élémentaires*, p. 598.
8. Almond and Verba, *Civic Culture* and *Civic Culture Revisited*. On this entire debate, see Badie, *Culture et politique*.
9. Eckstein, *Division and Cohesion in Democracy*.
10. On this debate, see Badie, *Le Développement politique*.
11. Vatkiotis, *Nasser and His Generation*.
12. See Hardin, "Hobbesian Political Order."
13. Hobbes, *Leviathan*, p. 109.
14. Ibid., p. 112.
15. Ibid.
16. On these questions, see Badie, *Les Deux États*, p. 133.
17. See in particular Gaudemet, *Les Communautés*, and Badie, "Communauté, individualisme et culture," pp. 114ff.
18. Hobbes, *Leviathan*, p. 110.
19. See Baali, *Society, State and Urbanism*.
20. Geertz, *Meaning and Order*; Gellner, *Saints of the Atlas*.
21. Compare Chevrier, "L'État en Chine" and *Modernization in China*.
22. Chevrier, "L'État," pp. 8-11.
23. Fakkar, *Reflets de la sociologie pré-marxiste,* pp. 82ff.; Algar, "Freemasonry in Iran."
24. Gernet, *Le Monde chinois*, p. 517.
25. On Yan Fu, compare Schwartz, *In Search of Wealth and Power*; on Chen Duxiu, see Feigon, *Chen Duxiu*.
26. Allies, *L'Invention du territoire*; Jacobson, *Territorial Rights*; Asiwaju, *Partitioned Africans*; Baduel, *Le monde musulman*.
27. MacFarlane, *Origins of English Individualism*.

28. Elias, *La Dynamique de l'Occident*.
29. Hyden, *No Shortcuts to Progress*; Shaw, *Title to Territory in Africa*.
30. Meyer, "La crise sri-lankaise," pp. 57ff.
31. Meyer, "Cingalais et Tamouls," p. 160.
32. Yapp, *Modern Near East*, pp. 126ff.
33. See Flory, *Annuaire français de droit international*, p. 253.
34. See Claudot-Hewod, "Des États-nations contre un peuple."
35. Bourgeot, "L'identité touareg."
36. Piscatori, *Islam in a World of Nation-States*, p. 84.
37. Ibid., pp. 87–88.
38. See Heesterman, *Inner Conflict of Tradition*, pp. 175–82 and 21–24.
39. Gonda, *L'Hindouisme récent*, pp. 360; Jaffrelot, *Des nationalistes*.
40. Crawford, *Ram Mohan Roy*.
41. Osborne, *Before Kampuchea*, pp. 165–66.
42. See André-Vincent, "Le dialogue Las Casas-Vitoria," p. 42, and Villey, *La Formation de la pensée juridique moderne*.
43. See the opposed viewpoints of Northrop, *The Meeting of East and West*, and Bozeman, *The Future of Law*.
44. Gernet, *Le Monde chinois*, pp. 177ff. and 250ff.
45. Yapp, *Modern Near East*, pp. 44–46.
46. Gernet, *Le Monde chinois*, pp. 416ff.
47. Ibid., pp. 451ff., 477ff., and 502ff.
48. Giddens, *Nation State and Violence*.
49. Migdal, *Strong Societies and Weak States*.
50. Mayall, *Nationalism and International Society*, pp. 121ff.
51. Jackson, "Negative Sovereignty in Sub-Saharan Africa" and "Quasi States, Dual Regimes and Neo-classical Theories."
52. See I. M. Lewis, "Ogaden," and Gascon, "Les mouvements armés."
53. Interview with Maître Lahidji, by Patricia Pic-Sernaglia, October 27, 1990.
54. Evans-Pritchard, *Les Nuer*, and Leach, *Les Systèmes politiques*.

Chapter 3

1. On the modernization of the Ottoman empire, see Polk and Chambers, *Beginnings of Modernization*; B. Lewis, *Emergence of Modern Turkey*; and Baily, *British Policy*.
2. Farman-Farmayan, "Forces of Modernization"; Millspaugh, *Americans in Persia*; Richard, *Entre l'Iran*.
3. See Agnouche, *Histoire politique du Maroc*, pp. 307ff.

4. See Yapp, *Modern Near East*, p. 181.

5. See Cohen, "Thailand, Burma and Laos."

6. Ibid., pp. 200-201; Sarkisyang, *Buddhist Background*, pp. 95-110.

7. See Umegaki, *After the Restoration*, and Akamatsu, *Meiji*.

8. Kawano, "La Révolution française et Meiji Ishin," p. 52.

9. See, in particular, Beasley, *Meiji Restoration*.

10. Giannini, "La costituzione della Transgiordania." On the constitution of 1951, see *N.E.D.*, May 1952.

11. Abu-Hakima, *Modern History of Kuwait*; Gavrielides, "Tribal Democracy."

12. Kochanek, *Congress Party of India*.

13. On the construction of politics in India, see in particular Heesterman, *Inner Conflict of Tradition*.

14. Sen, *Reaping the Green Revolution*; Advani, *Influence of Socialism*.

15. Mandaza, *Zimbabwe*; Moyona, *Political Economy of Land*.

16. Yapp, *Modern Near East*, pp. 202-10.

17. Ibid., pp. 199-200.

18. Ibid., pp. 335ff.

19. See Khayr Ed-Din, *Essai*.

20. Lapidus, "Islam and Modernity," pp. 97ff.

21. Ibid., pp. 96ff.

22. Shamir, "Historical Traditions and Modernity," pp. 121ff.

23. Srinavas, "A Note."

24. Baduel, *Le monde musulman*, pp. 6-7.

25. Interview with Hajj Seyyed Javadi, October 25, 1990.

26. Aktar, *L'Occidentalisation de la Turquie*, pp. 50ff.

27. I refer here to the work of Irene Fenoglio, research fellow at the CEDEJ in Cairo.

28. Raouf, *Nouveau regard*, pp. 134-35.

29. Interview with Abol Hassan Banisadr, November 1990.

30. Banerjea, *Nation in the Making*.

31. On Radhakrishnan, see Samartha, *Introduction to Radhakrishnan*.

32. Sen, *History of Bengali Literature*.

33. Lavelle, *La pensée politique*, pp. 10-13; Najita, *Japan*.

34. Lavelle, *La pensée politique*, p. 14.

35. Interview with Abol Hassan Banisadr.

36. Jaffrelot, *Des nationalistes*.

37. Interviews by Pic-Sernaglia with two mujahideen militants (January and February 1991).

38. Addi, "Religion et politique."

39. See Richard, *L'Islam chiite*, pp. 93ff.
40. Mishra, *RSS*; Jaffrelot, *Des nationalistes*.
41. Goyal, *Rashtriya Swayamsewak Sangh*, pp. 156-57.
42. Ibid., pp. 162ff.
43. Nahnah, interview. See also Al Ahnaf, Botiveau, and Fregoli, *L'Algérie par ses islamistes*.
44. Burgat, *L'Islamisme au Maghreb*, p. 32.
45. Ibid., p. 68.
46. Interview with Abol Hassan Banisadr, November 1990.

Chapter 4

1. Lipset and Rokkan, "Cleavage Structures."
2. On this subject, see Badie, "L'Analyse des partis politiques."
3. Buijtenhuijs, "Des résistances aux indépendances," pp. 48ff.
4. See in particular Roberts, *Creation of Modern Syria*, pp. 18ff.
5. See Rudebeck, *Party and People*.
6. Coulon, "Religions et politique," p. 91.
7. Tordoff, "Political Parties in Zambia."
8. See Leca and Vatin, *L'Algérie politique*, p. 35.
9. Hinnebusch, "Political Parties in the Arab States."
10. Tordoff, "Political Parties in Zambia," p. 177.
11. Thanks to Guy Hermet for this analysis.
12. World Bank, *Rapport*, p. 149.
13. Darbon, "Administration et société," p. 175.
14. Darbon, "Le Paradoxe administratif," p. 98.
15. Martin, *Tanzanie*, pp. 96ff.
16. Le Roy, "Les usages politiques du droit," p. 119.
17. Riggs, "Bureaucrats and Political Development," pp. 148-49. See also La Palombara's introduction to *Bureaucracy and Political Development*.
18. Bugnicourt, "Action administrative et communication."
19. Banfield, *Moral Basis*.
20. Darbon, "Administration et société," p. 56.
21. Hyden, *No Shortcuts to Progress*; Martin, *Tanzanie*, p. 175.
22. Darbon, "Le Paradoxe administratif," pp. 232ff. On the example of Senegal, see also Waterbury and Gersovitz, *Risk and Choice in Senegal*.
23. See Ayubi, *Bureaucracy and Politics in Contemporary Egypt*.
24. Martin, "Par-delà le boubou et la cravate."
25. Mousseron, "La réception," pp. 38ff.
26. David, *Les Grands systémes*, pp. 516-18.

27. Le Roy, "Les usages politiques du droit," p. 113.
28. Mozaffari, *La Naissance*, pp. 11 and 16-17.
29. Gernet, *Le Monde chinois*, pp. 549-50.
30. David, *Les Grands systémes*, pp. 547ff.; Moitry, *Le Droit japonais*.
31. Pons, "Consensus et idéologie," p. 58.
32. Lavelle, *La pensée politique*, pp. 41-42.
33. Ibid., p. 72.
34. Pons, "Consensus et idéologie," p. 53.
35. Lavelle, *Les Textes*.
36. Apter, *Pour l'État contre l'État*, pp. 195ff.
37. Le Roy, "Les usages politiques du droit," pp. 117-18.
38. Mousseron, "La réception," pp. 63-65.
39. Ibid., pp. 70-72.
40. On Egypt, see Botiveau, "Faits de vengeance." On sub-Saharan Africa, see Le Roy, "Les usages politiques du droit."
41. See Badie, "Démocratie et religion."
42. See Hermet, *Le Peuple contre la démocratie*.
43. Mozaffari, "La problématique," pp. 707ff.

Part Three

1. Bayart, *L'État en Afrique*, pp. 27ff.

Chapter 5

1. Fauré, "Éléments d'analyse," pp. 33ff.
2. On the new social movements, see Offe, "New Social Assessments"; Melucci, "Symbolic Challenge of Contemporary Movements."
3. Mozaffari, *La Naissance*, pp. 34-35.
4. Zghal, "Le retour du sacré," p. 61.
5. See Botiveau, "De nouveaux modes de contestation."
6. Jaffrelot, "Les émeutes."
7. Ibid.; Banerjee, "Hindutva."
8. Rajakovic, "Yougoslavie."
9. Coulon, "La sharia dans tous ses États."
10. Bouissou, "Mécontentement, désaccord et stabilité," p. 245.
11. Baduel, "Le front de l'État," p. 149.
12. See Whitten, *Cultural Transformations*, and Le Bot, "Le destin de l'Amérique latine."
13. Bach, "Les frontières du régionalisme."

14. Le Guennec-Coppens and Caplan, *Les Swahili entre Afrique et Arabie*.
15. Constantin, "Communautés musulmanes."
16. Majul, "Iranian Revolution," pp. 277ff.
17. Ramazani, "Iran's Export of the Revolution," p. 48.
18. Walder, *Communist Neo-traditionalism*.
19. See Lafont, *Les Frontières du Vietnam*, pp. 15-16.
20. On these questions, see in particular Purcell, *The Chinese in Southeast Asia*, and Trolliet, "Les Chinois."
21. As seen by Geertz. See Geertz, *Agricultural Involution* and *Old Societies and New States*.
22. Darbon, *L'Administration et le paysan*.
23. Leca and Vatin, "Social Structure and Political Stability."
24. Germani, *Authoritarianism, Fascism and National Populism*; Touraine, *La Parole et le Sang*.
25. On the populist movements in Latin America, see Castro Rea, Ducatenzeiler, and Faucher, "La tentación."
26. On the Philippines, see particularly Burton, *Impossible Dream*.
27. Regarding Burkino Faso, see Otayek, "Rectification."
28. Hermet, "L'Amérique latine."
29. See Jaffrelot, "La place de l'État."
30. Jelavich, *History of the Balkans* and "Balkan Intellectuals."
31. Baduel, "Le front de l'État," p. 148.
32. Van Bruinessen, "Kurdish Society," p. 51.
33. *Le Monde*, January 25, 1992.
34. See Chabal, *Political Domination in Africa*.
35. See Diamond, "Nigeria," pp. 56ff.
36. Zghal, "Le retour du sacré," p. 63.

Chapter 6

1. Rosenau, *Turbulence in World Politics*; Zacher, "Decaying Pillars."
2. Badie and Smouts, *Le Retournement du monde*.
3. Nordenstreng and Schiller, *National Sovereignty and International Communication*.
4. See in particular Boyd-Barrett, "Cultural Dependency and the Mass-media."
5. See in particular Uche, *Mass-media*.
6. Hamelink, *Cultural Autonomy in Global Communications*.
7. On India, see Malik, *Traditional Forms*.
8. Engineer, "Tragedy of Baghalpur Riots" and "Making of the Hyderabad Riots."

9. "Saudi Arabia," in Piscatori and Harris, *Law, Personalities and Politics*.

10. Lafont, *Les Frontières du Vietnam*, pp. 17-23; Dharma, "Les frontières du Campà," pp. 128ff.

11. Rawls, *A Theory of Justice*.

12. See Baduel, "La guerre contestataire."

13. On these mobilizations, see Burgat, "La part des islamistes," in *L'Islamisme au Maghreb*, pp. 75-78.

14. In just the most recent literature on this subject, see Roff, *Islam,* and Hunter Shiren, *Politics of Islamic Revivalism*.

15. See Flory, *Annuaire français de droit international*, pp. 102-3.

16. See Balta, *Le Grand Maghreb*, and Sadik, *Le Grand Maghreb*.

17. See Postel-Vinay, "L'Asie dans l'amphithéâtre japonais," p. 26.

18. See Bouissou, "La puissance politique," pp. 451ff., and Postel-Vinay, "Anachronique dépendance diplomatique," p. 22.

19. Bozarslan, "Turquie," pp. 46ff.

20. Ibid., pp. 37-46.

21. See Leca and Vatin, "Social Structure and Political Stability," and Birnbaum, *Dimensions*.

22. See "Des ethnies," in Baduel, *Revue du monde musulman et de la Méditerranée*.

23. On these questions, see Bloom, *Personal Identity*, particularly chaps. 2 and 5.

Bibliography

Abu-Hakima, A. *The Modern History of Kuwait*. London: Luzac, 1983.
Adda, J., and M.-C. Smouts. *La France face au Sud*. Paris: Karthala, 1989.
Addi, L. "Religion et politique dans le nationalisme algérien: le rôle des oulemas." *Revue maghrébine d'études politiques et religieuses* (October 1988): 60-77.
Advani, B. *Influence of Socialism on Policies, Legislation and Administration of India Since Independence*. New Delhi: Sterling Publishers, 1975.
Agnouche, C. *Histoire politique du Maroc*. Casablanca: Afrique-Orient, 1987.
Akamatsu, P. *Meiji 1868: Révolution et contre-révolution au Japon*. Paris: Calmann-Lévy, 1968.
Aktar, O. C. *L'Occidentalisation de la Turquie*. Paris: L'Harmattan, 1985.
Al Ahnaf, M., B. Botiveau, and F. Fregoli. *L'Algérie par ses islamistes*. Paris: Karthala, 1991.
Algar, H. "An Introduction to the History of Freemasonry in Iran." *Middle East Studies* 6 (1978): 276-79.
Al-Kuwairi, Ali K. *Oil Revenues in the Gulf Emirates*. Boulder, Colo.: Westview Press, 1978.
Allies, P. *L'Invention du territoire*. Grenoble: Presses universitaires de Grenoble, 1980.
Almond, G., and S. Verba. *The Civic Culture: Political Attitudes and Democracy in Five Nations*. Boston: Little, Brown, 1963.
———, eds. *The Civic Culture Revisited*. Boston: Little, Brown, 1980.
Amin, A. *Impérialisme et sous-développement en Afrique*. Paris: Anthropos, 1988.
Amselle, Jean-Loup, and E. Mbokolo. *Au coeur de l'ethnie: ethnie, tribalisme et Etat en Afrique*. Paris: La Découverte, 1985.
André-Vincent, P. "Le dialogue Las Casas-Vitoria: Deux interprétations nouvelles

du droit des gens." In *De la dégradation du droit des gens dans le monde contemporain*, ed. J.-P. Charnay. Paris: Anthropos, 1981.

Apter, D. *Pour l'État contre l'État*. Paris: Economica, 1988.

Arasteh, R. *Education and Social Awakening in Iran*. Leiden: E. J. Brill, 1962.

Aron, Raymond. *Paix et guerre entre les nations*. Paris: Calmann-Lévy, 1962.

Asiwaju, A. I., ed. *Partitioned Africans: Ethnic Relations Across Africa's International Boundaries*. London: Hurst, 1985.

Ayubi, N. *Bureaucracy and Politics in Contemporary Egypt*. London: Ithaca, 1980.

Baali, F. *Society, State and Urbanism*. Albany: State University of New York Press, 1988.

Bach, D. "Les frontières du régionalisme: Le Nigéria en Afrique de l'Ouest." In *Nigéria, un pouvoir en puissance*, ed. D. Bach, J. Egg, and J. Philippe, pp. 195-218. Paris: Karthala, 1988.

Badie, Bertrand. "L'Analyse des partis politiques en monde musulman." In *Idéologies, partis politiques et groupes sociaux*, ed. Y. Dir Mény, pp. 271-87. Paris: PFNSP, 1989.

———. "Communauté, individualisme et culture." In *Sur l'individualisme*, ed. P. Birnbaum and J. Leca. Paris: PFNSP, 1986.

———. *Culture et politique*. Paris: Economica, 1986.

———. "Démocratie et religion: Logiques culturelles et logiques de l'action." *Revue internationale des sciences sociales* (August 1991): 545-56.

———. *Les Deux États*. Paris: Fayard, 1987.

———. *Le Développement politique*. Paris: Economica, 1988.

Badie, Bertrand, and M.-C. Smouts. *Le Retournement du monde*. Paris: PFNSP, 1992.

———. "Le front de l'État." In *Le monde musulman à l'épreuve de la frontière*, ed. P. R. Baduel. Aix: Édisud, 1988.

Baduel, P. R. *Maghreb: État des lieux*. Aix: IREMAM, 1989.

———. "La guerre contestataire." In *Crise du Golfe, la logique des chercheurs*, ed. P. R. Baduel. Special issue of *Revue du monde musulman et de la Méditerranée*. 1991.

———, ed. *Crise du Golfe, la logique des chercheurs*. Special issue of *Revue du monde musulman et de la Méditerranée*. 1991.

Baily, F. E. *British Policy and the Turkish Reform Movement*. Cambridge, Mass.: Harvard University Press, 1962.

Balta, P. *Le Grand Maghreb*. Paris: La Découverte, 1990.

Banerjea, S. N. *A Nation in the Making*. London: Oxford University Press, 1963.

Banerjee, S. "Hindutva: Ideology and Social Psychology." *Economic and Political Weekly*, January 19, 1991, pp. 97-101.

Banfield, E. *The Moral Basis of a Backward Society*. New York: The Free Press, 1958.

Banisadr, Abol Hassan. Interview. November 1990.

Bayart, J. F. *L'État en Afrique*. Paris: Fayard, 1989.
Beasley, W. G. *The Meiji Restoration*. Stanford, Calif.: Stanford University Press, 1972.
Beauge, G., and A. Roussillon. *Le Migrant et son double*. Paris: Publisud, 1988.
Beblawi, H., and G. Luciani, eds. *The Rentier State*. London: Croom Helm, 1987.
Bell, D. *The End of Ideology*. Glencoe, Ill.: The Free Press, 1960.
Birnbaum, P. *Dimensions du pouvoir*. Paris: PUF, 1985.
Bloom W., *Personal Identity, National Identity and International Relations*. Cambridge, Mass.: Cambridge University Press, 1990.
Botiveau, B. "De nouveaux modes de contestation dans le monde arabe." *Cultures et Conflits*, no. 5 (1992).
———. "Faits de vengeance et concurrence de systèmes de droit." *Peuples méditerranés* 41-42 (October 1987): 153-66.
Bouissou, J.-M. "La puissance politique: Une enquête inachevée." In *L'expansion de la puissance japonaise*, ed. J.-M. Bouissou, G. Faure, and Z. Laidi. Paris: Complexe, 1992.
———. "Mécontentement, désaccord et stabilité: La vie politique dans le Japon contemporain." In *Japon: Le Consensus: mythe et réalitiés*, ed. A. Touraine. Paris: Economica, 1984.
Bourgeot, A. "L'identité touareg: De l'aristocratie à la révolution." *Études rurales*, December 1990, pp. 129-62.
Boyd-Barrett, J. "Cultural Dependency and the Mass-media." In *Culture, Society and the Media*, ed. M. Gurevitch, T. Bennett, J. Curran, and J. Woollacott. London: Methuen, 1982.
Bozarslan, H. "Turquie: Un défi permanent." In *La question Kurde*, ed. E. Picard, pp. 37-46. Paris: Complexe, 1991.
Bozeman, Al. *The Future of Law in a Multinational World*. Princeton, N.J.: Princeton University Press, 1975.
Bugnicourt, J. H. "Action administrative et communication avec les administrés en Afrique." *Revue française d'administration publique* 2 (1977): 145-66.
Buijtenhuijs, R. "Des résistances aux indépendances." In *Les Afriques politiques*, ed. C. Coulon and D. C. Martin. Paris: La Découverte, 1991.
Bull, H. *Anarchical Society*. New York: Columbia University Press, 1977.
Burgat, F. *L'Islamisme au Maghreb*. Paris: Karthala, 1988.
Burton, S. *Impossible Dream*. New York: Warner, 1959.
Callaghy, T. "The State as Lame Leviathan: The Patrimonial Administrative State in Africa." In *The African State in Transition*, ed. Z. Ergas, pp. 87-116. Basingstoke, U.K.: Macmillan, 1987.
Camau, M. *La Tunisie*. Paris: PUF, 1989.
Cardoso, F. "Associated Dependent Development: Theoretical and Practical Implications." In *Authoritarian Brazil*, ed. A. Stepan. New Haven, Conn.: Yale University Press, 1973.

———. *Politique et développement dans les sociétés dépendantes*. Paris: Anthropos, 1971.
Cardoso, F., and E. Faletto. *Dependency and Development in Latin America*. Berkeley: University of California Press, 1979.
Castro Rea, J., G. Ducatenzeiler, and P. Faucher. "La tentación populista: Argentina, Brasil, México y Peru." *Foro Internacional* (Mexico City), 31, no. 2 (1990).
Chabal, P. *Political Domination in Africa: Reflections on the Limits of Power*. New York: Cambridge University Press, 1986.
Chazan, N. "Patterns of State Society Incorporation and Disengagement in Africa." In *The Precarious Balance: State and Society in Africa*, ed. D. Rotchild and N. Chazan, pp. 121–48. Boulder, Colo.: Westview Press, 1988.
Chevrier, Y. "L'État en Chine: Paradoxes et polarités." *Rapport pour le 3e Congrès de l'AFSP*, Bordeaux, October 1988.
———. *Modernization in China. Historical Trends and Recent Developments*. London: Hurst, 1992.
Chrétien, J. P., and G. Prunier. *Les ethnies ont une histoire*. Paris: Karthala, 1989.
Claudot-Hewod, H. "Des États-nations contre un peuple, le cas des Touaregs." *Revue de l'Occident musulman et la Méditerranée* 44 (1987): 48–63.
Cohen, E. "Thailand, Burma and Laos: An Outline of the Comparative Social Dynamics of Three Theravada Buddhist Societies in the Modern Era." In *Patterns of Modernity*, ed. S. Eisenstadt, pp. 192–216. London: Pinter, 1987.
Compagnon, D. "Somalie, de l'État en formation à l'État en pointillé." In J. F. Médard, "Le rapport de clientèle: Du phénomène social à l'analyse politique." *Revue française de science politique* (February 1976): 205–40.
Constantin, F. "Communautés musulmanes et appareils d'État en Afrique orientale: Illusions organisatrices et aventurisme politique." Report presented to the ATP, *Islam, État et société en Afrique noire*. London, December 1987.
———. "Les relations internationales." In C. Coulon and D. C. Martin, *Les Afriques politiques*. Paris: La Découverte, 1991.
Coulon, C. "La sharia dans tous ses États." Report presented to the ATP, *Islam, État et société en Afrique noire*. London, December 1987.
———. "Religions et politique." In *Les Afriques politiques*, ed. C. Coulon and D. C. Martin. Paris: La Découverte, 1991.
Crawford, S. *Ram Mohan Roy, Social, Political and Religious Reforms in 19th Century India*. New York: Paragon House, 1987.
Darbon, D. "Administration et société." In *Les Afriques politiques*, ed. C. Coulon and D. C. Martin. Paris: La Découverte, 1991.
———. "Administration et société en Afrique." In *États et sociétés en Afrique francophone*, ed. D. Bach and A. Kirk-Greene. Published in English under the title *The State and Society in Francophone Africa Since Independence* (New York: St. Martin's Press, in association with St. Anthony's College, Oxford, 1995).

———. *L'Administration et le paysan en Casamance.* Paris: Pédone, 1988.
———. "Le Paradoxe administratif: Perspective comparative autour de cas africains." Ph.D. diss., University of Bordeaux, 1991.
David, R. *Les Grands systémes de droit contemporains.* Paris: Dalloz, 1982.
Défis au Sud. Rapport de la Commission Sud. Paris: Economica, 1990.
"Des ethnies aux nations en Asie centrale." *Revue du monde musulman et de la Méditerranée,* no. 59-60 (1991).
Dharma, Po. "Les frontières du Campà."
Diamond, L. "Nigeria: Pluralism, Statism and the Struggle for Democracy." In *Democracy in Developing Countries: Africa,* ed. L. Diamond, J. Linz, and S. M. Lipset. Boulder, Colo.: Lynne Rienner, 1988.
Durkheim, Emile. *The Division of Labor in Society.* Trans. George Simpson. Glencoe, Ill.: The Free Press, 1933.
———. *Les Formes élémentaires de la vie religieuse.* Paris: PUF, 1968.
Eckstein, H. *Division and Cohesion in Democracy. A Study of Norway.* Princeton, N.J.: Princeton University Press, 1966.
Ehrenberg, V. *L'État grec.* Paris: Maspero, 1976.
Elias, N. *La Dynamique de l'Occident.* Paris: Calmann-Lévy, 1975.
Engineer, A. A. "Making of the Hyderabad Riots." *Economic and Political Weekly,* February 9, 1992, pp. 271-74.
———. "Tragedy of Baghalpur Riots." *Economic and Political Weekly,* February 10, 1990, pp. 305-7.
Evans-Pritchard, E. E. *Les Nuer.* Paris: Gallimard, 1968.
Fakkar, R. *Reflets de la sociologie pré-marxiste dans le monde arabe.* Paris: Geuthner, 1974.
Farman-Farmayan, H. "The Forces of Modernization in 19th-Century Iran: A Historical Survey. In *The Beginnings of Modernization in the Middle East,* ed. W. R. Polk and R. L. Chambers. Chicago: University of Chicago Press, 1968.
Fauré, Y. "Éléments d'analyse à propos de l'expérience récente en Côte-d'Ivoire." *Politique africaine* 43 (October 1991): 33ff.
Feigon, L. N. *Chen Duxiu.* Princeton, N.J.: Princeton University Press, 1983.
Field, M. *The Merchants: The Big Business Families of Saudi Arabia and the Gulf States.* Woodstock, N.Y.: Overlook Press, 1985.
Flory, M., comp. *Annuaire français de droit international,* 1975.
Flory, M., et al. *Les Régimes politiques arabes.* Paris: PUF.
Frank, A. G. *Le développement du sous-développement.* Paris: Maspero, 1970.
Fukuyama, F. *La Fin de l'histoire et le dernier homme.* Paris: Flammarion, 1992.
Galtung, J. "A Structural Theory of Imperialism." *Journal of Peace Research* 8, no. 2 (1971): 81-117.
Gascon, A. "Les mouvements armés dans la Corne de l'Afrique et au Soudan: L'éclatement des États centraux." *Études Polémologiques* 51 (1989): 61-78.
Gaudemet, J. *Les Communautés familiales.* Paris: M. Rivière, 1963.

Gavrielides, N. "Tribal Democracy: The Anatomy of Parliamentary Elections in Kuwait." In *Elections in the Middle East*, ed. L. Layne. Boulder, Colo.: Westview Press, 1987.
Geertz, C. *Agricultural Involution*. Berkeley: University of California Press, 1963.
———. *Meaning and Order in Moroccan Society*. Cambridge: Cambridge University Press, 1979.
———. *Old Societies and New States*. New York: The Free Press, 1963.
Gellner, E. *Saints of the Atlas*. London: Weidenfeld & Nicolson, 1969.
Germani, G. *Authoritarianism, Fascism and National Populism*. New Brunswick, N.J.: Transaction Books, 1978.
Gernet, J. *Le Monde chinois*. Paris: A. Colin, 1972.
Giannini, A. "La costituzione della Transgiordania." *Orient Moderno* 2 (1931): 117-31.
Giddens, A. *The Nation State and Violence*. Cambridge: Polity Press, 1985.
Gilpin, R. *War and Change in World Politics*. Cambridge: Cambridge University Press, 1973.
Gonda, J. *L'Hindouisme récent*. Paris: Payot, 1965.
Good, R. "The Congo Crisis: A Study of Post-colonial Politics." In *Neutralism and Non-alignment*, ed. L. W. Martin. New York: Praeger, 1962.
Goyal, D. R. *Rashtriya Swayamsewak Sangh*. New Delhi: Radha Krishna, 1979.
Hamelink, C. *Cultural Autonomy in Global Communications*. New York: Longman, 1983.
Hardin, R. "Hobbesian Political Order." *Political Theory* 3, no. 2 (May 1991).
Heesterman, J. C. *The Inner Conflict of Tradition*. Chicago: University of Chicago Press, 1985.
Herald Tribune, December 3, 1990.
Hermet, G. "L'Amérique latine entre démocratie et populisme." *L'Année internationale*, 1990-1991: 211-16.
———. *Le Peuple contre la démocratie*. Paris: Fayard, 1989.
Hinnebusch, R. A. "Political Parties in the Arab States." In *Beyond Coercion*, ed. A. Dowisha and W. Zartman. London: Croom Helm, 1988.
Hobbes, T. *Leviathan*. Paris: Sirey, 1971.
Hobsbawm, E. *Les Primitifs de la révolte*. Paris: Fayard, 1966.
Horowitz, D. L. *Ethnic Groups in Conflict*. Berkeley: University of California Press, 1985.
———, ed. *The Creation of Tribalism in Southern Africa*. London: J. Currey, 1989.
Hunter Shiren, T. *The Politics of Islamic Revivalism*. Bloomington: Indiana University Press, 1988.
Hyden, G. *No Shortcuts to Progress: African Development Management in Perspective*. London: Heinemann, 1983.
Jackson, R. "Negative Sovereignty in Sub-Saharan Africa." *Review of International Studies* 12 (October 1986): 247-64.

———. "Quasi States, Dual Regimes and Neo-classical Theories." *International Organizations* 41 (Fall 1987): 519-50.

———. *Quasi States: Sovereignty, International Relations and the Third World*. Cambridge: Cambridge University Press, 1990.

Jacobson, J. R. *The Territorial Rights of Nations and Peoples*. Lewiston, N.Y.: E. Mellen Press, 1989.

Jaffrelot, C. *Des nationalistes en quête d'une nation. Les partis nationalistes hindous au XXe siècle*. Paris: IEP, 1991.

———. "La place de l'État dans l'idéologie nationaliste hindoue." *Revue française de science politique* 39 (December 1989): 840-41.

———. "Les émeutes entre hindous et musulmans: Essai de hiérarchisation des facteurs culturels, économiques et politiques." *Cultures et Conflits*, no. 5 (1992).

Javadi, Hajj Sayyed. Interview. October 25, 1990.

Jelavich, Barbara. *History of the Balkans*. Cambridge: Cambridge University Press, 1983.

———. "Balkan Intellectuals and the New States." Paper presented at the IPSA Congress, Washington, D.C., 1988.

Katz, E., and G. Wedell. *Broadcasting in the Third World: Promise and Performance*. Cambridge, Mass.: Harvard University Press, 1977.

Kawano, K. "La Révolution française et Meiji Ishin." *Revue internationale des sciences sociales* (February 1989).

Kay, D. *Dependent Development: The Alliance of Multinational State and Local Capitalism in Brazil*. Princeton, N.J.: Princeton University Press, 1979.

Khayr Ed-Din. *Essai sur les réformes nécessaires aux États musulmans*. Aix-en-Provence: Édisud, 1987.

Kochanek, S. A. *The Congress Party of India*. Princeton, N.J.: Princeton University Press, 1968.

Lafont, P. B. *Les Frontières du Vietnam: Histoire des frontières de la péninsule indochinoise*. Paris: L'Harmattan, 1989.

———. "La guerre contestataire." In *Crise du Golfe, la logique des chercheurs*, ed. P. R. Baduel, pp. 54-56. Special issue of *Revue du monde musulman et de la Méditerranée*. 1991.

Laitin, D., and S. Samatar. *Somalia: Nation in Search of a State*. Boulder, Colo.: Gower, 1987.

———. "L'analyse des partis politiques en monde musulman." In *Ideologies, partis politiques et groupes sociaux*, ed. Y. Meny, pp. 271-87. Paris: PFNSP, 1989.

Lapidus, I. "Islam and Modernity." In *Patterns of Modernity*, ed. S. Eisenstadt. London: Pinter, 1987.

Lavelle, P. *La pensée politique de Japon contemporain*. Paris: PUF, 1990.

———. *Les Textes et les thèmes fondamentaux de l'idéologie officielle du Japon impérial*. Paris: INALCO, 1981.

Leach, E. *Les Systèmes politiques des hautes terres de Birmanie*. Paris: Maspero, 1972.

Le Bot, Y. "Le destin de l'Amérique latine." *Le Monde*, December 29, 1991.
Leca, J., and J. C. Vatin. *L'Algérie politique*. Paris: PFNSP, 1975.
———. "Social Structure and Political Stability: Comparative Evidence from the Algerian, Syrian, Iraqi Case." In *Beyond Coercion*, ed. A. Dowisha and W. Zartman, pp. 164-202. London: Croom Helm, 1988.
Le Guennec-Coppens, F., and P. Caplan. *Les Swahili entre Afrique et Arabie*. Paris: Karthala, 1991.
Lemarchand, R. "The State, the Parallel Economy and the Changing Structure Systems." In *The Precarious Balance: State and Society in Africa*, ed. D. Rotchild and N. Chazan, pp. 149-70. Boulder, Colo.: Westview Press, 1988.
Le Monde, December 5 and 7, 1990; April 9 and 10, 1991; January 25, 1992.
Lenin, V. I. *Imperialism, the Highest Stage of Capitalism*. 1939. Revised translation. New York: International Publishers, 1993.
Le Roy, Étienne. "Les usages politiques du droit." In *Les Afriques politiques*, ed. C. Coulon and D. C. Martin. Paris: La Découverte, 1991.
Leveau, R. "État, société et rente pétrolière au Moyen-Orient." In *Droit, institutions et systèmes politiques*. Paris: PUF, 1987.
Lewis, B. *The Emergence of Modern Turkey*. London: Oxford University Press, 1961.
Lewis, I. M. "The Ogaden and the Fragility of Somali Segmentary Nationalism." *African Affairs* 88 (October 1989): 573-79.
Lipset, S. M., and S. Rokkan. "Cleavage Structures, Party Systems and Voter Alignments." In *Party Systems and Voter Alignments*. New York: The Free Press, 1967.
Lubeck, P. *The African Bourgeoisie*. Boulder, Colo.: Lynne Rienner, 1987.
Luxemburg, Rosa. *Imperialism and the Accumulation of Capital*. Trans. Rudolf Wichmann. London: Penguin, 1972.
MacFarlane, A. *The Origins of English Individualism*. Cambridge: Cambridge University Press, 1978.
Mahdavy, H. "The Patterns and Problems of Economic Rent in Rentier States: The Case of Iran." In *Studies in the Economic History of the Middle East*, ed. M. A. Cook, pp. 429-67. London: Oxford University Press, 1970.
Majul, C. A. "The Iranian Revolution and the Muslims in the Philippines." In *The Iranian Revolution: Its Global Impact*, ed. J. L. Esposito. Gainesville: Florida University Press, 1990.
Malik, M. *Traditional Forms of Communication and the Mass-media in India*. Paris: UNESCO, 1980.
Mandaza, I. ed. *Zimbabwe: The Political Economy of Transition, 1980-1986*. London: Codestria, 1986.
Martin, D. C. *Tanzanie: L'invention d'une culture politique*. Paris: PFNSP, n.d.
———. "Par-delà le boubou et la cravate: Pour une sociologie de l'innovation politique en Afrique noire." *Revue canadienne des études africaines* 20, no. 1 (1986): 4-35.

Mayall, J. *Nationalism and International Society*. Cambridge: Cambridge University Press, 1990.
Médard, J. F. "L'État néo-patrimonial." In *Etats d'Afrique Noire*, ed. J. F. Médard. Paris: Karthala, 1992.
———. "Le rapport de clientèle: Du phénomène social à l'analyse politique." *Revue française de science politique* (February 1976).
Melucci, A. "The Symbolic Challenge of Contemporary Movements." *Social Research* 52, no. 4 (1985): 789-816.
Meyer, E. "Cingalais et Tamouls en Asie du Sud." In *Inde: L'un et le multiple*, ed. J. A. Bernard et al. Paris: CHEAM, 1986.
———. "La crise sri-lankaise: Enjeux territoriaux et enjeux symboliques." *Hérodote*, no. 49 (April-June 1988).
Migdal, J. *Strong Societies and Weak States: State-Society Relations and Capabilities in the Third World*. Princeton, N.J.: Princeton University Press, 1988.
Miller, W. G. "The Dowreh and Iranian Politics." *Middle East Journal* 23, no. 2 (Spring 1969): 159-76.
Millspaugh, A. C. *Americans in Persia*. Washington, D.C.: The Brookings Institution, 1946.
Mishra, D. N. *RSS: Myth and Reality*. Delhi: Vikas Publishers, 1980.
Moitry, J. H. *Le Droit japonais*. Paris: PUF, 1988.
Moore, C. H. "Clientelist Ideology and Political Change: Fictitious Networks in Egypt and Tunisia." In *Patrons and Clients in Mediterranean Societies*, ed. E. Gellner and J. Waterbury. London: Duckworth, 1977.
Morgenthau, H. *Politics Among Nations: The Struggle for Power and Peace*. New York: Knopf, 1948.
Mousseron, J. M. "La réception au Proche-Orient du droit français des obligations." *Revue internationale de droit comparé* 1 (1968).
Moyona, H. V. *The Political Economy of Land*. Gweru, Zimbabwe: Mambo Press, 1984.
Mozaffari, M. *La Naissance de la bourgeoisie commerçante en Iran*. Aarhus, Denmark: Publication de l'université d'Aarhus, 1981.
———. "La problématique de la république et de l'islam chiite." *Revue juridique et politique* (1980): 707ff.
———. *Le Régime de la propriété en Iran*. Aarhus, Denmark: Publication de l' université d'Aarhus, 1981.
Nahnah, M. Interview. *Horizons*, April 9, 1989, p. 2.
Najita, T. *Japan: The Intellectual Foundations of Modern Japanese Politics*. Chicago: University of Chicago Press, 1974.
Najmabadi, A. "Depolitization of a Rentier State: The Case of Pahlavi Iran." In *The Rentier State*, ed. H. Beblawi and G. Luciani. London: Croom Helm, 1987.
N.E.D., no. 1613 (May 1952).

Nordenstreng, K., and H. I. Schiller. *National Sovereignty and International Communication*. Norwood, N.J.: Ablex, 1979.

Northrop, F.S.C. *The Meeting of East and West*. New York, 1972.

O'Donnell, G. *Modernization and Bureaucratic Authoritarianism: Studies in South-American Politics*. Berkeley: University of California Press, 1973.

Offe, C. "New Social Assessments: Challenging the Boundaries of Institutional Politics." *Social Research*, no. 32-34 (1985): 817-68.

Osborne, M. *Before Kampuchea: Preludes to Tragedy*. Sydney: G. Allen & Unwin, 1979.

Otayek, R. "Rectification." *Politique africaine* (March 1989): 2-10.

Pahlavi, M. R. *Réponse à l'Histoire*. Paris: Albin Michel, 1979.

Parsons, T. *Société*. Paris: Dunod, 1973.

Pic-Sernaglia, P. Interview with two "mujahideen" militants. January and February, 1991.

Piscatori, J. *Islam in a World of Nation-States*. London: Cambridge University Press, 1986.

Piscatori, J., and G. Harris, eds. *Law, Personalities and Politics in the Middle East*. Washington, D.C.: MEI, 1987.

Polk, W. R., and R. L. Chambers, eds. *The Beginnings of Modernization in the Middle East*. Chicago: University of Chicago Press, 1968.

Pons, P. "Consensus et idéologie." In *Japon: Le Consensus: Mythe et réalités*, ed. A. Touraine. Paris: Economica, 1984.

Postel-Vinay, K. "Anachronique dépendance diplomatique du Japon." *Le Monde diplomatique* (April 1991).

——. "L'Asie dans l'amphithéâtre japonais." *Le Monde diplomatique* (January 1991).

Prebisch, R. *The Economic Development of Latin America and Its Principal Problems*.

Purcell, V. *The Chinese in Southeast Asia*. London: Oxford University Press, 1965.

Quarterly Digest of Statistics. Harare: Republic of Zimbabwe, 1985.

Rajakovic, N. "Yougoslavie: L'absence de mouvements de contestation ou l'anatomie d'une dérive nationaliste." *Cultures et Conflits*, no. 5 (1992).

Ramazani, R. K. "Iran's Export of the Revolution." In *The Iranian Revolution: Its Global Impact*, ed. J. L. Esposito. Miami: Florida University Press, 1990.

Raouf, W. *Nouveau regard sur le nationalisme arabe*. Paris: L'Harmattan, 1984.

Rasler, K., and W. R. Thompson. *War and State-making*. Boston: Unwin Hyman, 1990.

Rapport Mondial sur le développement humain. New York: United Nations, PNUD, 1991.

Rawls, J. *A Theory of Justice*. Cambridge: Harvard University Press, 1971.

Richard, Y. *Entre l'Iran et l'Occident*. Paris: Éditions de la M.S.H., 1989.

———. *L'Islam chiite*. Paris: Fayard, 1991.
Riggs, F. "Bureaucrats and Political Development." In *Bureaucracy and Political Development*, ed. J. La Palombara. Princeton, N.J.: Princeton University Press, 1963.
Roberts, D. A. *The Ba'ath and the Creation of Modern Syria*. London: Croom Helm, 1987.
Roff, W. R. *Islam and the Political Economy of Meaning*. London: Croom Helm, 1987.
Rosenau, James. *Turbulence in World Politics: A Theory of Change and Continuity*. Princeton, N.J.: Princeton University Press, 1990.
Rudebeck, L. *Party and People. A Study of Political Change in Tunisia*. Stockholm: Almqvist & Wiksel, 1967.
Sadik, A. *Le Grand Maghreb: Intégration et systèmes économiques comparés*. Casablanca: Afrique Orient, 1989.
Samartha, S. J. *Introduction to Radhakrishnan: The Man and His Thought*. New York: Association Press, 1964.
Sandbrook, R. *The Politics of Africa's Economic Stagnation*. Cambridge: Cambridge University Press, 1985.
Sarkisyang, E. *Buddhist Background to the Burmese Revolution*. The Hague: M. Nijhoff, 1965.
"Saudi Arabia, Culture Change and the International Legal Order." In *Law, Personalities and Politics in the Middle East*, ed. J. Piscatori and G. Harris. Washington: MEI, 1987.
Schumpeter, J. *Impérialisme et classes sociales*. Paris: Éditions de Minuit, 1972.
Schwartz, B. *In Search of Wealth and Power, Yen-Fu and the West*. Cambridge, Mass.: Harvard University Press, 1964.
Sen, S. *History of Bengali Literature*. New Delhi: Sahitya Akademi, 1960.
———. *Reaping the Green Revolution*. Maryknoll, N.Y.: Orbis Books, 1975.
Shamir, S. "Historical Traditions and Modernity in the Belief Systems of the Egyptian Mainstream." In *Patterns of Modernity*, ed. S. Eisenstadt. London: Pinter, 1987.
Shaw, M. *Title to Territory in Africa*. Oxford: Clarendon Press, 1986.
Smith, S. "L'Afrique poubelle." *L'État du monde*, 1989.
Smith, W. *European Imperialism in the Nineteenth and Twentieth Centuries*. Chicago: Nelson, 1982.
Srinavas, M. N. "A Note on Sanskritization and Westernization." In *Class, Status and Power*, ed. R. Bendix and S. M. Lipset. New York: The Free Press, 1966.
Strange, S. *States and Markets*. New York: Blackwell, 1988.
Szyliowicz, J. S. *Education and Modernization in the Middle East*. Ithaca: Cornell University Press, N.Y., 1973.
Théobald, F. *Corruption, Development and Underdevelopment*. London: Macmillan, 1990.

Tilly, C. "War-making and State-making as Organized Crime." University of Michigan, 1982.
Tordoff, W. "Conclusion." In *Political Parties in the Third World*, ed. V. Randall. London: Sage, 1988.
———. "Political Parties in Zambia." In *Political Parties in the Third World*, ed. V. Randall. London: Sage, 1988.
Touraine, A. *La Parole et le Sang: Politique et société en Amérique latine.* Paris: Odile Jacob, 1988.
Troliett, P. "Les Chinois en Asie du Sud-Est." *Hérodote* 2 (1981): 62–82.
Uche, L. U. *Mass-media, People and Politics in Nigeria.* Concept: New Delhi, 1989.
Umegaki, M. *After the Restoration. The Beginnings of Japan's Modern State.* New York: New York University Press, 1988.
Vail, L., ed. *The Creation of Tribalism in Southern Africa.* London: J. Currey, 1989.
Van Bruinessen, M. "Kurdish Society, Ethnicity, Nationalism and Refugee Problems." In *The Kurds: A Contemporary Overview*, ed. P. Kreuensbroek and S. Sperl. London and New York: Routledge, 1992.
Vatkiotis, P. J. *Nasser and His Generation.* London: Croom Helm, 1978.
Villey, M. *La Formation de la pensée juridique moderne.* Paris: Montchrestien, 1975.
Wade, R. *Governing the Market Economy: Theory and the Role of Government in East Asian Industrialization.* Princeton, N.J.: Princeton University Press, 1990.
Walder, A. *Communist Neo-traditionalism.* Berkeley: University of California Press, 1986.
Waterbury, J., and M. Gersovitz. *The Political Economy of Risk and Choice in Senegal.* London: Frank Cass, 1987.
Weber, M. *The Protestant Ethic and the Spirit of Capitalism.* Trans. Talcott Parsons. London: HarperCollins Academy, 1991.
Wesseling, H. L., ed. *Expansion and Reaction.* Leiden: Leiden University Press, 1978.
Whitten, N. E. *Cultural Transformations and Ethnicity in Modern Ecuador.* Urbana: University of Illinois Press, 1981.
World Bank. *Rapport sur le développement dans le monde.* Washington, D.C., 1991.
Yapp, M. E. *The Making of the Modern Near East, 1792–1923.* London: Longman, 1987.
Zacher, N. W. "The Decaying Pillars of the Westphalian Temple: Implications for International Order and Governance." In *Governance without Government: Order and Change in World Politics*, ed. E. D. Czempiel and J. Rosenau. Cambridge: Cambridge University Press, 1992.
Zghal, A. "Le retour du sacré: La nouvelle demande idéologique des jeunes scolarisés. Le cas de la Tunisie." *Annuaire de l'Afrique du Nord* 18 (1979).

Index

Abbas, Ferhat, 126
Abbasid empire, 74; *dar al islam* and, 59
Abdel Aziz, 106
Abdel Madjid I, *Khatt-e-Sharif* and, 105
Abd el-Malik, Caliph, 74
Abduh, 124, 129, 162
Abdul Hamid II, 97
Accommodation, 41, 42, 43
Adaptation, 2, 144
Afghani, Djamal ed-Din Al-, 124, 129, 161
Aflak, Michel, 119
AFP, 205
African Independence Party of Guinea-Bissau (PAIGC), 134
Aga Khan, 118
Agricultural sector, 17-18, 103, 145, 187
Ahval, Terjumani, 119
Akbar III, 69
Akhbaris, politics and, 126
Al-Barzani, Mustafa, 225
Al-Bustani, Boutros, 120

Al-Fassi, Allal, 67
Algerian People's Party, 125
Allegiance, 64, 175, 202-3, 230
Allende, Salvador, 36
Al-Mahdi, Sadik, 67
Almond, Gabriel, 51
Al-Sabah, Abdallah al-Salem, 101
Al-Sabah family, 29
Al-Sayyadi, Abdul Khoda, 97
Amane, Nishi, 122
Amnesty International, 85
Amr, importance of, 126
Andean Pact, 222
Anglo-Iranian Company, nationalization of, 19
AP, 205
Appeal to Youth (Chen Duxiu), 57
Apter, David, 151
Aquino, Corazon, 192
Arabism, 124, 126, 129
Arab League, 82, 183, 217
Arab nationalism, 108, 109
Arab Socialist Union (USA), 137
Arab Syrian Congress, 120
Armenian issue, 62, 110, 209, 230

Aron, Raymond, 12; interstate model by, 58
Arya Samaj sect, 69, 70
ASEAN, 222
Asian culture, Western culture and, 118
Association for Human Rights, 85
Association of Cantonese Merchants, 77
Association of Democratic Jurists, 85
Association of Lawyers, 85
Association of Turk Derneye, 120
Association of Writers, 85
Associative networks, rise of, 196–97
Authoritarianism, 52, 139, 197; dependence and, 21
Authority: importation of, 169; legitimacy and, 101
Avadi resolution (1955), 103
Avoidance logic, 154, 155
Ayan, 100, 194
Ayodhia temple, 174, 174n
Azawed Liberation Front, 65

Ba'ath Party, 67, 115, 120, 133, 138, 139, 140, 156; Alaouite minority and, 15; Taef accords and, 226
Bakhtiar, Shapur, government by, 161
Bandung conference, 193
Banerjea, Surendranath, nationalism and, 121
Banfield, on clientelism, 16
Banisadr, Abol Hassan, 121, 130; on Khomeini, 124
Barre, Siad, 195
Baule summit, 106
Bayart, Jean-François, hypothesis of, 167
Bazargan, Nehdi, 117, 117n
BBC, impact of, 206
Bell, Daniel, 49
Benahdj, FIS and, 200

Ben Ali, President, price increases by, 44
Ben Badis, Abdelhamid, 125, 126
Ben Bella, 156, 157
Ben Salah, Ahmed: socialist development and, 44
Bentham, Jeremy, 123, 147
Bharatiya Janta Party (BJP), 128, 178, 179, 209, 219; identity-based demands and, 176
Bhutto, populism and, 190
Bilateralism, 27, 37, 41, 42, 43, 221
BJP. *See* Bharatiya Janta Party
Bouissou, Jean-Marie, 179
Boumédienne, political populism of, 192
Bourgeot, André, on nomadic movements, 65
Bourguiba, Habib, 18, 84, 158; Bizerte and, 19; Destour reform and, 134, 137; political populism of, 192; PSD and, 140; socialist development and, 44
Brady plan, 42–43
Brahmo Samaj sect, 69
British-Persian treaty (1814), internal affairs and, 37
Brussels Commission, resolution and, 42
Buddhism: reintroduction of, 97–98; Tamils and, 61; *Theravada*, 160
Bull, Hedley, on anarchic society, 35
Bureaucracy: access to, 142–43; imported, 146; nationalist behavior and, 109; social life and, 143; universal/abstract rationality and, 141; universal/particularist conflict and, 145; Weberian concept of, 145; westernizing, 109
Bush, George, 39, 42–43

CACU, model for, 104

Callaghy, formula of, 14
Capitalism, 10, 11, 36, 150
Captured peasantry, 144
Cardoso, 11, 16, 20, 22
Carter, Jimmy, 106
Castro, Fidel, 216
Catholic Church, 60, 160, 180
Cavadia, Marie, 120
Cavallo, Domingo, 191
CDT, 173
Chadli, political populism of, 192
Charlemagne, 74
Charter Act (1833), 146
Chen Duxiu, 57
Chevrier, Yves, 55
Chiang Kai-shek, Song bank and, 149
Chikao, Fujisawa, on Hitler/Confucianism, 151
Chimborazo Indians, 180
China: dependence and, 39; Gulf crisis and, 38-40; as international force, 76; revolution in, 149; sociopolitical reality and, 54; Western treaties and, 76-77. *See also* Sino-American relations
Chinguiti oasis, dispute over, 63-64
Chomin, Nakae, 123
Christianity, 108, 196; contradictory experiences of, 159-60
Chukoku-Ha sect, 175
Chulalongkorn, 97
Citizenship, 60, 66, 178; allegiance and, 54, 202; crisis of, 171, 179, 181, 208, 227; forced/artificial, 196; free mobility and, 154; identification and, 177, 180, 202; imported idea of, 185; rejection of, 65
Civic integration, model of, 50
Civil codes, 149, 150, 152, 153
Civil obedience, universalism and, 154
Civil procedure, codes of, 147, 149, 150
Civil society, 53, 59, 84, 114, 182, 197, 222-23; clientelist bonds and, 224; constitution of, 84; fragmenting of, 80; innovation and, 198; missing, 83-87; social spaces and, 49, 79; territoriality and, 59
Clientelism, 24, 26, 27, 29, 38, 47, 54, 86, 185, 187, 189, 204, 205, 208, 214; American/Soviet, 25; civil society and, 224; dependence and, 33-34; precariousness and, 16
Client sovereignty, strategy of, 34
Client states: influence of, 26; patron states and, 24-34
Code of Commerce (1850), 148
Code of Inheritance and Alimony (1951), 153
Codes, 146, 147, 148; creation of, 149-50
Cohong monopoly, 77
Collectivities, identification toward, 184
Collor plan, 43
Colonialism, 11, 34, 61, 113; end of, 1; nationalist behavior and, 110; political mechanisms and, 12
Colonization, 7, 38, 98, 142
Commercial codes, 148, 149, 150
Commercial Procedure Code (1860), 148
Common law, 152, 153; Muslim, 146; in sub-Saharan Africa, 147-48
Communal culture, 60, 65-66; territorial affiliation for, 63
Communalization: effects of, 108; liberation of modes of, 132; political, 188, 220; redefinition of, 157; regional, 220
Communes, 66, 170
Communication, 3, 36, 183, 202, 205, 217; mastery of, 35; social networks and, 136
Communitarianism, 55, 111, 160, 206,

229; fusional, 150, 151; institutionalization of, 181; pan-Islamic, 209; residual, 83
Community, 15; identity and, 60; international, 215, 217; of pain, 220; territory and, 60-61; of usefulness, 220
Comte, Auguste, 95
Conference of Non-Aligned States (1973), 205
Congress of Baku, 13
Congress of Berlin, Africa and, 12
Congress Party, 128, 133, 140, 156, 157, 179; agricultural socialization and, 103; importation and, 174; intellectuals in, 121; nationalism and, 102, 203; third-world diplomacy of, 216
Conservative modernization, 94, 97, 111, 114-15; Meiji revolution and, 98, 99-100
Constantin, François, on associative movement, 181
Constitutional law, 152; social crises and, 156
Convention of Beijing (1860), 77
Coulon, Christian, 177; on countersociety, 136
Counsel of Ministers (Brussels Commission), resolution by, 42
Counterlegitimacy, 152, 172, 187
Countermobilization movements, 68, 215; identity-based, 210
Countersocialization, 36, 158
Cultural alienation, 214; logic of, 228; protest wars and, 216
Cultural dependence, 3, 208; dominators/dominated and, 234; international order and, 233
Cultural dissonance, 91, 131, 153
Cultural identity, 182, 221, 223, 229, 231; Islam and, 199; sovereignty and, 86
Cultural inflows, 35-36, 219

Culturalism: developmentalism and, 157-58, 159, 163-64; universalism and, 235
Cultural models, 47, 169; diffusion of, 204
Cultural neonationalism, political/social, 207
Cultural Revolution, 185
Cultural spaces, 50, 183, 224, 226; emergence of, 227; individualization and, 228
Culture: civic, 51; dependence and, 233; displacement of, 50; of government, 234; individual and, 229; mobilization of, 183; political, 50; primordialist vision of, 228. *See also* Communal culture
Curiel, Henri, 120, 204

Daimyo, 99, 111
Dar al harb, 66, 74
Dar al islam, 59, 66, 219; identification through, 230
Darbon, Dominique, on bureaucratic model, 142
Darwin, Charles, 56
Datsua Nyuo, doctrine of, 223
Datta, Michael Madhusudana, 121
Datta, Ramesh Chandra, 121-22
Dawle, Vosuq, 120
Decentralization, 95, 115, 137, 193, 194, 227; independence and, 142
Decolonization, 2, 7, 63, 73, 214, 228
De Gaulle, Charles, 169
Delegitimation, 19, 171
Democracy, 157, 158, 159, 160
Democratic Party of Guinea (PDG), 137, 140
Democratic Party of Independence, 139
Democratic Party of the Ivory Coast (PDCI), 137, 158, 170

Democratization, 106, 159, 161, 169
Deng Xiaoping, 55
Dependence, 10, 13-14, 21, 23, 26, 29, 80, 105, 131, 138, 155, 196, 202, 204, 233; clientelist, 33-34; components of, 32, 37; democracy and, 160; domination and, 48; effective/dynamic, 7, 48; globalization and, 3; importation and, 140, 151, 153; indirect effects of, 203; legitimation of, 43; logic of, 12, 27, 30, 39, 40, 46, 47; mechanism of, 11, 21; neopatrimonialism and, 149; political foundations of, 12-13, 20, 24, 42, 47; protest and, 233-34; reinforcing, 31, 146; resistance to, 104; socioeconomic functions and, 41; source of, 93-94; sovereignty and, 86; state, 13-24, 34-37; symbolism of, 77. *See also* Cultural dependence; Economic dependence
Dependentist ideology, 20, 32, 116; "development from underdevelopment" thesis and, 22
Derozio, Henry Louis Vivian, 69
Destourian Socialist Party (DSP): formation of, 44, 137; reform of, 134
Development: accommodation and, 42; financial support for, 141; neopatrimonialism and, 19; political strategy of, 22-23; rentier economy and, 31; socialist, 44. *See also* Economic development
Developmentalism, 1, 51-52; culturalism and, 157-58, 159, 163-64; political alienation and, 188; Western models and, 131
"Development from underdevelopment" thesis, 22
Dickens, Charles, 120
Differentiation, 115; strategy of, 197
Diplomacy, 37, 220; deception of, 38; foreign policy and, 39, 40; international order and, 210; non-Western, 214; particularism and, 211
Disorder: logic of, 207-9; strategies of, 214-18
Division of Labor in Society (Durkheim), 50-51
Djamali, Mahamed Fadel, 67
Djevdet Pasha, *Medjelle* and, 146
Djeza'ara school, 200
Dominant, 234; clientelist relation and, 214; dominated and, 13, 81; supremacy of, 233
Dominated, 182, 234; cultural alienation/exclusion and, 214; dominant and, 13, 81
Domination, 67; dependence and, 48; populism and, 190
Doubling, 9, 155, 184-85
Dowlat-e islami, 163
Dowreh, 15
Dragoumis, Ion, 193
DSP. *See* Destourian Socialist Party
Dual society, 85, 186
Durkheim, Emile, 50-51, 113

East and West in Religion (Radhakrishnan), 121
Eastern Religion and Western Thought (Radhakrishnan), 121
East-West relations, 73, 81
Eckstein, Harry, 51
Economic dependence, 19, 208; resource precariousness and, 16
Economic development, 229; anti-imperialist discourse and, 102; democracy and, 157; elites and, 19; political dependence and, 23
Economic theory: failure of, 10-13; Islamic, 129
Edict of Caracalla, 59
Effendi, Mazhar, 95
Effendi, Mustafa, 95

Effendi, Reshvan, 95
Efkyar, Tasviri, 119
Egalitarianism, 190, 191
Egyptian Central Security Force, 173
Elias, Norbert: on feudalism, 58
Elite, 30, 32, 224; economic development and, 19; immigrant, 30; importation/subjugation and, 112; masses and, 13; nationalist, 109, 110; political, 19, 169; rivalries among, 136; socialism and, 103; technocratic, 115; Westernization and, 113, 114
Eminescu, Mikhail, 194
Enlightenment, 1, 56, 83
En-Nadah, identity-based demands and, 176
Essafsaf oasis, 221
European Community, 45, 221, 230; integration and, 26
Exclusion, 212, 213, 214
Exportation, 41, 86; economy of, 22; negative impact of, 91; tribal culture and, 87

Fables (La Fontaine), 122
Fauré, Yves, on Ivory Coast elections, 170
Federal party, evolution of, 61
Fengtian government, 54, 55
Feudal logic, territory and, 58, 59
FIS, 162; Benahdj and, 200; identity-based demands and, 176; political debate and, 158
FLN, disappearance of, 115
Foreign policy, 34, 82–83; Chinese, 39, 40; clientelist logic and, 32; diplomatic sovereignty and, 39, 40
Formes élémentaires (Durkheim), 51
FOSS, 195
France 2, 204
Francis I, Süleyman treaty with, 37, 75
Freemasonry, 56, 57, 119, 203

FRELIMO, 134
French Club, 204
Fujimori, Alberto, 21, 191; Cambio 90 movement and, 180; election of, 189
Fukuyama, Francis, 49
Fukuzawa, Yukichi, 121, 123; Western civilization/Japan and, 122n

Gadhafi, Muammar, 184, 193; on urban society, 194
Galtung, 13, 27
Gandhi, Indira, 128, 158; Congress Party and, 140; personalization of power by, 103; populism of, 190
Gandhi, Mohandas, 128, 193
Gandhi, Rajiv, 103–4; assassination of, 127
Garcia, Alan, 189
Geertz, Clifford, 54
Gellner, Ernest, 54; on clandestine self-administration, 145
Gemayel, Pierre, Phalanges and, 133
Getulism, 115; populism and, 190
Ghanushi, 121, 129
Globalization, 1–2, 7, 12, 34, 235; dependence and, 3; economic, 201; forced, 91; singularity and, 3
Golwalkar, Madhav Sadashiv, 127, 128
Governed states, governing states and, 168
Greek city, growth of, 48
Green March, 78
Guarani Indians, 180
Gulf crisis/Gulf War, 213, 215; diplomacy during, 29, 38–40, 216–17; Kurdish refugees and, 226; populism and, 214; Saudi Arabia and, 32; United Nations and, 73
Gulf money, denouncing, 174, 176
Gunder-Frank, André, 20

Hadj, Messali, 126

Hague convention (1907), piracy and, 78
Hamid, Abd al-Haqq, 120
Hamid, Abdul, 107, 109
Hamidiyya, creation of, 109
Han empire, Funan and, 74
Harare parliament, Land Acquisition Bill and, 17
Hassan II, Green March and, 68
Havel, Vaclav, 117
Hawiye, CSU and, 195
Hedgewar, 127
Hegel, Friedrich, 182
Hegemony, 91; American, 11, 35; economic development and, 10; populism and, 190
Hermet, Guy, populism of, 192–93
Hinduism, 69, 86, 178
Hindu Marriage Act (1955), 147
Hindu nationalism, territorialization and, 68
Hiroyuki, Katoa, 122
History: end of, 1, 49; varied/contradictory directions for, 2
Hitler, Adolf, 150; Confucianism and, 151
Hobbes, Thomas, 123; hypothesis of, 52–53; on reason, 56; universalism of, 55
Hobsbawm, Eric, 21
Home Rule, 61
Hong Kong, cession of, 76
Horizontal alliances, 15, 27, 198
Horizontal solidarities, 83, 132, 157
Houphouët-Boigny, Félix, 18, 52, 84, 133; PDCI and, 137
Hugo, Victor, 120
Human rights, 49, 84
Hume, Allan Octavian, Congress Party and, 102
Hussein (martyr), 117
Hussein, Ahmad, Young Egypt Party and, 133

Hussein, Saddam, 28, 173, 175, 184, 193, 202, 231; Ba?ath party and, 140; demonstration of consensus by, 161; Kuwait and, 68; populism and, 190, 214; territorial expansion/popular mobilization and, 68
Hybridization, 151, 154, 163, 186, 188; forced, 2; logic of, 167, 174
Hyden, Goran, 59; captured peasantry and, 144

Ibn Khaldun, on communal groups, 54
IBRD. *See* International Bank of Reconstruction and Development
Identification: allegiance and, 175; citizenship and, 177, 180, 202; formation of, 109; multiple, 230; political, 58; transnational, 182
Identity, 50, 51, 60–62, 114, 155, 196; affirmation of, 176; communal, 54, 60, 227; as instrument of political action, 234; Islamic, 173, 176; particularist, 83, 84; populism and, 190; political, 18, 20, 58, 177; quest for, 234; rediscovery of, 190; rejection/recomposition of, 174; socialist, 135; state and, 49; threat to, 167; Westernization and, 120. *See also* Cultural identity
Identity-based expression, 173, 174, 226; officialization of, 181–82
Identity-based mobilization, 186, 187, 193, 202; populism and, 190
Identity parties, 175, 207; function of, 177–78; irruption of, 177, 179
IGOs, 220
IHD. *See* Indicators of human development
IMF. *See* International Monetary Fund
Imperialism, 12, 13, 35, 36, 124; capitalism and, 10; economic theory of,

10; market effects of, 11; recourse to, 183-84; struggle against, 19-20

Importation, 118, 123, 125, 150, 156-64, 174, 177, 186; conservation and, 94-101; dependence and, 140, 151, 153; effects of, 168; functioning and, 142; logic of, 86, 93; revolutions and, 101-5; social movements and, 172; strategies, 94, 203; subjugation and, 112; tribal culture and, 87; westernization and, 112

Imported state, European state and, 195

Importing class, creation of, 112-16

Incorporation, 9; forced, 13

Independence, 18, 98, 141, 154; decentralization and, 142; nationalism and, 156; Western influence and, 101

India: crisis of legitimacy in, 174; socialism in, 18

Indian Association, 121

Indian identity, 69, 70

Indian law, 156; British juridicial culture and, 147

Indian nationalism: Congress Party and, 102; intellectuals and, 121

Indian Union, 230

Indicators of human development (IHD), GNP and, 31

Individualism, 26, 55, 155, 229

Individualization, 58; cultural spaces and, 228; natural law and, 72

Industrial sector, 10, 124; socialization of, 103; in Zimbabwe, 17-18

Industries Act, state licensing and, 103

Inequality: dependence and, 46; symbolism of, 77

Infitah, 116, 116n

Innovation, 2, 200; civil society and, 198; localism and, 199

Institutionalization, 12, 46, 75, 182, 183, 186, 204

Intellectuals: importing, 116-23; westernized, 116, 120; Western models and, 93

Internal affairs, 201; intervening in, 37

International Bank of Reconstruction and Development (IBRD), 41

International Confederation of Human Rights, 85

International Court of Justice, Chinguiti group and, 63

International disorder, 210, 214, 231; terrorist movements and, 232

Internationalism, 27, 222

International law, 40, 75, 76, 79, 214; birth of, 70-71; invoking, 210; Iran and, 211; transcultural, 73; universalization of, 71, 74, 85

International Monetary Fund (IMF), 41, 45, 135, 142; adjustment policies of, 191; Algeria and, 221; dependence and, 42; Tunisia and, 43

International order: critique of, 212, 213; cultural dependence and, 233; diplomatic action and, 210; division of, 219; durability of, 232; forced westernization of, 213; innovation for, 220; loss of meaning for, 201; security and, 210

International relations: obligation in, 72; power and, 9; principles of, 78; state model and, 80; universalization of, 218

International system: apprenticeship of, 74-75; interstate system as, 80

Interstate system, 80, 211; construction of, 77-78; universalization of, 85

Invention, 168, 218

Iran. *See* Islamic Republic of Iran

Iranian revolution (1906), 118, 172

Iranian revolution (1979). *See* Islamic revolution

Iron law, 143

Islam: orthodox/mystical, 97; universalist orientation of, 67
Islamic Conference, 183, 219; charter stipulations of, 220
Islamic culture: universality and, 87; Western culture and, 235
Islamic law, 153, 210
Islamic modernity, Western modernity and, 158
Islamic movements, 128, 157, 178, 216, 217; countermobilization strategies and, 68; foundation of, 179; microcommunitarian solidarity/mutual help and, 194; sovereignty and, 66; state models and, 129-30
Islamic Party of the Republic (PRI), 138, 139
Islamic Republic of Iran: confrontation with, 217; constitutional referendum by, 160; constitution of, 184; executive class of, 35; international law and, 211; Kurdish rebellion against, 225
Islamic revivalism, 69, 162, 200
Islamic revolution (1979), 116, 117n, 118, 124-25, 172-73
Islamic Salvation Movement, 129; NLF and, 135
Ispahan Opium Company, 148
Istiqlal, 156
Italian Fascist Party, 133
Ivory Coast: elections in, 170; price regulation in, 16

Jackson, Robert: on quasi-nations/negative sovereignty, 80
Jacobins, 152, 227
Jana Sangh, 124, 128; RSS and, 158
Japan, 111-12, 223
Japanese constitution (1889), Prussian model and, 99
Javadi, Hajj Seyyed, 85; itinerary of, 116-17; on nationalism, 119; on secularism, 118
Jus loci, jus sanguinis and, 60

Kabir, Amir, 96
Kabisig, Aquina and, 192
Kameiny, Ayatollah, 117n
Karpatri, Dharma Sangh de Svami, 124
Katt-e Homayyun, 106
Kaunda, President, 140
Keita, Modibo, 133
Kelsenian normativism, 73
Kemal, Mustafa, 141
Kemalist party, 157; Kurdish question and, 226
Khatt-e-Sharif (Abdel Madjid I and Rashid Pasha), 105
Khayred-Din, 120; importation by, 112
Kher, Amy, 120
Khomeini, Ayatollah, 25, 66, 121, 124, 127, 139, 184, 200; fundamentalism and, 130; imported institutions and, 162-63; Iranian revolution and, 116; Javadi and, 117
Kimbanguism, political debate and, 158
Koenkai, 179
Kokka, 151
Kokusaika, 222
Komeito, 157, 213; foundation of, 179; political debate and, 158
Koussi and Theophilatkos, monopoly by, 148
Kurdish identity, 61-62, 63, 225; Hamidiyya and, 109
Kurdish issue, 85, 209, 225, 226-27; elimination/marginalization of, 63
Kurdish movement, 79, 110-11, 225
Kurdish Republic of Mahabad, 225
Kurdish state, 111, 196
Kurdistan, 62-63, 111
Kurds, 208; Ottoman empire and, 195;

tribalism among, 108; United Nations and, 226
Kushans, Han empire and, 74

Lahidji, Association for Human Rights and, 85
Lancaster House accords, 104
Land Acquisition Bill (1992), 17
Lapidus, Ira: on Ottoman empire/westernization, 112-13
Las Casas, Bartolomé de, 71
Latin America: domination of, 9; importation by, 91; populism in, 189
Law: administrative, 152; imported, 146-56; jacobinization of, 152; of practice, 147; religious, 177; return to, 162; social, 152; valorization of, 212; westernization of, 148, 149-50. *See also* Common law; International law
Lawyers Association, 197
LDP. *See* Liberal Democratic Party
Lebanese Christians, Taef accords and, 226
Legitimacy, 152, 159; authority and, 101; crisis of, 174; developmentalist political science and, 52; rational-legal, 49
Lenin, Vladimir, 10-11, 26
Le Play, Frédéric, 113, 113n
Le Roy, Étienne, 143, 152
Leviathan (Hobbes), 52
Liberal Democratic Party (LDP), 179
Liberalism, 36, 44-45
Li Jiachen, 185
Localism, 193, 194, 199
Louisiana Constitution (1950), Article 372 of, 147
Louisiana penal code, Napoleonic influence on, 147
"Lumpen-nomadic" collectivity, 65
Luxemburg, Rosa, 11

Macaulay, Lord, 147
MacBride, Sean, 205
Maga, Hubert, 133
Mahabharata, translation of, 122
Mahasabha, 124
Mahatir, Prime Minister, 67
Mahmoud II, 94; *sheykh-al-islam* and, 107
Maitatsine sect, 135
Malian Adrar, autonomy of, 65
Malinke, 140
Mamichi, Tsuda, 122
"Man and Liberty" (Nasser), 120
Manchu dynasty, 75, 76
Mandingo people, 202
Maraboutism, 135, 173
Mardom Party, 139
Maritime law (1864), 148
Marja' taqlid, 126
Martin, Denis, 144
Marxism, 18, 115
Masses: elites and, 13; nationalist ideologies and, 109
Mawdudi, 124
Media imperialism thesis, problems with, 206-7
Medjelle, 146, 155
Mehemet-Ali, 94, 95
Meiji period, 94, 111, 121, 203; conservative modernization during, 98, 99-100; imperialism during, 223; westernization in, 96-97
Melli Party, 139
Mendès France, Pierre, 117
Menem, Carlos, 21, 191; Brady plan and, 43
Mercosur, 222
Messianism, 194, 196
Microcommunitarian solidarities, 184-85, 187, 198, 209; economies of, 16
Microdecisions, 199, 202

Midhat Pasha, financial crisis and, 106
Migdal, Joel, 79
Mill, John Stuart, 56, 95, 123
Mindon Min, King: Western influence and, 98
Minorities, 209, 226; Muslim, 208, 226; in Ottoman empire, 108
Mitterand, François, Baule summit and, 106
Mobilization, 171-78, 207, 215, 228, 231; electoral, 132, 170; identity, 186, 190, 193, 202, 234; political, 131; populist, 28; social, 109
Mobutu, President, 156
Modernization, 18, 50, 96, 212; acceptance of, 51; Hindu, 158; ideology, 192; Islamic, 158; Western models of, 55, 206. *See also* Conservative modernization
Mongkut, 97
Montesquieu, 56, 117, 123
Morgenthau, Hans, 12
Mossadegh, 118; Anglo-Iranian Company and, 19; nationalization by, 30-31; ouster of, 116
Movement for Liberty and People's Rights, 121
Movement of Nonaligned Nations, 79
MPLA. *See* People's Movement for the Liberation of Angola
MPS, 195
MTI, 158, 173, 176
Mugabe, Robert: Marxist discourse/symbolism and, 105; ZANU and, 104, 134
Muhammad, Prophet, 74
Multilateralism, 35, 221, 222, 235; patron states and, 41; socioeconomic functions and, 43
Multiparty system, 106, 161, 179; in Egypt, 139
Muslim brotherhoods, 127, 162, 196, 208, 216; identity-based demands and, 176
Muslim minorities, 208, 226
Mustafa IV, assassination of, 95
Mzali, Prime Minister, 192

Nahnah, Mahfoud: on state, 129
Naidu, Sarojini, 121
Nakamura, 123
Nanking regime, codes of, 149
Napoleonic Civil Code, 146
Naqshbandi order, common bond for, 62
Naseredin Shah, elite and, 96
Nasser, Gamal Abdel, 16, 28, 35, 82, 120, 137, 184; agrarian reforms and, 187; on feudalism/imperialism, 52; nationalist diplomacy of, 216; pan-Arab movement of, 101; populism and, 190; socialism and, 18; Suez canal and, 19, 68
National Development Council, 103
National Farmer Association of Zimbabwe (NFAZ), 104
Nationalism, 21, 35, 110n, 129, 132, 150; Arab, 108, 109; colonialism and, 110; independence and, 156; in India, 68, 102, 121, 203; in Japan, 151; in Ottoman empire, 108; populism and, 190; symbols of, 30-31; variations of, 192; Western construction of, 119
Nationalism (Tagore), 121
Nationality: challenging, 229; cultural/political, 126
Nationalization, 30, 103, 105
National League for the Defense of Human Rights, 117
National sovereignty, 9, 160; illusion of, 10; state sovereignty and, 80
Nation in the Making, A (Banerjea), 121

Nation-state logic, transnational logic and, 168
Nation-state model, reproduction of, 78-79
Natural law, 73; individualization and, 72
Ndebele, Shona and, 134, 198
Negotiation, principle of, 78
Nehru, Jawahrlal, 35, 156; agrarian revolution and, 187; Congress Party and, 102; Goa and, 19; Planning Commission and, 103; socialism and, 18
Neighborhood movements, 151
Neo-Destour, 134; Sahelians and, 15; transformation of, 44, 137
Neoliberalism, 41, 43, 44, 115, 153
Neopatrimonialism, 14-15, 16, 22, 24, 30, 163, 193, 197, 198; civil servants and, 188; dependence and, 149; development and, 19
Neopopulism, 129, 171
Neotraditionalism, 185, 219
New Caledonia, United Nations and, 25
Newly industrializing nations (NINs); economic transformations of, 23; rise of, 21-22
NFAZ. *See* National Farmer Association of Zimbabwe
NGOs. *See* Nongovernmental organizations
Nichiren, 177
NINs. *See* Newly industrializing nations
Nkomo, Josué: ZAPU and, 134
Nkrumah, Nkwame, 28; client sovereignty and, 34; symbols of struggle and, 19
NLF, 45, 126, 138, 156; as intermediary organization, 139; Islamic Salvation Movement and, 135; Leninist model and, 134

Nomads, dilemma for, 64-65
Nonalignment, 193, 214, 214
Nongovernmental organizations (NGOs), 196, 220; limitations on, 19; professional associations and, 84
Noninterference, principle of, 79
Noriega, Manuel, 218
North, 3; defined, 2n; elites of, 13; models from, 46; South and, 13, 14, 73
North African Star, 125
Northcote-Trevelyan report (1854), 141
NSDAP, 133

O'Donnell, Guillermo: authoritarianism and, 21
Ogodenis, opposition by, 82, 195
Oil: dependence situations and, 29; nationalization of, 30
Omeyyad empire, *dar al islam* and, 59
ONG, 145-46
"Open Letter to the Army" (Javadi), 117
Ottoman empire, 94; importation by, 112-13; international system and, 108; Kurds and, 63, 195; nationalism in, 108; Westernization and, 96, 99, 100, 112
Ovid, 121

Pacta sunt servanda, 74
Padri movement, 113
Pahlavi dynasty, 108, 130
PAIGC. *See* African Independence Party of Guinea-Bissau
Pan-Arab movement, 101
Panchayati-raj, 184, 193
Pan-Hindu movement, identity-based protest and, 181
Pan-Islamism, 230; denunciation

of, 209; Hindu reaction to, 174; identity-based protest and, 181; rise of, 176

Pan-Turkism, 184, 219, 230

Particularism, 15, 94, 181, 182, 185, 193, 219, 228, 229, 234; communal, 84; diplomatic discourse and, 211; exclusion and, 12; glorification of, 168; infra-state, 219; revitalization of, 220

Parti démocratique de Guinée équatoriale, 158

Parti démocratique gabonais, 158

Parties: in developing countries, 139-40; functional deficit for, 138; identity for, 134-35; as instruments of rupture, 136; in noncompetitive system, 138

Partisanship, 132, 138, 140, 179

Patrimonialism, 15, 24, 48, 149. *See also* Neopatrimonialism

Patronage, 26, 139-40, 170; adjustment policies and, 42; American, 33, 35

Patron states: client states and, 24-34, 41

Paz Zamora, President, 180

PDCI. *See* Democratic Party of the Ivory Coast

PDG. *See* Democratic Party of Guinea

Peace of Westphalia (1648), 12, 60, 77, 210

Penados, Prospero, 36

Penal codes, 147, 150

People's Agrarian Movement, reconstruction of, 139

People's Movement for the Liberation of Angola (MPLA), 134

Peripheral societies: adaptation by, 2; awakening of, 233; loss of power in, 11; political production of, 167

Peronism, 115, 189, 190

Persia, westernization in, 95-96

Persian revolution (1906), 118, 172

Pirnia, 118

Planning Commission (India), five-year plans and, 103

PME, 45

Political communalization, 188, 220

Political debate, 234; democracy and, 159

Political dependence, 42, 224; economic transformation and, 23

Political innovation, 51, 62, 168; blocking, 164

Political order: overcoming, 102; transformation of, 11

Political space, 83; social actors and, 198; unification of, 113

Politics, 188; administration and, 140-41; contradictory forces of, 28; dependence relations and, 20; imported, 131-36; instrumental/functional conception of, 20; recomposition of, 170-71

Populism, 21, 188-93, 194, 218; secular, 32; tribune-based, 129. *See also* Neopopulism

Positivism, 56, 72, 95; in Egypt, 113; in Turkey, 119

Power, 91; concentration of, 139; confrontation of, 81; effective/dynamic, 48; equality of, 196; international relations and, 9; neopatrimonial construction of, 14; state monopoly on, 95; territory and, 36-37

Power actors, described, 93-94

PPA, 126

Press agencies, quasi-monopoly for, 205

PRI. *See* Islamic Party of the Republic

Private space, public space and, 225

Privatization, 43, 135, 198; adaptation and, 144; Algeria and, 221; corrup-

tion and, 144; in Mahgrebian states, 45
Professional associations, NGOs and, 84
Property code, 149
Protest, 123, 215, 218, 232; authoritarian nature of, 172; dependence and, 233-34; identity-based, 181; internal, 201; Islamic, 124; tribunes and, 217
Protestant Ethic, The (Weber), 50
Protesters, 123-30
Protest wars, 215, 216
Providence states, rise of, 31
PSD, 140
Public law, 152, 155, 205
Public services, 42
Public space, 37, 49, 112, 119, 182; Arab nationalism and, 109; private space and, 225; Western law and, 154
Pye, Lucian, 51

Qadi, 181
Qadjar dynasty, 107-8, 195
Quian Quichen, 39

Radhakrishnan, Sarvepalli, 121
Radio Free Europe, 204
Radwan, Fathi, 133
Rama I, 9, 128, 174n, 178; Buddhism and, 97
Ramayana, translation of, 121
Rao, Narasimha, 104
Rashid Pasha, *Khatt-e-Sharif* and, 105
Rashtriya Swayamsewak Association (RSS), 127-28, 157, 158, 178, 179, 193; identity-based demands and, 176; Jana Sangh and, 158
Rassemblement démocratique africain (RDA), 132, 156
Rassemblement démocratique centrafricain, 158
Rassemblement démocratique du peuple camerounais, 158
Rassim, Georges, 120
Rationality, 123, 217
Rawls, John, 212
RDA. See *Rassemblement démocratique africain*
Readjustment, patron states and, 41
Reappropriation, populist strategies of, 207
Reason, 118; Hobbes on, 56
Recommunalization, 228
Reformation, 98, 160; Renaissance and, 71
Regionalization, 218, 219-27
Relations: inequality of, 25-26; verticality of, 26-27
Religion of Man, The (Tagore), 121
Renaissance: market capitalism in, 57; Protestant Reformation and, 71
Rentier state, 32; allocation/distribution and, 31
Representative government, development of, 160
Republic of Geneva, 160
Republic of Mahabad, 63
Resolution 618 (Security Council), China and, 39
Resolution 678 (Security Council), China and, 39-40
Restructuration, policies of, 43
Reuters, 205
Review of Year Six (Arinori), 122
Revivalist movements, 187, 215, 219, 229
Revolutions, 194; importation and, 101-5
Reza Shah, 117
Rida, Rashid, 124
Rifah party, 187
Rifai Alep order, 97
Riza, Ahmed, 119

Rokkan, Stein, 131
Rosenau, James, 35, 202-3
Rousseau, Jean-Jacques, 117, 120, 123
Roy, Ram Mohan, 69
RSS. *See* Rashtriya Swayamsewak Association

Sadat, Anwar: *infitah* and, 116n; liberalization policies by, 116; multiparty system and, 106, 139, 161
Sadequiyyeh branch, 126
Sadiqiyya, 134
Safavids, 118, 195
Saharan State, Libyan myth of, 65
Sahel, 140
Sahrawi identity, 64
Saint-Simonism, 56, 57, 113, 141; in Egypt, 95, 119
Salar, Sepah, 96
Saltaneh, Qavam, 120
Samurai, 99, 111
Sankara, populism and, 190
Sanrizuka movement, 151
Sassanid Persians, Tang dynasty and, 74
Scientism, 95
Sebastiani, Bastien, 94, 94n
Secularization, 107
Security, international order and, 210
Seigo, Nakono, 150
Self Help (Smiles), 123
Selim III, 94, 95
Serasvati, Dayananda, 69
Serrano, Jorge: election of, 180
Sève, Captain, 94
Seventh-Day Adventists, 175
SEZ. *See* Special economic zones
Shakespeare, William, 121
Sharia, 129, 176; revolution and, 172
Shari'at Madari, Ayatollah, 127
Sharif Pasha, 111
Shillal, 15

Shingalese nationalists, antiminority sentiments of, 61
Shinkichi, Uesugi, 150
Shiva, 128, 178
Shona, Ndebele and, 134, 198
Siam, Westernization and, 97-99
Sikhs, 208
Sinasi, Ibrahim, 119, 120
Singh, Bharatiya Lok Dal de Charan, 124
Singularity, globalization and, 3
Sino-American relations, 39. *See also* China
Sismondi, Jean, 149, 149n
Sixth Plan (1981), liberalization in, 43
Siyaad, President, 82
Smiles, Samuel, 123
Smith, Adam, 11, 149n
Smith, Ian, 187
SNSP. *See* Syrian National Socialist Party
Social bonds, 54, 183
Social Contract (Rousseau), 123
Social Democratic Populist Party, 226
Socialism, 18, 115, 116, 192; egalitarian principles and, 102-3
Socialization, 157; control of, 205
Social justice, 160, 199
Social movements, 124; identity-based expression of, 175, 176; importation and, 172; in India, 174-75; legitimacy for, 170-71
Social networks, communication and, 136
Social order, 23, 91
Social relations, individualization of, 14-15, 53, 83, 132
Social spaces, 114, 155; civil society and, 79; empty, 186-88; internal, 24; political communalization and, 188; private, 83, 228; suburban, 187
Société générale of Iran, 148

Society of Getul, 133n
Society of Year Six, 122
Society of Young Arabs, 108
Socioeconomic functions, 41, 46
Socioeconomic structures, homogenization of, 45
Sociological hypothesis, 52
Sociology, 50, 52
Solidarities: horizontal, 83, 132, 157; microcommunitarian, 16, 184–85, 187, 198, 209; transnational, 202, 224; vertical, 132, 144
Suleyman the Magnificent, François I treaty with, 37, 75
Song bank, Chiang Kai-shek and, 149
South, 2, 3; elites of, 13; North and, 13, 14
Sovereignty, 38, 79, 81, 118; cultural identity and, 86; deceptions of, 37–47; dependence and, 86; national, 9, 10, 80, 160; natural right to, 75; negative, 80; principle of, 72, 80, 205; rupture of, 228; spaces of, 209; state and, 80, 86, 204–5, 208
Special economic zones (SEZ), 222
Spencer, Herbert, 56
Srinavas, M. N.: on Sanskritization, 114
State: cultural spaces and, 227; dependence by, 13–24, 34–37; identity and, 49, 83; legitimacy and, 49; violence and, 78; Western model of, 96–97
State logic, territory and, 59–60
State model, international relations and, 80
State order, imperial order and, 183–84
State sovereignty, 86; national sovereignty and, 80; principle of, 204–5; shrinkage of, 208
Stere, Constantin, 194
Strange, Susan: on global power, 34

Structural adjustment, 115, 116
Substitution: formulas of, 167; legitimacy of, 189
Suez canal, 19, 68, 214
Sufi sects, 97; common bond for, 62
Sukarno, Ahmed, 18, 28, 35; symbols of struggle and, 19
Symbolism: anti-imperialist, 19, 21; Western-style, 114
Syrian National Socialist Party (SNSP), 133
System of meanings, 66

Tagore, Rabindranath, 121
Tahtawi, Minister, 95, 120; importation by, 112
Takriti clan, 15, 140
Taleqani, 200
Tamanrasset, peace accord at, 65
Tamils, 60–61, 63, 85, 225
Tamil United Liberation Front, 61
Tang dynasty, 54; Sassanid Persians and, 74
Territorial identity, 60; absence of, 62
Territoriality, 58–70, 100, 142, 183; civil society and, 59; Islamic model and, 66–67; Western model of, 66
Territorialization, 66, 69, 110, 227; effects of, 108; Hindu nationalism and, 68; nomadic populations and, 64–65; Western rural society and, 59
Territorial logic, 60–62, 100, 111
Territorial organization, 142, 143
Territory: allegiance and, 64, 67–68; community and, 60–61; feudal logic and, 58; invention of, 59; power and, 36–37; state logic and, 59–60
Terrorism, 81, 210; international disorder and, 232
Theravada Buddhism, society and, 160
Third International, imperialism issue at, 13

Third world: defined, 2n; formation of, 1; looting of, 24
Third-world diplomacy, 216
Third-worldist view, 7
Thomism, 160
Tigreens, 82
Tocqueville, Alexis de, 123
Tohokai Party, 150
Totalitarianism, 1; democracy and, 158
Touré, Ahmed Sékou: local revolutionary powers and, 143; PDG and, 137, 140; symbols of struggle and, 19
Transnational flows, 37, 204, 229; growth of, 34-35
Transnational groups: identification of, 180; mobilization of, 81
Transnationalization, 168, 208
Transnational solidarities, 202, 224
Trash state, 25
Treaty of Erzerum (1847), Kurds and, 62
Treaty of Marrakech (1989), 221
Treaty of Nanking (1842), 76
Treaty of Sèvres (1920), 110, 110n; Kurdish territory and, 63
Treaty of Shimonoseki (1904), 77
Treaty of Tianjin (1858), 77
Tribalism, 15, 84; importation/exportation and, 87; resurgence of, 21; universality and, 83
Tribunals, 213, 218; establishment of, 153; protest role for, 217
Tuaregs, dilemma for, 64-65
Tubus, armed conflict for, 65
Tudeh Party, Javadi and, 117
Turkish minorities, 225, 226

UAM. *See* Union of Arabic Maghreb
UGTM, 173
Ulama, 95, 113, 126, 176; revolution and, 172
Ulama Association, 125, 126, 127
Ulema, 196
Umma, 40, 66, 67, 124, 125
UNESCO, 205
Unification, 1-2; by law, 70-77
Union démocratique du peuple malien, 158
Union of Arabic Maghreb (UAM), 221, 222, 224; Moroccan foreign policy and, 26
United Independence Party (UNIP), 137, 139
United Nations: Gulf crisis and, 73; Kurdish refugees and, 226; New Caledonia and, 25; sovereignty and, 9; universalization and, 78
Universal city, invention of, 48-57
Universalism, 7, 57, 68, 181; civil obedience and, 154; ulturalism and, 235; Hobbesian, 55; state, 81; Western rationalism and, 69
Universality, 48, 83, 155, 216; crisis of, 231; Islamic culture and, 87; of the sovereign, 80
Universalization, 3, 51, 77, 84; forced, 203, 208-9; propensity toward, 73; United Nations and, 78
Universal village thesis, problems with, 206-7
Urabi Pasha, 110; Nationalist Movement and, 110n
Urbanization, 109; patron-client relation and, 189
Urban society, Gadhafi criticism on, 194
USA. *See* Arab Socialist Union
Usuli, 126

Valis, integration by, 62
Vargas, Getúlio, 133n
Vattel, work of, 72
Veka'i, Takvimi, 119
Velayat-e-fakih, 130

Verba, Sidney: on civic culture, 51
Vertical solidarities, 27, 132, 144
Violence: communitarian, 209; control of, 78, 107; individual/universal, 77; state use of, 82
Vitoria, work of, 71-72
Von Moltke, Helmuth, 94, 94n; Ottoman army and, 95

Wallerstein, Immanuel, 20
Waqf, institution of, 107
Weber, Max, 50, 210
Western culture, 32, 36; Asian culture and, 118; Islamic culture and, 235
Westernization, 7, 57, 93, 96, 100, 101, 111, 115, 224; cultural backwardness and, 118-19; elite and, 113, 114; forced, 105-6, 118, 208, 213, 234; identity and, 120; importation and, 112; increase in, 55; intellectuals and, 116; limitations on, 168; process of, 96-97, 121; protest and, 123
Western law: conformity with, 153; expansion of, 148; importation of, 151; public space and, 154
Western model, 28, 51, 100-101, 111, 113, 152, 202, 205, 206, 235; crisis of, 182 diffusion of, 96; importation of, 91, 93, 100, 101-7, 177, 186, 204; universalization of, 85, 87, 203, 208-9

What is to be Done? (Chernyshevsky), 127
Workers Party, Young Egypt Party and, 133
World Bank, 45; adjustment policies of, 191; Algeria and, 44, 221; China and, 39
Writers Association, 197

Yan Fu, 56
Yassin, Abdessalem, 129
Young Bengal movement, 69
Young Egypt Party, 133
Young Turks, 113, 120; Postivism and, 56; westernization and, 112

Zain (President Zain Al Abidin), land confiscation by, 44
ZANU. *See* Zimbabwe African National Union
ZAPU, 134
Zghal, Abdelkadar, 173, 199
Zimbabwe, 114: agriculture in, 17, 114, 145, 187; external commerce for, 17-18, 104; importation in, 104; Marxism in, 18 Zimbabwe African National Union (ZANU), 105, 134, 180; agrarian reform and, 104-5; colonial order and, 135; land collectivization in, 187
Zsitva Torok Treaty (1606), 75